Java Quiz Book

A Compendium of over 1,200 questions, with answers and programs

S.R. Subramanya

Exskillence
San Diego, USA

Java Quiz Book

Table of Contents

Preface v
Unique features of this book vi
Who could benefit from this book? vi
   Notes vii
  Questions 1
  A. Java Basics 3
    True/False Questions 3
    Fill-in the-blanks Questions 10
    Essay-type Questions 25
  B. Control Structures 29
    True/False Questions 29
    Fill-in the-blanks Questions 30
    Essay-type Questions 32
  C. Arrays and Arraylists 38
    True/False Questions 38
    Fill-in the-blanks Questions 39
    Essay-type Questions 41
  D. Classes, Objects, Methods 49
    True/False Questions 49
    Fill-in the-blanks Questions 63
    Essay-type Questions 69
  E. Inheritance and Polymorphism 72
    True/False Questions 72
    Fill-in the-blanks Questions 77
    Essay-type Questions 78
  F. Exception Handling 84
    True/False Questions 84
    Fill-in the-blanks Questions 88
    Essay-type Questions 91
  G. Files and I/O 95
    True/False Questions 95
    Fill-in the-blanks Questions 96
  H. Programming Problems 100
  Answers 113
  A. Java Basics 115
    True/False Questions 115
    Fill-in the-blanks Questions 128
    Essay-type Questions 153
  B. Control Structures 160
    True/False Questions 160
    Fill-in the-blanks Questions 162
    Essay-type Questions 164
  C. Arrays and Arraylists 176
    True/False Questions 176
    Fill-in the-blanks Questions 178

Essay-type Questions 182
D. Classes, Objects, Methods 191
  True/False Questions 191
  Fill-in the-blanks Questions 217
  Essay-type Questions 226
E. Inheritance and Polymorphism 231
  True/False Questions 231
  Fill-in the-blanks Questions 239
  Essay-type Questions 242
F. Exception Handling 252
  True/False Questions 252
  Fill-in the-blanks Questions 258
  Essay-type Questions 262
G. Files and I/O 268
  True/False Questions 268
  Fill-in the-blanks Questions 271
H. Programming Problems 275
  Books on Java 313

Preface

Java has been one of the most widely used programming language in numerous real-world applications. Although it was originally designed/developed for use in embedded systems, it quickly grew in popularity in programming for Web and mobile applications, and is now used in many domains. Java is an object-oriented language, along with numerous control features of C family of languages. Java language is supported with several libraries and routines. Java source code is compiled to an intermediate language called Java Bytecode, which is further compiled to native machine code. This makes Java programs to be highly portable.

Java is also a programming language of choice for introductory programming courses in numerous institutions. For a student who is currently taking (or has already taken) a course on Java programming, there are no comprehensive resources to facilitate a quick assessment/testing of the understanding of the features/facilities of Java, and for analyzing and writing Java code. This book aims to fill that need. It is intended to be a quick assessment book / quiz book. It has a vast collection of over 1,200 questions, along with answers and programs.

This book covers questions on all the major topics of Java programming typically covered in an introductory course. The topical coverage includes data types, control structures, arrays, classes, objects, and methods, inheritance and polymorphism, exception handling, and stream and text I/O.

Unique features of this book

- Over 1,200 short questions, with answers and programs.
- Question types consist of (a) True/False (b) sentence completion, (c) program (segment) analysis, and (c) developing programs.
- Questions have a wide range of difficulty levels.
- Questions are designed to test a thorough understanding of various aspects of Java.
- Questions and programs can help in internship / job interview preparation.

Who could benefit from this book?

- Students who are currently taking a course on Java Programming.
- Students who have already completed a course on Java Programming, and are preparing to take written exams and/or interviews for industry/companies.
- Professionals trying to make a switch to Computing/IT industry could use it as a source of self–assessment in Java.
- Participants and quiz masters in quiz competitions.

Notes

- The terms 'object' and 'instance' are used interchangably.

- The terms 'reserved word' and 'keyword' are used synonymously.

- Occasionally, but rarely, a question is posed in a couple of different ways.

- Relational operators are (<, <=, !=, ==, >=, >)

- Logical operators are ! (negation), && (conjunction: AND), || (disjunction: OR), ^ (exclusive OR)

- The operators '&' and '|' are used both as non-short-circuit logical operators, as well as bitwise operators.

- The datatypes of variables (ex. 'x', 'y', etc.), if unspecified, are assumed to be of the valid types based on the context of expressions.

- The exhaustive coverage of all possible features of Java will be available in the language reference manual. The intent here is to give the reader an opportunity for self assessment with regard to some of the basic, and commonly used features and constructs of Java.

- The questions on programming are intended to provide samples of several aspects of algorithmic thinking and problem solving. It draws upon a variety of problems, of varying difficulties.

Questions

Java Quiz Book

A. Java Basics

True/False Questions

A1 A `.class` file is not created if compilation of a class has no errors, but there are warnings. _____

A2 Java is dynamically typed. _____

A3 All the letters in a Java keyword is in lowercase. _____

A4 Java keywords may be used as variable names. _____

A5 $amount is a valid identifier. _____

A6 $6,379 is a valid identifier. _____

A7 52_83 is a valid integer. _____

A8 3.1_4 is a valid real number. _____

A9 _738 is a valid integer. _____

A10 `class` is a valid identifier. _____

A11 `74Points` is a valid identifier. _____

A12 `total-count` is a valid identifier. _____

A13 `current_sum` is a valid identifier. _____

A14 The "_" (underscore character) can be used as digit separator for intergers or floating point numbers. _____

A15 The following assignment statements are not equivalent. _____

    a.   `i = j = k = 1;`

    b.   `i = 1; j = 1; k = 1;`

A16 The value of $1 - 0.1 - 0.1 - 0.1 - 0.1 - 0.1 - 0.1 - 0.1 - 0.1$ may not exactly be 0.2. _____

A17   Floating point arithmetic does not cause overflow. _____

A18   Integer computations do not cause rounding errors. _____

A19   Arithmetic overflow causes a run-time error. _____

A20   A Java character takes up 2 bytes of space. _____

A21   Local variables must be initialized before their values are used in an expression. _____

A22   Java requires all variables to have a type before they can be used in a program. _____

A23   In Java, string is a primitive type. _____

A24   In Java, a string is treated as an array of characters. _____

A25   Nothing can be added or deleted from a string. _____

A26   A 'double' to 'float' promotion of primitive type is allowed to occur. _____

A27   The operands of an operator are always evaluated from left to right. _____

A28   A Package is a group of related classes and interfaces. _____

A29   Java does not allow overloading of primitive (ex. '+', '*') operators. _____

A30   An **enum** constructor cannot be overloaded. _____

A31   Recursion is often more efficient than iteration. _____

A32   Recursion often is preferable to iteration because it models the problem more logically. _____

A33   Java compiler is a multipass compiler. _____

A34   In Java, a 'subpackage' is always contained within its 'parent' package. _____

A35   Java does not support the pointer type. _____

A. Java Basics

A36 The 'int' datatype has different variations in Java. _____

A37 In Java, there are no operators or methods for explicit deallocation of objects. _____

A38 An array may contain only primitive types. _____

A39 The sub-expressions are executed from left to right. _____

A40 Java does not have built-in exponentiation operator. _____

A41 Java guarantees left–to–right evaluation of operands. _____

A42 Java is a type-safe language. _____

A43 Java bytecode can only be compiled, and not interpreted, into native code at run time. _____

A44 Java does not have array-bounds checks. _____

A45 Java does not have a pre-processor. _____

A46 Java does not support macros. _____

A47 Java has no pointer data type. _____

A48 In Java, whenever a variable of non-primitive type is declared, a block of memory of the required size is allocated. _____

A49 Java byte code does not hide machine-specific details. _____

A50 In Java, call-by-value is not used. _____

A51 A garbage collection mechanism is supported by the Java Virtual Machine (JVM). _____

A52 The default value for data field of a boolean type is _____

A53 The default value for data field of a numeric type is _____

A54 The default value for object type is _____

A55 Local variables do not have default values. _____

A56 Local variables are initialized with default values when they are declared. _____

A57 A reference type does not store an object. _____

A58 An **int** value can be assigned to a reference variable. _____

A59 Use of an uninitialized variable in statement does not give compilation error. _____

A60 Java requires declaration of variables before use. _____

A61 Variables declarations can be anywhere a statement can be. _____

A62 A variable in a nested block can have the same name as a variable in the enclosing block. _____

A63 Java supports multiple-selection statement. _____

A64 Arrays are not initialized at the time of allocation. _____

A65 Array index range checks are not done in Java. _____

A66 String is a primitive type in Java. _____

A67 Java does not support enumeration types. _____

A68 Java supports concurrency. _____

A69 Java has built-in garbage collection. _____

A70 Java supports only widening assignment coercions. _____

A71 Java does not have implicit type conversions (coercions). _____

A72 Java does not support explicit type conversions (casts). _____

A73 Java supports short circuit evaluation of Boolean expressions. _____

A74 Short circuit evaluation of Boolean expressions cannot be overridden in Java. _____

A. Java Basics

A75 Java does not have the **goto** control structure. _____

A76 Java has predefined overloaded subprograms. _____

A77 In Java, the control expression must be Boolean. _____

A78 Java does not allow mixed-mode expressions. _____

A79 Java supports parameterized ADTs. _____

A80 Java has built-in support for exception handling. _____

A81 Local variables must be initialized before their values are used in an expression. _____

A82 Java requires all variables to have a type before they can be used in a program. _____

A83 In Java, **string** is a primitive type. _____

A84 An expression cannot be an argument to a method. _____

A85 The **++** and **--** operators can be applied to a 'char' variable. _____

A86 The ++ and -- operators are binary operators. _____

A87 A string variable is a primitive variable. _____

A88 The '%' operator is not valid on floating point numbers. _____

A89 Relational operators are (generally) used for primitive types. _____

A90 There is no value of x for which the expression **(x < 10) && (x > 10)** would be true. _____

A91 There is no value of x for which the expression **(x < 10) || (x > 10)** would be false. _____

A92 The value of the expression **(x <= y ^ x >= y)** would always be true. _____

A93 The value of the expression **(x < y ^ x > y)** would always be true. _____

A94 The value of the expression **((x%y == 0) ^ (y%x == 0))** would always be true. _____

A95 For integers x and y, the value of the expression **(x/y == 0 ^ y/x == 0)** would always be true. _____

A96 For integers x and y, the value of the expression **(x/y == 1 ^ y/x == 1)** could never be false. _____

A97 For integers x and y, the value of the expression **(x/y == 0 ^ x/y != 0)** is always true. _____

A98 The value of **(x < y || x > y)** is always true. _____

A99 The value of **(x <= y && x >= y)** is always true. _____

A100 The value of **(x < y && x > y)** is always false. _____

A101 The value of **(x == y || x != y)** is always true. _____

A102 The value of **(x == y && x != y)** is always false. _____

A103 The value of **(x == y ^ x != y)** is always true. _____

A104 The value of **(x % y == y % x)** is always false. _____

A105 For integer values of x and y, the expression **(x/y == y/x)** would never be true. _____

A106 In Java, arithmetic overflow does not result in run-time error. _____

A107 When x ≠ y, it is never the case that **x % y** is 0. _____

A108 For integers (positive or negative) x, y, when x < y, it is always the case that **x / y** is 0. _____

A109 For integers (positive or negative) x, y, when x < y and x ≠ 0, it is never the case that **x % y** is 0. _____

A. Java Basics

A110 For integer values of x and y, when x ≥ y, it is always the case that **x / y** is not 0. _____

A111 When x ≠ y, it is never the case that **x % y** and **x / y** are equal. _____

A112 **(x != y)** is equivalent to **!(x == y)**. _____

A113 **!(x < y)** is equivalent to **(x >= y)**. _____

A114 **(x > y || x < y)** is equivalent to **(x == y)**. _____

A115 The value of the expression **(x < y ^ x > y)** would always be true. _____

A116 Integer arithmetic is always gives the correct result. _____

A117 All integer values in the range supported are accurately represented. _____

A118 Floating point arithmetic is always accurate. _____

A119 If 's' and 'i' are vaiables of type string and integer, respectively, then **s = i;** will automatically perform type conversion of the sequence of digits to a string. _____

A120 If 's' and 'i' are vaiables of type string and integer, respectively, then **s = i + "";** will automatically perform type conversion of the sequence of digits to a string. _____

A121 For any two strings s1 and s2, the value of the expression **s1.equalsIgnoreCase(s2) == s2.equals(s1)** is always true. _____

A122 For any strings s1 and s2, the value of **s1.contains(s2) && s2.contains(s1)** is never true. _____

A123 An Integer instance can be cast to a Double instance. _____

A124 **Integer i = 4.5** is a valid assignment. _____

A125 **Double i = 4.5** is a valid assignment. _____

A126 `Object i = 4.5` is a not valid assignment. _____

A127 `Number i = 4.5` is a not valid assignment. _____

A128 The String class implements Comparable method. _____

A129 The Double class does not implement Comparable method. _____

A130 Even if two Random objects have the same seed, the sequence of the random numbers obtained from these two objects may not be identical. _____

A131 What are the values of the following expressions?

```
int a = 2, b = 3, c = 5;

a > b || c > b                              _____

b < a + 2 && c <= a + b                     _____

(b > c - a) || (a < c / b + 1)              _____

b == b % c || a + b > c                     _____

(b <= c) && (b + c % a == 0)                _____
```

IOIOIOIOIOIOIOIOIOIOIOIOIOIOIOIOIOIOIOIOIOIOIOIOI

Fill-in the-blanks Questions

A1 The high-level language code / program written by the programmer is known as _____ code.

A2 The code / program executed by the computer is known as _____ code.

A3 The software which translates high-level language program into machine language program is known as _____

A. Java Basics

A4 The software which manages various resources and activities in a computer is known as the _____

A5 A(n) _____ provides facilities such as editing, compiling, running, and debugging during program development.

A6 A program which does not compile is said to have _____ error(s).

A7 A program which compiles without error(s) but terminates abnormally when run is said to have _____ error.

A8 A program which compiles without error(s) but produces incorrect result(s) is said to have _____ error.

A9 The extension of a Java source code file is _____

A10 The extension of a Java bytecode file is _____

A11 A Java class **public class Test { ... }** must be defined in a file named _____

A12 A block is enclosed between _____

A13 In Java, the Boolean literals are _____ and _____

A14 The software that interprets Java bytecode is known as _____

A15 A set of separate programs for developing and testing Java programs, is collectively known as _____

A16 _____ contains predefined classes and interfaces for developing Java programs.

A17 Java compiler translates Java source code into _____

A18 The signed integer types supported by Java are, _____, _____, _____, and _____

A19 In Java, whenever a variable of non-primitive type is declared, a(n) _____ is allocated.

A20   In Java, a _____ is a collection of classes.

A21   After compilation of an interface without errors, a _____ file is created for the interface.

A22   Every statement in a Java program must end with a _____

A23   The starting character of an identifier could only be _____, _____, or _____.

A24   The _____ can be used as digit separator for intergers or floating point numbers.

A25   The declaration of a constant ARR_SIZE inside a method with value 100, is _____

A26   The result of 4 / 5 is _____

A27   The result of (double) (4 / 5) is _____

A28   The result of (double) 4 / 5 is _____

A29   The result of 4 / (double) 5 is _____

A30   The result of 4.0 / 5 is _____

A31   The result of 4 / 5.0 is _____

A32   The result of 19 / 5 is _____

A33   The result of 19 / 5.0 is _____

A34   The result of (double)19 / 5 is _____

A35   For **x** % **n** to be 0 for all values of **x**, the value of **n**, should be _____

A36   The result of 5 % 1 is _____

A37   The result of 17 % 3 is _____

A38   The result of 3 % 17 is _____

A39   The result of 25 % 5 is _____

A. Java Basics

A40   The result of 5 % 1 is _____

A41   The result of 5.2 % 3.7 is _____

A42   The result of 3.7 % 5.2 is _____

A43   The result of (int)(12.345 * 100) / 100.0 is _____

A44   The result of (int)(12.345 * 100 / 100) is _____

A45   The result of (int)(12.345) * 100 / 100.0 is _____

A46   The value of (double)(7/3) is _____

A47   The value of x for which the expression **(x <= 10) && (x >= 10)** would be true is _____

A48   The value of x for which the expression **(x < 10) || (x > 10)** would be false is _____

A49   Given x = 5, the value of **(x << 5)** would be _____

A50   Given x = 84, the value of **(x >> 3)** would be _____

A51   The value of **(x == y && x != y)** is always _____

A52   The value of **(x == y || x != y)** is always _____

A53   When x ≠ y, the value of the expression **(x <= y && x >= y)** would always be _____

A54   The value of **(x <= y || x >= y)** is always _____

A55   The value of **(x == y || x != y)** is always _____

A56   The value of **(x == y ^ x != y)** is always _____

A57   When x ≠ y, the value of the expression **(x < y ^ x > y)** would always be _____

A58   The value of **(x == y && x != y)** is always _____

Java Quiz Book

A59 The value of **(x <= y && x >= y)** is true only under the condition _____

A60 The value of **(x < y ^ x > y)** is false only under the condition _____

A61 The value of **(x >= 0) || (x < 0)** is always _____

A62 The value of **(x < y && x > y)** is always _____

A63 The value of **(x == y ^ x != y)** is always _____

A64 For integer values of x and y, the expression **(x/y == y/x)** would be true only under the condition _____

A65 **(true) && (false)** evaluates to _____

A66 **(true) || (false)** evaluates to _____

A67 The value of **(x > 0) || (x < 0)** is always **true** except when x is _____

A68 The value of **(x > 0) && (x < 0)** is always _____

A69 The value of **!(x > 0) && (x > 0)** is always _____

A70 The value of **(x != 0) || (x == 0)** is always _____

A71 The expression to check if the value of **age** is at least 18 is _____

A72 The expression to check if the value of **age** is between 18 and 65 (inclusive) is _____

A73 The expression to check if the value of x is at least 3 and at most 10 is _____

A74 The expression to ckeck if x is evenly divisible by 3 and 7 is _____

A75 The expression to check if the value of **count** is not in the range 25 to 35 (inclusive) is _____

A. Java Basics

A76 The value of **Math.round(1.49)** is _____

A77 The value of **Math.round(1.5)** is _____

A78 The value of **Math.rint(1.49)** is _____

A79 The value of **Math.rint(1.5)** is _____

A80 The value of **Math.ceil(1.01)** is _____

A81 The value of **Math.ceil(1.99)** is _____

A82 The value of **Math.floor(1.99)** is _____

A83 The value of **Math.floor(1.01)** is _____

A84 Given i=12, j=3, k=9, the value of **Math.min(i, Math.min(j,k))** is _____

A85 Given i=12, j=3, k=9, the value of **Math.min(i, Math.max(j,k))** is _____

A86 Given i=12, j=3, k=9, the value of **Math.abs (j-k-i)** is _____

A87 Given x = 3 and y = 7, the value of y after evaluating the expression **(x >= 3) && (y-- > 5)**, is _____

A88 Given x = 3 and y = 7, the value of y after evaluating the expression **(x > 3) && (y-- > 5)**, is _____

A89 Given x = 3 and y = 7, the value of y after evaluating the expression **(x > 3) & (y-- > 5)**, is _____

A90 Given x = 5 and y = 9, the value of y after evaluating the expression **(x > 5) || (y++ >= 12)**, is _____

A91 Given x = 5 and y = 9, the value of y after evaluating the expression **(x >= 5) || (y++ >= 12)**, is _____

A92 Given x = 5 and y = 9, the value of y after evaluating the expression **(x >= 5) | (y++ >= 12)**, is _____

Java Quiz Book

A93 Given x = 3 and y = 7, the value of the expression **(x >= 3) && (y-- <= 6)**, is _____

A94 Given x = 3 and y = 7, the value of the expression **(x >= 3) && (y-- == 6)**, is _____

A95 Given x = 3 and y = 7, the value of the expression **(x >= 3) && (y-- >= 7)**, is _____

A96 Given x = 3 and y = 7, the value of the expression **(x >= 3) && (y-- == 7)**, is _____

A97 Given x = 3 and y = 7, the value of the expression **(x >= 3) && (--y <= 6)**, is _____

A98 Given x = 3 and y = 7, the value of the expression **(x++ == 3) && (y-- == 7)**, is _____

A99 Given x = 3 and y = 7, the value of the expression **(++x >= 4) && (--y == 6)**, is _____

A100 Given x = 3 and y = 7, the value of the expression **(x++ > 3) && (y-- == 7)**, is _____

A101 Given x = 5 and y = 9, the value of the expression **(x > 5) || (y++ > 9)**, is _____

A102 Given x = 5 and y = 9, the value of the expression **(x > 5) || (++y > 9)**, is _____

A103 Given x = 3 and y = 7, the value of the expression **(x > 3) && (--y <= 6)**, is _____

A104 The _____ primitive type is never promoted to another type.

A105 To improve readability and maintainability, you should declare _____ instead of using literal values such as 3.14159.

A106 The size in bytes of the data type long is ____, short is ____, byte is ____, and int is ____.

A107 The default initial value of a String instance variable is _____

A. Java Basics

A108 The default value of a reference is _____

A109 The number of parameters of a default constructor is _____

A110 The expression to increment element of array **numlist** at index **i** is _____

A111 The declaration of a constant PI inside a method with value 3.14159265358979, is _____

A112 When a literal which is too large to be stored in a Byte is assigned to a variable which has the size of a Byte causes _____ error.

A113 The Java statement to compute $3.2^{4.5}$ is _____

A114 **Math.pow(3,4)** evaluates to _____

A115 **Math.pow(9,1/2)** evaluates to _____

A116 **Math.pow(9,1.0/2)** evaluates to _____

A117 **Math.pow(25, 1/2.0)** evaluates to _____

A118 The _____ method evaluates to a^b.

A119 The statement to assign a variable **d** of type double to a float variable **f**, is _____

A120 A Java character is stored in _____ bytes.

A121 **(int)(Math.random() * (100))** returns a random number between _____ and _____

A122 **(int)(Math.random() + 0.5)** generates random integer _____ or _____.

A123 Write a statement that generates random integers in the range 18 to 65. _____

A124 **(char)('a' + Math.random() * ('z' - 'a' + 1))** returns a random character between _____

A125 Unary arithmetic operators are _____

A126 Unary logical operator is _____

A127 The just one statement to assign to x the larger of the values of x and y, is _____

A128 A collection of classes that have been grouped together into a folder is known as a _____

A129 The datatype of the result of adding an int, a byte, a long, and a double, is _____

A130 The method in the Random class which returns the next random int value is _____

A131 The method in the Random class which returns the next random double value is _____

A132 The statement to declare a constant ARR_SIZE of value 25 as a class member, is _____

A133 In the statement **System.out.println(num)**, **System** refers to _____, **out** refers to _____, **println** refers to _____, refers to a _____

A134 Methods and variables that are not declared as **static** are known as _____ methods and _____ variables.

A135 Java's _____ variables act as global variables.

A136 The value returned by **(int)Math.random()** is _____

A137 The possible range of values returned by **(int)(Math.random() * 10)** is between _____ and _____

A138 The method which immediately terminates a program is _____

A139 The short-circuit operators are _____ and _____

A. Java Basics

A140 The difference between the computed value in a program and the exact mathematical value is known as _____ error.

A141 In Java, the variables declared in methods are, by default, of type _____

A142 The keyword used for method declaration to indicate that the method cannot be overridden by subclasses is, _____

A143 A class that cannot be subclassed must be declared _____

A144 Only _____ types are not objects.

A145 The statement to display the character whose Unicode is stored in variable **x** is _____

A146 The output of `System.out.println(5)` is _____

A147 The output of `System.out.println('5')` is _____

A148 The output of `System.out.println('A')` is _____

A149 The output of `System.out.println((int)'A')` is _____

A150 The output of `System.out.println('Z'-'A'+1)` is _____

A151 The output of `System.out.println('A'+7)` is _____

A152 The output of `System.out.println((char)'A'+7)` is _____

A153 The output of `System.out.println((char)('A'+7))` is _____

A154 The output of `System.out.println((int)('H'))` is _____

A155 The output of `System.out.print ('1');` is _____

A156 The output of `System.out.print ('1' + 1);` is _____

A157 The output of `System.out.print ((char)('1' + 16));` is _____

A158 The output of **System.out.print ((char) ('1' + 1));** is _____

A159 Given a sring s1 to be "Example", the value of **s1.length()** is _____

A160 Given a sring s1 to be "Example", the value of **s1.charAt(2)** is _____

A161 Given a sring s1 to be "In" and s2 to be "habit", the value of **s1.concat(s2)** is _____

A162 Given a sring s1 to be "Example" and s2 to be "example", the value of **s1.equals(s2)** is _____

A163 Given a sring s1 to be "Example" and s2 to be "EXAMPLE", the value of **s1.equalsIgnoreCase(s2)** is _____

A164 Given a sring s1 to be "antelope" and s2 to be "zebra", the value of **s1.compareTo(s2)** is _____

A165 Given a sring s1 to be "Antelope" and s2 to be "Zebra", the value of **s1.compareTo(s2)** is _____

A166 Given a sring s1 to be "Antelope" and s2 to be "ZEBRA", the value of **s1.compareTo(s2)** is _____

A167 Given a sring s1 to be "antelope" and s2 to be "ZEBRA", the value of **s1.compareTo(s2)** is _____

A168 Given a sring s1 to be "antelope" and s2 to be "Zebra", the value of **s1.compareTo(s2)** is _____

A169 Given a sring s1 to be "Antelope" and s2 to be "zebra", the value of **s1.compareTo(s2)** is _____

A170 Given a sring s1 to be "zebra" and s2 to be "ZEBRA", the value of **s1.compareToIgnoreCase(s2)** is _____

A171 For any string s1, the value of **s1.compareTo(s1)** is _____

A. Java Basics

A172 Given a sring s1 to be "venture", the value of **s1.startsWith("vent")** is _____

A173 Given a sring s1 to be "Inhabit", the value of **s1.endsWith("habit")** is _____

A174 For any string s1, the value of **s1.startsWith(s1)** is _____

A175 For any string s1, the value of **s1.startsWith(s1) && s1.endsWith(s1)** is _____

A176 For any string s1, the value of **s1.contains(s1)** is always _____

A177 For any strings s1 and s2, the value of **s1.concat(s2).contains(s1)** is always _____

A178 Given a sring s1 to be "Inhabit", the value of **s1.substring(0)** is _____

A179 Given a sring s1 to be "Inhabit", the value of **s1.substring(2)** is _____

A180 Given a sring s1 to be "Transportation", the statement using **substring** which returns "sport" is _____

A181 Given a string s to be "Java Programming", the statement to return "Program" is _____

A182 The value of **"HABITAT".substring(0, 5)** is _____

A183 The value of **"HABITAT".substring(4, 4)** is _____

A184 The value of **"HABITAT".substring(2, 5)** is _____

A185 The value of **"example".substring(2)** is _____

A186 The value of **"upper".toUpperCase()** is _____

A187 The value of **"uPpEr".toUpperCase()** is _____

Java Quiz Book

A188 The value of **"UPPER".toUpperCase()** is _____

A189 The value of **"lower".toLowerCase()** is _____

A190 The value of **"LoWeR".toLowerCase()** is _____

A191 The value of **"LOWER".toLowerCase()** is _____

A192 For any two strings s1 and s2, the value of the expression **s1.equals(s2) == s2.equals(s1)** is always _____

A193 For any two non-null strings s1 and s2, the value of the expression **s1.equals(s2) != s2.equals(s1)** is always _____

A194 The expression **"Desire"+2+"Learn"** evaluates to _____

A195 The statement to access the last character a string **str** is _____

A196 Given a string s to be "Java Programming", the value of **s.startsWith("Java")** is _____

A197 Given a string s to be "Java Programming", the value of **s.endsWith("ing")** is _____

A198 Given a string s to be "Java Programming", the value of **s.indexOf("Java")** is _____

A199 Given a string s to be "Java Programming", the value of **s.lastIndexOf("gram")** is _____

A200 Given a string s to be "Java Programming", the value of **s.charAt(9)** is _____

A201 Given a string s to be "Java Programming", the value of **str.indexOf('m')** is _____

A202 Given a string s to be "Java Programming", the value of **str.lastIndexOf('m')** is _____

A203 For any string s, the value of **s.startsWith(s)** is _____

A. Java Basics

A204 Given **String str = "Java C++ Python Ruby"**, the value of **str.matches("Python")** is _____

A205 Given **String str = "Java C++ Python Ruby"**, the value of **str.matches(".*Python.*")** is _____

A206 Given **String str = "Java C++ Python Ruby"**, the value of **str.replaceAll(" ", ", ", ")** is _____

A207 Given **String str = "Java, C++, Python; Ruby;"**, the value of **str.replaceAll("[,;]", "")** is _____

A208 Given char[] chArr = {'c','h','a','r','a','r','r','a','y'}, the statement to return a string from the content of charr is _____

A209 Given s is "Example", the statement to convert the string to an array of characters is _____

A210 Given s is " example ", the statement to remove leading and trailing spaces and return a new string "abc" is _____

A211 Given s1 is "Example", **s1.replace("Ex", "S")** returns _____

A212 Given s1 is "Sample", **s1.replace('a', 'i')** returns _____

A213 Given s1 is "Example", **s1.replace("Ex", "S").replace('a', 'i')** returns _____

A214 **String.valueOf(12.34).replace('.', '\')** returns _____

A215 Given the following declarations,

```
String s1 = "Java is fun";
String s2 = s1;
```

The value of **(s1 == s2)** is _____

A216 Given the following declarations,

```
String s1 = new String("Java is fun");
String s2 = new String("Java is fun");
```

The value of **(s1 == s2)** is _____

A217 Given the following declarations,

```
String s1 = new String("Java is fun");
String s2 = new String("Java is fun");
```

The value of **(s1.equals(s2))** is _____

A218 The output of **System.out.print ("1" + 1);** is ___

A219 The output of **System.out.print ("1" + 1 + 1);** is _____

A220 The output of **System.out.print ("1" + (1+1));** is _____

A221 Given int i = 3, j = 5, The output of **System out.println ("i + j is " + i + j)** is _____

A222 Given int i = 3, j = 5, The output of **System out.println ("i + j is " + (i + j))** is _____

A223 The output of **System.out.printf("%.2f", 1234.567)** is _____

A224 The output of **System.out.printf("%.3e", 1234.56)** is _____

A225 The output of **System.out.printf("%3d", 123456)** is _____

A226 The method to parse a string **s** to an int value is _____

A227 The method to parse a string **s** to a double value is _____

A. Java Basics

A228 The (decimal) value of `Integer.parseInt("1001", 2)` is
      _____

A229 The (decimal) value of `Integer.parseInt("1001", 10)` is _____

A230 The (decimal) value of `Integer.parseInt("1A", 16)` is
      _____

A231 The (decimal) value of `Integer.parseInt("359")` is
      _____

IOIOIOIOIOIOIOIOIOIOIOIOIOIOIOIOIOIOIOIOIOIOIOIOIOIOI

Essay-type Questions

A1 Give examples of syntax errors.

A2 Give examples of run-time errors.

A3 Give examples of logical errors

A4 What is the role of Java package?

A5 What are Java's primitive types?

A6 What was the first application for Java?

A7 Analyze the following code segment:

```
boolean a, b, c;
a = (5 < 7); b = (5 == 6);
c = (a < b);
```

A8 What is the output of the following code segment:

```
boolean a, b, c;
a = (5 < 7); b = (5 == 6);
c = (a == b);
System.out.format("%b %b %b\n", a, b, c);
```

A9 What is the output of the following code segment?

```
int n = 09;
System.out.println("n = " + n);
```

A10 What is the output of the following code segment?

```
int n = 99;
System.out.println("n = " + n);
```

A11 What is displayed by the following code segment?

```
int j = 0;
int i = ++j + j * 5;
System.out.println("i = " + i);
```

A12 What is displayed by the following code segment?

```
int j = 0;
int i = j++ + j * 5;
System.out.println("i = " + i);
```

A13 What is displayed by the following code segment?

```
int x = 1;
int y = x++ + x;
System.out.println("y is " + y);
```

A14 What is displayed by the following code segment?

```
int x = 1;
int y = ++x + x;
System.out.println("y is " + y);
```

A15 What is displayed by the following code segment?

```
int x = 1;
int y = x + x++;
System.out.println("y is " + y);
```

A16 Give examples of two operators that are not associative.

A. Java Basics

A17 What are the values of **a** and **n** after the execution of the following statements?

```
a = 2; n = a++; a = n++; n = a++;
```

A18 What are the values of **a** and **n** after the execution of the following statements?

```
a = 2; n = a++; a = ++n; n = a++;
```

A19 What are the values of **a** and **n** after the execution of the following statements?

```
a = 2; n = ++a; a = n++; n = ++a;
```

A20 What are the values of **a** and **n** after the execution of the following statements?

```
a = 2; n = ++a; a = ++n; n = ++a;
```

A21 What is the difference between coercion and cast?

A22 What is an overloaded operator?

A23 What is short-circuit evaluation?

A24 What is the output of the following code segment?
```
int n = 1000 * 1000 * 2000;
System.out.println("n = " + n);
```

A25 What is the output of the following code segment?
```
int n = 1000 * 1000 * 3000;
System.out.println("n = " + n);
```

A26 What is the output of the following code segment?
```
int n = 1000 * 1000 * 5000;
System.out.println("n = " + n);
```

IOIOIOIOIOIOIOIOIOIOIOIOIOIOIOIOIOIOIOIOIOIOIOIOIOI

Java Quiz Book

B. Control Structures

True/False Questions

B1 The 'for' loop is more powerful (in terms of controlling the flow of statement executions) than a 'while' loop. _____

B2 The **for** statement can be rewritten as a **while** loop. _____

B3 The **for**, **while**, and **do-while** loops do not have equivalent expressive power. _____

B4 Any of the **for**, **while**, and **do-while** loops can be transformed to the other having the same effect. _____

B5 The **do-while** loop always executes at least once. _____

B6 The **while** loop always executes at least once. _____

B7 The **for** loop always executes at least once. _____

B8 The index variable of a **for** loop cannot be of type double. _____

B9 **for (; ;);** is equivalent to **for (; true;);** _____

B10 The **switch** statement cannot be rewritten by using multiple **if-else** statements. _____

B11 The **break** statement inside an inner loop of a nested loop will pass control out of the all the nested loops to the statement outside of the outermost loop. _____

B12 The **break** statement inside a loop of a nested loop will pass control out of the entire loop. _____

B13 Assignment statements always produce side effects. _____

B14 An Iterator is a method. _____

B15 An Iterator can be used to loop through an array. _____

B16 All the three expressions of the 'for' statement are optional. _____

B17 The **exp1** in **for (exp1; exp2; exp3)** can be executed more than once. _____

B18 The **exp1** in **for (exp1; exp2; exp3)** cannot consist of multiple statements. _____

B19 The **exp3** in **for (exp1; exp2; exp3)** can consist of multiple statements. _____

B20 The **continue** control statement transfers control to the the outermost loop. _____

B21 The **continue** control statement transfers control to the start of the loop, ignoring further statements after the **continue**. _____

IOIOIOIOIOIOIOIOIOIOIOIOIOIOIOIOIOIOIOIOIOIOIOI

Fill-in the-blanks Questions

B1 Statement that is used to modify the order of execution is known as _____ statement.

B2 A control statement together with its associated block of statements is known as _____

B3 A loop whose number of iterations is determined by the numeric value of a variable is known as _____ loop.

B4 A loop whose number of iterations is determined by the Boolean condition of an expression is known as _____ loop.

B5 In a _____ loop control structure, the loop body is executed at least once.

B6 It is more natural to use the _____ loop when the number of iterations is known *a priori* (before hand).

B. Control Structures

B7 The statement block in a _____ (or _____) control structure is executed at least once.

B8 The _____ construct allows the selection of one of a number of statements or statement groups.

B9 _____ causes a (compound) statement to be executed zero or more times.

B10 The _____ control statement transfers control out of the smallest enclosing loop.

B11 The _____ control statement transfers control to the control mechanism of the smallest enclosing loop.

B12 An optional **else** clause in an **if–then** [**–else**] statement resulting in nested conditionals being ambiguous is known as _____ problem.

B13 The effect of the statement **for (; ;)** ; is _____

B14 The numbet of times the **STATEMENT BLOCK** is executed in the following loop is _____

```
for (int i=23; i <= 47; i++) {
    STATEMENT BLOCK
}
```

B15 The numbet of times the **STATEMENT BLOCK** is executed in the following loop is _____

```
for (int i=51; i > 36; i--) {
    STATEMENT BLOCK
}
```

IOIOIOIOIOIOIOIOIOIOIOIOIOIOIOIOIOIOIOIOIOIOIOIOIOIOI

Essay-type Questions

B1 Do the `while`, `do-while`, and `for` loops have different expressive powers?

B2 What is the difference between `break` and `continue` statements (of C-family) of languages?

B3 What are the two broad categories of control statements?

B4 Briefly describe the two categories of loops.

B5 When is it beneficial have the `if` and multiple `else if` statements in a certain order?

B6 The following loop was intended to compute $1/2 + 2/3 + 3/4 + \ldots + 99/100$. What is the error and what is a fix?.

```
double sum = 0;
for (int i = 1; i <= 99; i++) {
   sum += i / (i + 1);
}
```

B7 Do the following loops result in the same value of sum?

```
for (int i = 1; i <= 10; ++i) {
   sum += i;
}

for (int i = 1; i <= 10; i++) {
   sum += i;
}
```

B8 What is flaw with the following segment? How could it be overcome?

```
double sum = 0;
double n = 0;
while (n != 10.0) {
   n += 0.1;
   sum += n;
```

}

B9 The following code which was intended to print 1, 2, ... 10 has a flaw. What does it print? What is the correction required?

```
int i;
for (i = 1; i <= 10; i++);
    System.out.println(i);
```

B10 How many times does the **while** loop execute in the following code segment?

```
int x = 0;
while (x < 5)
   x++;
```

B11 How many times does the **while** loop execute in the following code segment?

```
int x = 10;
while (x < 5)
   x++;
```

B12 How many times does the **while** loop execute, and what will be the value of **sum** after the loop has finished?

```
double n = 0, sum = 0;
while (n <= 1.0) {
   n += 0.1;
   sum += n;
}
```

B13 Does the following code segment result in an infinite loop?

```
int x = 0;
while (x >= 0)
   x++;
```

B14 What is the output of the following code segment?

```
int i=0, x = 0;
while (x >= 0) {
```

```
    x++;
    i++;
}
System.out.println("i=" + (i-1) + " x=" + x);
```

B15 What is the output of the following code segment?

```
int x = 0;
while (x < 5)
   x++;
System.out.println("x = " + x);
```

B16 Rewrite the following code segment using a **for** loop with the same effect.

```
int x = 0;
while (x < 5)
   x++;
System.out.println("x = " + x);
```

B17 Convert the following 'for' loop to 'while' loop.

```
for (int i=low; i <= high; i++) {
   STATEMENT BLOCK
}
```

B18 Convert the following 'while' loop to 'do-while' loop, assuming low ≤ high.

```
int i=low;
while (i <= high) {
   STATEMENT BLOCK
   i++;
}
```

B19 What is the output of the following code segment?

```
double sum = 0;
while (sum != 10)
   sum += 0.1;
System.out.println(sum);
```

B20 What is the output of the following code segment?

```
    double sum = 0;
    while (sum < 10)
       sum += 0.1;
    System.out.println(sum);
```

B21 What is the output of the following code segment?

```
    double sum = 0, incr = 0.01;
    for (int i=1; i<=100; i++)
       sum += incr;
    System.out.println(sum);
```

B22 What is the output of the following code segment?

```
    double sum = 0, incr = 0;
    for (int i=1; i<=100; i++){
       incr += 0.01;
       sum += incr;
    }
    System.out.println(sum);
```

B23 What is the output of the following code segment?

```
    double sum = 0, decr = 1;
    for (int i=1; i<=100; i++){
       sum += decr;
       decr -= 0.01;
    }
    System.out.println(sum);
```

B24 What is the output of the following code segment?

```
double sum = 0, incr = 0, decr = 1.0;
for (int i=1; i<=50; i++){
  incr += 0.01;
  sum = sum + incr + decr;
  decr -= 0.01;
}
System.out.println(incr);
System.out.println(sum);
```

B25 What error does the following code segment have?

```
int x;
double d = 1.5;

switch (d) {
  case 1.0: x = 1;
  case 1.5: x = 2;
  case 2.0: x = 3;
}
```

B26 What error does the following code segment have?

```
int x;
double d = 1.5;

switch ((int)d) {
  case (int)1.0: x = 1;
  case (int)1.5: x = 2;
  case (int)2.0: x = 3;
}
```

B27 What error does the following code segment have, if any?

```
int x;
double d = 1.5;

switch ((int)d) {
  case (int)1.5: x = 1;
  case (int)2.5: x = 2;
  case (int)3.5: x = 3;
}
```

B28 What is the output of the following program?

```
public class Main {

  public static void main(String[] args) {
    int i, j;
    for (i=1; i<=3; i++) {
      for (j=1; j<=3; j++) {
        if ((i+j) % 4 == 0) {
          System.out.println("\nIteration (" + i + "," + j
  + ") is not done");
          break;
        }
```

```
            else
                System.out.print("("+ i + ", " + j + ") is done
    ");
        }
        System.out.println();
      }
    }
}
```

B29   What is the output of the following program?

```
public class Main
{
  public static void main(String[] args) {
    int i, j;
    for (i=1; i<=3; i++) {
      for (j=1; j<=3; j++) {
        if ((i+j) % 4 == 0) {
          System.out.println("\nIteration (" + i + "," + j +
    ") is not done");
          continue;
        }
        else
          System.out.print("("+ i + ", " + j + ") is done ");
      }
      System.out.println();
    }
  }
}
```

B30   What is the output of the following program?

```
public class Main {
  public static void main(String[] args) {
    for (int i = 0; i < 10; i++){
      for (int j = 0; j < 10; j++){
        if ((i+j) % 3 == 0)
          break;
        System.out.print("(" + i + "," + j + ") ");
      }
      System.out.println();
    }
  }
}
```

IOIOIOIOIOIOIOIOIOIOIOIOIOIOIOIOIOIOIOIOIOIOIOIOIOIOIOIOIOI

C. Arrays and Arraylists

True/False Questions

C1 An array cannot be passed as argument to a method. _____

C2 When an array is passed to a method, the method receives a copy of the array. _____

C3 The parameter passing mechanisms of arrays and array elements are the same. _____

C4 Arrays cannot be returned from methods. _____

C5 Multidimensioal arrays cannot be returned from methods. _____

C6 The elements of an array of primitive type can be heterogeneous. _____

C7 The elements of an array for instances of a class should be instances of that same class. _____

C8 When an array is created using the 'new' statement, the element values are automatically initialized to 0. _____

C9 The size of an array can be changed after it is created. _____

C10 The datatype of an array must be specified at the time of declaration. _____

C11 An array of a generic type can be declared. _____

C12 The datatype of an array could be changed during run time. _____

C13 An array is an instance of a class. _____

C14 An ArrayList is an instance of a class. _____

C15 The size of an ArrayList can change (shrink/grow) after its creation. _____

C. Arrays and Arraylists

C16 Methods for common operations on ArrayList are available via APIs. _____

C17 The elements of an ArrayList can be heterogeneous. _____

C18 An ArrayList can contain elements of primitive (ex. int, double) types. _____

C19 An ArrayList can be declared to be of 'generic' type. _____

C20 Given the declaration `int i1`, the value of `i1` is a reference to an integer. _____

C21 Given the declaration `Integer i2`, the value of `i2` is a an integer. _____

C22 Given the declaration `int[] i3`, the value of `i3` is `null`. _____

C23 Given the declaration `int[] i3 = new int[3]`, the value of `i3` is `null`. _____

C24 Given the declaration `int[] i4 = {1, 2, 3}`, the value of `i4` is not `null`. _____

IOIOIOIOIOIOIOIOIOIOIOIOIOIOIOIOIOIOIOIOIOIOIOIOIOI

Fill-in the-blanks Questions

C1 When an array is returned from a method, _____ is returned.

C2 When an array is passed to a method, the method receives _____

C3 The parameter passing mechanism used, when arrays are passed as arguments to methods, is _____

C4 The parameter passing mechanism used, when array elements are passed as arguments to methods, is _____

C5   The parameter passing mechanism used, when primitive types are passed as arguments to methods, is _____

C6   The parameter passing mechanism used, when objects are passed as arguments to methods, is _____

C7   In Java, arrays are always allocated on _____

C8   Given int[] a = {12, 9, 5, 14, 25}, a.length is _____

C9   Given int[] a = {12, 9, 5, 14, 25}, element 14 is accessed using _____

C10 Given double[][] x = new double[4][5], x.length is _____

C11 Given double[][] x = new double[4][5], x[2].length is _____

C12 The number of objects created by the following code is _____

```
double[] a = new double[10];
double[] b;
b = a;
```

C13 Given the following code segment, the number of elements of x is _____

```
boolean[][] x = new boolean[3][];
x[0] = new boolean[1]; x[1] = new boolean[2];
x[2] = new boolean[3];
```

C14 Given `int[][] x = {{1, 2}, {3, 4}, {5, 6}, {7, 8}}`, `x.length` is 4 and `x[0].length` is _____

C15 Given int[][] x = {{1}, {2, 3}, {4, 5, 6}}, the values of `x.length`, `x[0].length`, `x[1].length`, and `x[2].length` are ____, ____, ____, and ____

C16 Given the declaration `int i1`, the data type of `i1` is _____

C17 Given the declaration `int[]` `i2`, the data type of `i2` is _____

C18 Given the declaration `int[] i2`, the value of `i2` is _____

C. Arrays and Arraylists

C19 Given the declaration `int[] i3 = new int[3]`, the value of `i3` is _____

C20 Given the declaration `int[] i3 = new int[3]`, the values of the elements of the array of 3 integers referenced by `i3` are _____

C21 A statement to remove all elements in an ArrayList list is _____

C22 Assuming ArrayList pcolor of type String is [Red, Blue], a statement to make it [Red, Green, Blue] is _____

C23 Assuming ArrayList pcolor of type String is [Red, Green, Cyan, Blue], a statement to make it [Red, Green, Blue] is _____ or _____

C24 A statement to return the last element in an ArrayList list is _____

C25 Assuming ArrayList list of type Integer is [10, 11, 12], a statement to add 13 as the new element at the end of the list is _____

C26 Given an ArrayList list contains {"red", "green", "blue", "red", "yellow", "blue"}, the list after list.remove("red") would be _____

IOIOIOIOIOIOIOIOIOIOIOIOIOIOIOIOIOIOIOIOIOIOIOIOIOIOI

Essay-type Questions

C1 What is the output of the following code segment?

```
int[] a = new int[5];
int i;
for (i = 0; i < a.length; i++)
   a[i] = i+1;
System.out.print(a[i] + " ");
```

C2 What is the output of the following code segment?

```java
int[] a = new int[5];
int i;
for (i = 0; i < a.length; i++) {
    a[i] = i+1;
    System.out.print(a[i] + " ");
}
```

C3 What is the output of the following code segment?

```java
int[] list = {1, 2, 3, 4, 5};
for (int i = list.length - 2; i >= 0; i--) {
    list[i+1] = list[i];
}
for (int e: list)
    System.out.print(e + " ");
```

C4 What is the output of the following code segment?

```java
int[] list = {1, 2, 3, 4, 5};
for (int i = list.length - 1; i > 0; i--) {
    list[i-1] = list[i];
}
for (int e: list)
    System.out.print(e + " ");
```

C5 What is the output of the following code?

```java
int[] list = {1, 2, 3, 4, 5};
for (int i = 1; i < list.length; i++) {
    list[i-1] = list[i];
}
for (int e: list)
    System.out.print(e + " ");
```

C6 What is output of the following code segment?

```java
public class Base {
    public static void main(String[] args) {
        int x = 25, y = 025;
        System.out.println("x = " + x + " y = " + y);
    }
}
```

C7 What is the output of the following code segment?

```
final int i=10;
i=12;
System.out.println (i);
```

C8 What is the output of the following code segment?

```
final int[] a = {1, 2, 6, 4, 5};
System.out.println (a[2]);
a[2] = 3;
System.out.println (a[2]);
```

C9 What is the output of the following code segment?

```
int[] a = {1, 2, 3, 4, 5};
System.out.println (a[2]);
a = new int[5];
System.out.println (a[2]);
```

C10 What is the output of the following code segment?

```
final int[] a = {1, 2, 3, 4, 5};
System.out.println (a[2]);
a = new int[5];
```

C11 What is the output of the following code segment?

```
int[] x = {1, 2, 3, 4, 5};
int[] y = x;
x = new int[]{5, 6, 7, 8, 9};
for (int i = 0; i < y.length; i++)
    System.out.print (y[i] + " ");
```

C12 What is the output of the following code segment?

```
int[] x = {1, 2, 3, 4, 5};
int[] y = x;
x[0]=5; x[1]=6; x[2]=7; x[3]=8; x[4]=9;
for (int i = 0; i < y.length; i++)
    System.out.print (y[i] + " ");
```

C13 What is the output of the following code segment?

```
    int[] x = {1, 2, 3, 4, 5};
    int[] y = x;
    y[0]=5; y[1]=6; y[2]=7; y[3]=8; y[4]=9;
    for (int i = 0; i < x.length; i++)
        System.out.print(x[i] + " ");
```

C14 What is the output of the following code segment?

```
int[] x = {1, 2, 3, 4, 5}, y = {6, 7, 8, 9};
int[] z = new int[9];
System.arraycopy(y, 0, z, 0, y.length);
System.arraycopy(x, 0, z, 4, x.length);
for (int i = 0; i < z.length; i++)
  System.out.print(z[i] + " ");
```

C15 What is the output of the following program?

```
public class Test {
  public static void main(String[] args) {
    int[] x = {1, 2, 3, 4, 5};
    increment(x);
    int[] y = {1, 2, 3, 4, 5};
    increment(y[0]); increment(y[1]);
    increment(y[2]); increment(y[3]);
    increment(y[4]);

    for (int i=0; i<x.length; i++)
      System.out.print(x[i] + " ");
    System.out.println();
    for (int i=0; i<y.length; i++)
      System.out.print(y[i] + " ");
  }
  public static void increment(int[] a) {
    for (int i = 0; i < a.length; i++)
      a[i]++;
  }
  public static void increment(int a) {
    a++;
  }
}
```

C16 What is the output of the following code segment?

44

C. Arrays and Arraylists

```
ArrayList<String> list = new ArrayList<String>();
String s1 = new String("Example");
String s2 = new String("Example");
list.add(s1);
list.add(s2);
System.out.println(list.get(0) == list.get(1));
System.out.println (list.get(0).equals(list.get(1)));
```

C17 What is the output of the following code segment?

```
ArrayList<String>list =
      new ArrayList<String>();
list.add(0,"red");list.add(1,"green");
list.add(2,"blue");list.add(3,"red");
for (int i = 0; i < list.size(); i++)
  System.out.print(list.get(i) + " ");
list.remove("red");
for (int i = 0; i < list.size(); i++)
  System.out.print(list.get(i) + " ");
```

C18 What is the output of the following code segment?

```
ArrayList<Integer>list =
      new ArrayList<Integer >();
for (int i = 0; i < list.size(); i++)
  list.add(i);
 System.out.println(list);
```

C19 Given an ArrayList `list` contains
[apple, pear, pear, banana, pear, pear, orange, pear, pear]
what is the list after executing the following code segment?

```
String fruit = "pear";
  for (int i = 0; i < list.size(); i++)
     if (list.get(i).equals(fruit))
        list.remove(fruit);
```

C20 Given an ArrayList `list` contains
[apple, pear, pear, banana, pear, pear, orange, pear, pear]
what is the list after executing the following code segment?

```
String fruit = "pear";
  for (int i = 0; i < list.size(); i++)
```

```
        if (list.get(i).equals(fruit)) {
          list.remove(fruit);
          i--;
        }
```

C21 Given an ArrayList **list** contains
[apple, pear, pear, banana, pear, pear, orange, pear, pear]
what is the list after executing the following code segment?

```
String fruit = "pear";
  for (int i = list.size()-1; i >= 0; i++)
    if (list.get(i).equals(fruit))
      list.remove(fruit);
```

C22 What is the output from the following code segment?

```
ArrayList<String> list1 = new ArrayList<String>();
list1.add("C++");
list1.add("Java");
java.util.ArrayList<String> list2 = list1;
list2.add("Python");
list2.add("Ruby");
System.out.println(list1);
System.out.println(list2);
```

C23 What is the output of the following code?

```
class Test<E> {
  E obj;
  Test(E obj) { this.obj = obj; }
  public E getObject()  { return this.obj; }
}

class Main {
  public static void main (String[] args) {
    Test <Integer> intObj = new Test<Integer>(25);
    System.out.println(intObj.getObject());
    Test <String> strObj = new Test<String>("Test of ArrayList");
    System.out.println(strObj.getObject());
  }
}
```

C24 What is the output of the following code?

C. Arrays and Arraylists

```java
class Test {
  static <T> void genericDisplay (T element){
    System.out.println(element.getClass().getName() + " "
      = " + element);
  }
  public static void main(String[] args) {
    genericDisplay(10);
    genericDisplay("Java is fun");
    genericDisplay(1.0);
  }
}
```

C25 What is the output of the following program? What does the program do in general?

```java
public class Test {
  public static void main(String[] args) {
    int[][] matrix = {{10, 4, 10, 18}, {12, 7, 2,
    11}};
    int x = matrix[0][0];
    for (int[] row : matrix)
      for (int e : row)
        if (x > e)
          x = e;
    System.out.print(x);
  }
}
```

C26 What is the output of the following program? What does the program do in general?

```java
public class Test {
  public static void main(String[] args) {
    int[][] matrix = {{12, 7, 5, 10}, {9, 16, 14,
    2}};
    for (int row = 0; row < matrix.length; row++)
    {
      System.out.print(max(matrix[row]) + " ");
    }
  }

  public static int max(int[] vec) {
    int e = vec[0];
    for (int i = 1; i < vec.length; i++)
```

```
      if (e < vec[i])
         e = vec[i];
   return e;
  }
}
```

IOIOIOIOIOIOIOIOIOIOIOIOIOIOIOIOIOIOIOIOIOIOIOIOIOI

D. Classes, Objects, Methods

True/False Questions

D1   The variables declared within a method's body can be used outside of the method. _____

D2   Explicit use of **this** reference is made to access a field that is shadowed by a local variable. _____

D3   The collection interfaces declare the operations that can be performed on each type of collection. _____

D4   A List is an ordered Collection. _____

D5   In Java, there are no standalone methods (subprograms). _____

D6   If the method is declared 'final', static binding occurs. _____

D7   When an argument is passed by reference, the called method can access the argument's value in the caller directly and modify that data. _____

D8   An array element used as an argument to a method is treated as call by reference. _____

D9   The private members of a class are directly accessible to the client of a class. _____

D10 An expression cannot be used as an argument to a method. _____

D11 The parameter list in the method header and the arguments in the method call must agree in number, order, and type. _____

D12 A method being called must appear after it its definition in the class. _____

D13 A 'static' method can call only other 'static' methods of the same class directly. _____

D14 The generic parameters of Java can be primitive types. _____

D15   Objects are accessed through reference variables. _____

D16   All objects (class instances) are heap dynamic. _____

D17   Redeclaring a method parameter as a local variable in the method's body causes a compilation error. _____

D18   Absence of a return statement in a method that should return a value causes runtime error. _____

D19   An overloaded method has the same name as another method, but different parameters (by number, types or order of the types). _____

D20   Method calls can be distinguished by return type. _____

D21   When a method or variable has package access, no access specifier need be specified. _____

D22   Java supports nesting of classes. _____

D23   Java does not (directly) support multiple inheritance. _____

D24   All local variables in the methods of Java are stack-dynamic. _____

D25   The variables declared within a method's body can be used outside of the method. _____

D26   An instance method can access instance variables and instance methods directly. _____

D27   An instance method cannot access static variables and static methods directly. _____

D28   A static method can access static variables and static methods directly. _____

D29   A static method can call instance methods directly. _____

D30   Each obect of a class has its own instance method in memory. _____

D31   The private modifier is used to encapsulate data fields. _____

D. Classes, Objects, Methods

D32 The current method executing is always the method whose activation record is at the top of the stack. _____

D33 The contents of an immutable object cannot be modified. _____

D34 All members of an immutable object must be private. _____

D35 All members of an immutable object must be of primitive types. _____

D36 An immutable object contains no mutator methods. _____

D37 A constructor may be static. _____

D38 A constructor may never be private. _____

D39 A constructor may invoke a static method. _____

D40 A constructor may invoke an overloaded constructor. _____

D41 A constructor which is private can be used to create (instances) objects of the class. _____

D42 To override a method, the method must be defined in the subclass using the same signature and compatible return type as in its superclass. _____

D43 Overloading a method is to provide more than one method with the same name but with different signatures to distinguish them. _____

D44 Overloaded methods always have the same name. _____

D45 It is a compile error if two methods differ only in return type in the same class. _____

D46 A private method can be overridden. _____

D47 A static method cannot be overridden. _____

D48 A method can be overloaded in the same class. _____

D49 A method can be overridden in the same class. _____

D50   Overloaded methods must have the same signature. _____

D51   Overloaded methods must have different return types. _____

D52   Overloaded methods must have the same return types. _____

D53   If a method overrides another method, these two methods must have the same signature. _____

D54   If a method overrides another method, these two methods could have different types. _____

D55   A method in a subclass can override *any* method in the superclass. _____

D56   An instance of a subclass can be passed to a parameter of its superclass type. _____

D57   The matching method based on the type, number, and order of the parameters is determined at run time. _____

D58   A method may not be implemented in several subclasses. _____

D59   The Java Virtual Machine dynamically binds the implementation of the method at runtime. _____

D60   Dynamic binding can apply to static methods. _____

D61   Dynamic binding cannot apply to instance methods. _____

D62   Static methods are bound at compile time. _____

D63   A class should always contain a no-arg constructor. _____

D64   In Java's Math class, all methods are static. _____

D65   The constructors must always be public. _____

D66   The constructors of a class may be protected. _____

D67   A reference variable is an object. _____

D68   A data field in a class can only be of a primitive type. _____

D. Classes, Objects, Methods

D69 A data field in a class can be of an object type. _____

D70 An abstract class will not have constructors. _____

D71 The constructors in an abstract class are of type 'protected'. _____

D72 The constructors in an abstract class are private. _____

D73 A 'final' abstract class may be declared. _____

D74 An interface may contain constructors. _____

D75 Actual data is stored in primitive variables. _____

D76 Primitive types are not reference types. _____

D77 Array types are reference types. _____

D78 Actual data is sometimes stored in a reference variable. _____

D79 A default constructor is automatically provided if no constructors are explicitly declared in the class. _____

D80 At least one constructor must always be defined explicitly for a class. _____

D81 Every class provides a default constructor. _____

D82 The default constructor is a no-arg constructor. _____

D83 Multiple constructors cannot be defined in a class. _____

D84 Constructors do not have a return type (including void). _____

D85 Constructors must have the same name as the class itself. _____

D86 **final class A {   } cannot be extended.** _____

D87 An instance of a subclass cannot be passed as a parameter of its superclass type. _____

D88 Cast is not required for widening conversion. _____

D89   An object cannot be treated as a type of its superclass or of any ancestor class. _____

D90   Treating an object as a type of its subclass requires a cast. _____

D91   A method may be implemented in several subclasses. _____

D92   Dynamic binding can apply to instance methods, _____

D93   When a method with an object argument is invoked, a copy of the object is passed. _____

D94   When a method with an object argument is invoked, the content of the object is passed. _____

D95   A public class can be accessed by a class in a different package. _____

D96   A protected method cannot be accessed by a subclass in a different package. _____

D97   A method with no visibility modifier cannot be accessed by a class in a different package. _____

D98   The value of a private instance variable cannot be changed inside the class definition. _____

D99   A private method cannot be accessed by a class in a different package. _____

D100 A private method cannot be invoked outside the class where it is defined. _____

D101 A derived class can define a method that invokes a private method of its base class. _____

D102 A method in a derived class can use an inherited public method of its base class that invokes a private method of the base class. _____

D103 If an interface compiles with warnings, a .class file is not created for the interface. _____

D. Classes, Objects, Methods

D104 If a class definition does not compile without errors, a .class file is not created for the class. _____

D105 If a class definition compiles with warnings, a .class file is not created for the class. _____

D106 A local variable and a formal parameter in a method cannot have the same name. _____

D107 Two variables with the same name cannot be declared in different methods in a class. _____

D108 A non-static method can be called from a static method. _____

D109 A static method can be accessed from a non-static method. _____

D110 The static method exists even before an object of a defined class is created. _____

D111 More than one variable-length parameter may be specified in a method. _____

D112 The variable-length parameter specified in a method must be the last parameter. _____

D113 The return type of a method could be a variable-length parameter. _____

D114 Local variables are not initialized. _____

D115 Methods cannot be overloaded based on the return types. _____

D116 Methods having the same signature cannot be overloaded. _____

D117 More than one variable-length parameter may be specified in a method. _____

D118 The variable-length parameter of a method must be the last parameter. _____

D119 The return type of a method can be a variable-length parameter. _____

D120 The 'main' method is always a 'void' method. _____

D121 A class cannot have a 'main' method if it is not run as a program. _____

D122 There cannot be statements after the 'return' statement in a method. _____

D123 Execution of the return statement ends a method's execution. _____

D124 A 'void' method may or may not have a return statement. _____

D125 A method cannot return more than one value. _____

D126 The scope of a variable declared in a class can extend beyond the class definition. _____

D127 The names of the formal parameters in a method definition, and names of the arguments in the method invocation must be the same. _____

D128 The types of the formal parameters in a method definition, and types of the arguments in the method invocation must be the same. _____

D129 The arguments passed in a method invocation can only be variables. _____

D130 Multiple values cannot be returned by a method. _____

D131 A class can be instantiated when the 'public' modifier is used on the constructor. _____

D132 A class cannot be instantiated when the 'static' modifier is used on the constructor. _____

D133 All Java methods must be contained in some class. _____

D134 The **main** method is always static. _____

D135 A variable of type **double** can be assigned an **int** variable (or an expression returning **int**) without cast. _____

D. Classes, Objects, Methods

D136 A variable of type **int** can be assigned a **double** variable (or an expression returning **double**) without cast. _____

D137 The cast of a floating point value (literal, variable, or expression) to an integer will round the value. _____

D138 Static variables must be declared with the private access specifier. _____

D139 The constructor method may have a return type. _____

D140 The default constructor has no argiments. _____

D141 A class definition must have a constructor definition. _____

D142 In the method calls (invocations), primitive types are passed by value. _____

D143 In the method calls (invocations), object references are passed by reference. _____

D144 In case of overloaded methods, the methods need not belong to the same class. _____

D145 The decision about the correct method to call among the overloaded methods is done at run time. _____

D146 Two or more methods with the same signatures but different return types can be overloaded. _____

D147 Two or more methods with different signatures but the return types cannot be overloaded. _____

D148 The default constructor could have arguments for initialization. _____

D149 Java automatically defines a default constructor when a class does not define any constructor methods. _____

D150 When none of the constructors defined in a class is a default constructor, Java automatically defines a default constructor. _____

D151 Constructor methods cannot be overloaded. _____

D152 A constructor cannot call another constructor. _____

D153 Instances can be created using the constructor of the abstract class. _____

D154 An abstract class cannot be extended. _____

D155 A subclass of a non-abstract superclass cannot be abstract. _____

D156 A subclass can override a concrete method in a superclass to declare it abstract. _____

D157 An abstract class cannot be used as a data type. _____

D158 A class that contains abstract methods must be abstract. _____

D159 An abstract class need not contain abstract methods. _____

D160 An abstract method cannot be contained in a nonabstract class. _____

D161 An abstract class must contain at least one abstract method. _____

D162 An abstract class cannot have nonabstract methods. _____

D163 A class containing at least one abstract method must be declared abstract. _____

D164 A data field may be declared abstract. _____

D165 The subclass of an abstract class cannot itself be an abstract class. _____

D166 Instances cannot be created for an abstract class. _____

D167 A class declared to be final has no subclasses. _____

D168 A 'final' class may contain any abstract methods. _____

D169 A class can be both 'abstract' and 'final'. _____

D. Classes, Objects, Methods

D170 A static method may reference an instance variable. _____

D171 A static method can directly call another static method. _____

D172 A static method cannot be invoked within a non-static method. _____

D173 A non-static method can never be invoked within a static method. _____

D174 A non-static method can reference any variable within its class. _____

D175 A class cannot contain both instance variables and static methods. _____

D176 A class can contain both static and non-static methods. _____

D177 A static variable can be referenced by name within the definition of a static method without class name and 'dot'. _____

D178 An instance variable can be referenced by name within the definition of a static method. _____

D179 Instance variables cannot be defined within an enumeration. _____

D180 Constructors and mehods cannot be defined within an enumeration. _____

D181 Given Car is a class and the declaration Car c1, c1 is an object of type Car. _____

D182 Given Car is a class and the declaration Car c1, the value of c1 is a reference to an object of type Car. _____

D183 Given Car is a class, the declaration required to make the value of c1 to be a reference to an object of type Car is _____

D184 A class need not have a parent class. _____

D185 Objects can be either stack dynamic or heap dynamic. _____

D186 Method bindings can only be dynamic. _____

Java Quiz Book

D187 The constructor methods must always be public. _____

D188 The methods or data members declared as *protected* are accessible within same package but not in sub classes in different package. _____

D189 The static method exists even before an object of a defined class is created. _____

D190 More than one variable-length parameter may be specified in a method. _____

D191 A variable-length parameter specified in a method must be the last parameter. _____

D192 The return type of a method could be a variable-length parameter. _____

D193 A non-static method can be called from a static method. _____

D194 A static method can be accessed from a non-static method. _____

D195 A static method may call an instance method. _____

D196 A static method may not access a private instance variable. _____

D197 Local variables are not initialized. _____

D198 Two methods can have the same name but different parameter types. _____

D199 Only public methods are made use of in encapsulation. _____

D200 Given 'Car' is a class, after the declaration **Car c1**, **c1** is an object of type 'Car'. _____

D201 Given 'Car' is a class, after the declaration **Car c1**, **c1** is a valid reference to an object of type 'Car'. _____

D202 Given 'Car' is a class, after the declaration **Car c1 = new Car()**, **c1** is an object of type 'Car'. _____

D. Classes, Objects, Methods

D203 Given 'Car' is a class, after the declaration **Car c1 = new Car()**, **c1** is a valid reference to an object of type 'Car'. _____

D204 Given a class Car and the declaration Car[] cars = new Car[1000], cars is an array of 1000 objects of type Car. _____

D205 Given a class Car and the declaration Car[] cars = new Car[1000], cars is reference to an array of 1000 objects of type Car. _____

D206 Given a class Car and the declaration Car[] cars = new Car[1000], cars is reference to an array of 1000 references to objects of type Car. _____

D207 A method parameter can be redeclared as a local variable in the method's body. _____

D208 Missing return statement in a method that should return a value results in a compilation error. _____

D209 Overloaded methods have the same name, but different parameters (by number, types or order of the types). _____

D210 Overloaded method calls can be distinguished by return type. _____

D211 Arrays cannot be passed as arguments to methods – each array element must be passed to the method separately. _____

D212 Every Java application is composed of at least one public class declaration. _____

D213 Two variables with the same name can be declared in different methods in the same class. _____

D214 A local variable of a method could have the same name as that of a formal parameter of the method. _____

D215 Two variables with the same name cannot be declared in a block. _____

D216 The class Integer is not immutable. _____

D217 The class BigInteger is immutable. _____

Java Quiz Book

D218 The class BigDecimal is immutable. _____

D219 Objects of String class are immutable. _____

D220 Given two reference variables s1 and s2, if s1 == s2 is true, s1.equals(s2) may not be true. _____

D221 Given two reference variables s1 and s2, if s1.equals(s2) is true, s1 == s2 may not be true. _____

D222 Given the following declarations, the value of s1 == s2 is _____
```
String s1 = "Apple";
String s2 = "Apple";
```

D223 Given the following declarations, the value of s1 == s2 is _____
```
String s1 = "Apple";
String s2 = new String ("Apple");
```

D224 Given the following declarations, the value of s1.equals (s2) is _____

```
String s1 = "Apple";
String s2 = new String ("Apple");
```

D225 An abstract method can be defined in a non-abstract class. _____

D226 An abstract class cannot define both abstract methods and non-abstract methods. _____

D227 The derived class of an abstract base class must be an abstract class. _____

D228 The child of an abstract parent class that does not override all of the parent's abstract methods must be declared to be abstract. _____

D229 A child class can extend a parent or implement an interface, but cannot do both. _____

D230 An interface cannot contain a method that returns a value. _____

D231 An interface cannot extend another interface. _____

D232 An interface can have the 'private' access modifier. _____

D. Classes, Objects, Methods

D233 There is no limit on the number of objects created in a program. _____

D234 One object named 'a' is created by the statement `Object a;` _____

D235 Only one object is created by the following statements. _____

```
Object a = new Object;
Object b = a;
```

D236 The access modifier must always be specified for class members. _____

D237 The return value of a method must be exactly the same type as the return type. _____

D238 Private methods are final. _____

D239 Protected methods are final. _____

D240 Class members must be assigned a value to before they are accessed. _____

D241 Accessing an uninitialized local variable of a method results in compile error. _____

IOIOIOIOIOIOIOIOIOIOIOIOIOIOIOIOIOIOIOIOIOIOIOIOIOI

Fill-in the-blanks Questions

D1 The signature of a method consists of _____ and _____

D2 All Java applications must have a method named _____ where the execution starts.

D3 A class instance creation is done using the _____ keyword.

D4 More than one reference variable referring to the same object, is known as _____

63

D5 The general order of declarations/descriptions in a class definition are _____, _____, and _____

D6 When the access modifier is not specified for a class member, it would have _____ modifier.

D7 Calling a method of another object requires the _____ separator.

D8 The values the method call passes to the method for the parameters are called _____

D9 Attributes of a class are also known as _____

D10 An instance of a class is known as _____

D11 An object is created by invoking a special method known as _____

D12 When an object is created, constructors are invoked using the _____ operator.

D13 The access specifiers keywords are _____, _____, and _____

D14 A member of a class with _____ specifiers is accessible only within the class itself.

D15 A member of a class with _____ specifiers is accessible anywhere the containing class is accessible.

D16 A member of a class with _____ specifiers is not accessible to another class in a different package, but is accessible to any of its subclass in any package.

D17 A member of a class with _____ access is accessible to code within all classes that are defined in the same package, but inaccessible outside of the package.

D18 The modifiers in order of increasing visibility are _____, _____, _____, and _____

D19 An instance variable with access specifier _____ is not accessible outside of the class definition.

D. Classes, Objects, Methods

D20 In Java, instance variables that are visible only in the class where they are defined are called _____

D21 In Java, instance variables that are visible everywhere are specified with access qualifier _____

D22 Instance variables that are visible in the class where they are defined and in all of the subclasses are specified with access qualifier _____

D23 A method that is associated with a specific class is known as _____ method.

D24 A method that is associated with an object of a class is known as _____ or _____ method.

D25 A simple but incomplete version of a method used while testing, is known as a _____

D26 The methods that allow a client of a class to assign values to a private instance variable, are known as _____ methods.

D27 The number of *parameters* of a default constructor is _____

D28 The _____ class variables are shared by all objects of a class.

D29 The _____ members cannot be accessed outside of the class.

D30 The classes and interfaces which comprise the collections framework are members of package _____

D31 A method should use the class's *set* and *get* methods to access the class's _____ data.

D32 A variable defined inside a method is referred to as _____

D33 A class cannot be instantiated when the _____ modifier is used on the constructor.

D34 The decision about the correct method to call, among the overloaded methods, is done by examining the method's _____

D35 The decision about the correct method to call among the overloaded methods is done at _____ time.

D36 _____ variables are shared by all objects of a class.

D37 A _____ method is invoked using a class name instead of an object name.

D38 Variables that are shared by every instances of a class are known as _____.

D39 All Java objects (class instances) are allocated on the _____.

D40 A method that is associated with an individual object is known as _____.

D41 The keyword used for referring to the current object in a method or constructor is _____.

D42 A constructor invokes its _____ constructor by default, if a constructor does not invoke an overloaded constructor or its superclass's constructor.

D43 A method that is defined to be _____ cannot be overridden in any descendant class.

D44 When a method with an object argument is invoked, _____ is passed.

D45 The keyword _____ is required to declare a class.

D46 Static methods are bound at _____ time.

D47 A matching method based on parameter type, number of parameters, and order of the parameters is found at _____ time.

D48 The arguments passed in a method invocation must match the formal parameters in the method definition in their _____, _____, and _____.

D49 A method that is associated with a specific class is known as _____ method.

D50 A method that is associated with an object of a class is known as _____ (or _____) method.

D. Classes, Objects, Methods

D51 The method name and parameter list, together are known as, the method's _____

D52 In a method's parameter list, a data type followed by a(n) _____ indicates that the method receives a variable number of arguments of that data type.

D53 Array passed as argument to a method uses the _____ parameter passing mechanism.

D54 An array element passed as argument to a method uses the _____ parameter passing mechanism.

D55 Using the _____ parameter passing, the called method can access the argument's value and can modify it.

D56 The operator to create an object, which is a class instance, is _____

D57 Calling a method of another object requires the _____

D58 At the time of method invocation (call), the variables/expressions used in place of the formal parameters of the method definition are known as _____

D59 The attributes of a class are known as _____

D60 The method that does not return any value has return type _____

D61 The signature of a method consists of _____ and _____

D62 All Java programs must have a method named _____

D63 The local variables and arguments of a method are stored the area of memory called _____

D64 A variable whose value is shared by all instances of a class is known as _____ variable.

D65 Methods with _____ modifier are usable outside of the class where they are defined.

D66 Methods with _____ modifier will not access objects of a class.

D67 _____ is a method which creates an object of a class.

D68 The method that has no return type, including **void**, is the _____

D69 A method which accesses values (of instance variables) in an object without altering the object is known as _____ method.

D70 A method which modifies the state of an object is known as _____ method.

D71 A method that performs operations for the whole class is known as _____ (or _____) method.

D72 A method that performs operations for the individual objects of a class is known as _____ method.

D73 Given 'Car' is a class, after the declaration **Car c1**, the value of c1 is _____

D74 A _____ variable is shared by all objects of a class.

D75 A class version of a primitive data type is known as a _____ class.

D76 Conversion of a primitive data type value to its wrapper object is facilitated by _____

D77 Conversion of a wrapper object to its primitive type value is facilitated by _____

D78 The program component that contains (only) the headings of several public methods is known as a(n) _____

D79 The _____, _____, and _____ of the arguments at method invocation should match those of the formal parameters in the method definition.

IOIOIOIOIOIOIOIOIOIOIOIOIOIOIOIOIOIOIOIOIOIOIOIOIOI

Essay-type Questions

D1 Given that the following methods are in the same class, what is the output of the following code segment?

```
public static double max(int x, double y){
  System.out.println("max(int, double) called");
  return (x > y) ? x : y;
}
public static double max(double x, int y){
  System.out.println("max(double, int) called");
  return (x > y) ? x : y;
}
public static void main(String[] args){
  System.out.println(max(2, 5));
}
```

D2 What is the output, if in the 'main' method of problem D1, the statement is `System.out.println(max(2.0, 5));` ?

D3 What is the output, if in the 'main' method of problem D1, the statement is `System.out.println(max(2, 5.0));` ?

D4 What is the output, if in the 'main' method of problem D1, the statement is `System.out.println(max(2.0, 5.0));` ?

D5 Given that the following methods are in the same class, what is the output of the following code segment?

```
public static int test (int x) {
  System.out.println("test(int) called");
  return x;
}
public static double test (double x) {
  System.out.println("test(double) called");
  return x;
}
public static void main(String[] args)  {
  System.out.println(test(5.0));
}
```

D6 What is the output, if in the 'main' method of the above problem, the statement is `System.out.println(test(5));` ?

D7   What is the output of the following code segment?

```java
String s1 = new String("Java");
String s2 = s1;
System.out.println(s1 == s2);
s1 += "Programming";
System.out.println(s1 == s2);
```

D8   What is the output the following code segment?

```java
String str = "Java C++ Python Ruby";
String[] words = str.split(" ");
for (int i = 0; i < words.length; i++)
   System.out.println(words[i] + " ");
```

D9   What is the output of the following program?

```java
public class Example {
  int i;
  static int s;

  public static void main(String[] args) {
    Example ex = new Example ();
    System.out.println ("i: " + ex.i + " s: " +
    ex.s);
    ex = new Example ();
    System.out.println ("i: " + ex.i + " s: " +
    ex.s);
    ex = new Example ();
    System.out.println("i: " + ex.i + " s: " +
    ex.s);
  }

  public Example() {
    i++; s++;
  }
}
```

D10 What is the output of the following code?

```java
public class Example {
  private int a = 5;
```

```
    public static void main(String[] args) {
      System.out.println (a);
    }
}
```

D11   What is the output of the following code?

```
public class Example {
  private int a = 5;
  public static void main(String[] args) {
    Example ex = new Example ();
    System.out.println (ex.a);
  }
}
```

D12   What is the output of the following program?

```
public class Example {
  static int i = 0, j = 0, k = 0;

  public static void main(String[] args) {
    int i = 2;
    {
      int j = 3;
      System.out.println ("i: " + i + " j: " + j + " k: " + k);
    }
    System.out.println ("i: " + i + " j: " + j + " k: " + k);
  }
}
```

IOIOIOIOIOIOIOIOIOIOIOIOIOIOIOIOIOIOIOIOIOIOIOIOIOIOIOI

E. Inheritance and Polymorphism

True/False Questions

E1 Inheritance models the 'is-a' relationship between two classes. _____

E2 A strong 'is-a' relationship describes a direct inheritance relationship between two classes. _____

E3 The 'is-a' relationship is not transitive. _____

E4 A weak is-a relationship cannot be represented using interfaces. _____

E5 Inheritance is the relationship between an interface and the class that implements it. _____

E6 A subclass will not contain more data or methods than in its superclass. _____

E7 A subclass of some class could be a superclass for some other class. _____

E8 A subclass inherits the public variables and methods of its superclass. _____

E9 A subclass does not inherit the private variables and methods of its superclass. _____

E10 A subclass can directly access the public instance variables of its superclass. _____

E11 A subclass cannot directly access the private instance variables of its superclass. _____

E12 A subclass cannot ever access the private instance variables of its superclass. _____

E13 A subclass cannot add new private instance variables. _____

E14 A subclass can add new public or private methods. _____

E. Inheritance and Polymorphism

E15 A subclass cannot add new static methods. _____

E16 A subclass inherits the constructors of its superclass. _____

E17 A subclass can inherit the private method of its parent class. _____

E18 A subclass cannot redefine a method that is inherited from its superclass. _____

E19 A private method of a class cannot be overridden by its subclass. _____

E20 A static method of a class can be overridden by its subclass. _____

E21 A subclass can call a private method defined in its parent class. _____

E22 A derived class can call a private method of the base class. _____

E23 A derived class can call a public method that in turn calls a private method when both the methods are in the base class. _____

E24 A derived class can define a method that invokes a private method of its base class. _____

E25 A subclass is more genalized than its superclass. _____

E26 Given 'Car' is a class, and 'ElectricCar' is a subclass of car, the declaration ElectricCar ec1 = new ElectricCar() is valid. _____

E27 Given 'Car' is a class, and 'ElectricCar' is a subclass of car, the declaration Car ec1 = new ElectricCar() is not valid. _____

E28 Given 'Car' is a class, and 'ElectricCar' is a subclass of car, the declaration ElectricCar ec1 = new Car() is not valid. _____

E29 A method definition with the **final** modifier may be overridden in a derived class. _____

E30 The correct method to choose at method invocation is determined by the type of the actual object. _____

E31 The correct method to choose at method invocation is determined by the type of the object reference. _____

E32 Method names cannot be overloaded within a derived class. _____

E33 The default modifier of a class makes it accessible to a class in the same package, but a class (including a subclass) in a different package cannot access it. _____

E34 Polymorphism does not work with static binding. _____

E35 Dynamic binding is necessary for polymorphism. _____

E36 Declaring the data fields to be private facilitates encapsulation. _____

E37 A class extending another class facilitates inheritance. _____

E38 A method defined in the subclass using the same signature and compatible return type as in its superclass can be overridden. _____

E39 Overloading is valid for methods with the same name but with different signatures. _____

E40 Methods in the same class differing only in the return types can be overridden. _____

E41 Methods in the same class differing only in the return type results in run time error. _____

E42 A private method can be overridden. _____

E43 A method defined in a subclass is unrelated to a method defined as private in its superclass. _____

E44 A static method can be overridden. _____

E45 A static method defined in the superclass gets hidden by a method redefined in a subclass. _____

E46 An object of a derived class cannot be cast to a type of its base class. _____

E. Inheritance and Polymorphism

E47   An object of a base class can be cast to a type of its derived class. _____

E48   A base class reference value cannot be assigned to a derived class variable. _____

E49   An object of a derived class cannot be assigned to a variable of any ancestor type. _____

E50   A subclass may not contain more functions than it's parent class. _____

E51   A subclass may contain more data members than its superclass. _____

E52   **`class A extends B`** means B is a subclass of A. _____

E53   The **super** keyword is used only for invoking the constructor, but not a method, of a superclass. _____

E54   A class that implements an interface must define the body for every method specified in the interface. _____

E55   A class that implements an interface can define any number of methods. _____

E56   More than one class may not implement an interface. _____

E57   An interface will not contain complete method definitions. _____

E58   All interfaces are abstract. _____

E59   An interface may contain instance variables. _____

E60   An interface is a reference type. _____

E61   A class that implements an interface may define more methods than declared in the interface. _____

E62   A class cannot implement more than one interface. _____

E63   Different classes can implement the same interface. _____

E64 An interface can be a formal parameter to a method. _____

E65 An interface can be passed as an argument to a method invocation. _____

E66 An object of a class implementing an interface can be passed as an argument to a method. _____

E67 It is not possible to have a method that is both overloaded and overridden. _____

E68 Invoking an overridden method from some ancesotor class, other than the direct parent class, is not permitted. _____

E69 An object of a derived class can be referenced by a variable whose type is any one of its ancestor classes. _____

E70 A direct subclass cannot be defined until its direct superclass has been defined. _____

E71 Polymorphism does not work with abstract classes. _____

E72 A variable of a subtype can be assigned to a variable of its supertype. _____

E73 Given x is a variable of a subtype, and y is a variable of a supertype, the assignment x = y is valid. _____

E74 A variable of a supertype can never be assigned to a variable of its subtype. _____

E75 An abstract class cannot have a concrete subclass. _____

E76 Given A is an abstract class, A a = new A() is not a valid statement. _____

E77 Casting object reference variable affects the contents of the object. _____

IOIOIOIOIOIOIOIOIOIOIOIOIOIOIOIOIOIOIOIOIOIOIOIOIOI

E. Inheritance and Polymorphism

Fill-in the-blanks Questions

E1   Only the _____ or _____ methods of a class may be overridden by its subclass.

E2   The _____ and _____ methods of a class cannot be overridden by its subclass.

E3   Different objects of different methods invoking the same method name, but with different actions, is known as _____

E4   A subclass using a call to a method of its superclass in order to override a method of the superclass is known as _____

E5   Method overriding in the subclass which retains a part of the inherited method from its superclass is known as _____

E6   A class which cannot be used as a base class to derive subclasses must be declared with the modifier _____

E7   A method that has been overridden in at least one subclass is known as _____

E8   Facilitating the calling (invocation) of the correct method for a subclass object during runtime is facilitated by _____

E9   A(n) _____ method has only header, and no implementation code.

E10 The correct method to choose at method invocation is determined at _____ time.

E11 Redefining/changing method in a subclass which was inherited from its superclass is known as _____

E12 Casting a superclass to a subclass is known as _____

E13 Conversion of an object to the type of its subclass is known as _____ conversion.

E14 Conversion of an object to the type of its superclass (or of any ancestor class) is known as _____ conversion.

E15 Method _____ occurs when a method in a base class is redefined in its derived class.

E16 Assigning a derived class reference to a base class variable is known as _____

E17 "**class A extends B**" means ____ is a subclass of ____

E18 Data field of a class referencing another object is known as _____

E19 The keyword for invoking a superclass constructor is _____

E20 _____ models the is-a relationship between two classes.

E21 A strong is-a relationship describes a _____ relationship between two classes.

E22 The access modifier required for a member variable of a class so that it is accessible by any subclasses of this class, but not by classes which are not members of the same package is _____

IOIOIOIOIOIOIOIOIOIOIOIOIOIOIOIOIOIOIOIOIOIOIOIOIOI

Essay-type Questions

E1 Noting the 'String' class is a descendent classes of the 'Object' class, is there a problem with the following statements? If so, what is a fix?

E2 Analyze the following code segment. Is there a problem, and if so, what is a fix?

```
class A { }
class B extends A {
  B (int a) {
    A (a);
```

E3 Analyze the following code segment.

```
class A {
  public A () { }
}
public class B extends A { }
```

E4 What is the error in the following code segment, and what is the fix?

```
class A {
  public A (int a) {
  }
}
public class B extends A { }
```

E5 What is the output of the following code?

```
public class Test {
  public static void main(String[] args) {
    printType (new PC ());
    printType (new Laptop ());
    printType (new Computer ());
    printType (new Object ());
  }

  public static void printType (Object x) {
    System.out.println(x. getType ());
  }
}

class PC extends Laptop {
  public String getType () {
    return "PC";
  }
}

class Laptop extends Computer {
  public String getType () {
    return "Laptop";
  }
```

```
}

class Computer extends Object {
   public String getType () {
      return "Computer";
   }
}
class Object {
   public String getType () {
      return "Object";
   }
}
```

E6   What is the output of the following code?

```
public class Test {
   public static void main(String[] args) {
      new Computer ().printType();
      new Laptop ().printType();
   }
}

class Laptop extends Computer {
   @Override
   public String getType() {
      return "Laptop";
   }
}

class Computer {
   public String getType() {
      return "Computer";
   }

   public void printType() {
      System.out.println(getType());
   }
}
```

E7   What is the output of the following code?

```
public class Test {
   public static void main(String[] args) {
```

```
        new Computer().printType();
        new Laptop().printType();
    }
}

class Laptop extends Computer {
    private String getType() {
        return "Laptop";
    }
}

class Computer {
    private String getType() {
        return "Computer";
    }

    public void printType() {
        System.out.println(getType());
    }
}
```

E8   Given the following classes and the declarations:

```
class A { }
class B extends A { }
class C extends B { }
class D extends A { }

A  a1 = new A();
A  a2 = new B();
A  a3 = new D();
B  b1 = new B();
B  b2 = new C();
```

Which of the following assignments are in error?

```
a1 = a2;
a2 = a1;
a1 = b1;
b1 = b2;
b2 = b1;
A a4 = a3;
```

E9 Consider the following statements:
```
String s = new String("Example");
Object o = s;
String t = (String) o;
```

E10 What is the output of the following code segment?
```
Object o1 = new Object();
Object o2 = new Object();
Object o3 = o1;
System.out.println(o1 == o2);
System.out.println(o1 == o3);
```

E11 What is the output of the following code segment?
```
Object o1 = new Object();
Object o2 = o1;
System.out.println(o1 == o2);
System.out.println(o1.equals(o2));
```

E12 What is the output of the following code segment?
```
Object o1 = new Object();
Object o2 = o1;
o1 = "Example";
System.out.println(o1 == o2);
System.out.println(o1.equals(o2));
```

E13 What is the output of the following code segment?
```
Object o1 = new Object();
o1 = "Example";
Object o2 = o1;
System.out.println(o1 == o2);
System.out.println(o1.equals(o2));
```

E14 What is the output of the following code segment?
```
Object o1 = new String("Example");
Object o2 = "Example";
System.out.println(o1 == o2);
System.out.println(o1.equals(o2));
```

E15 What is the output of the following code?

```java
public class Test {
  public static void main(String[] args) {
    Object o1 = new A();
    Object o2 = new A();
    System.out.println(o1.equals(o2));
  }
}

class A {
  int x;

  public boolean equals(Object o) {
    return this.x == ((A) o).x;
  }
}
```

E16 What is the output of the following code?

```java
public class Test {
  public static void main(String[] args) {
    Object a1 = new A();
    Object a2 = new A();
    System.out.println(a1.equals(a2));
  }
}

class A {
  int x;

  public boolean equals(A a) {
    return this.x == a.x;
  }
}
```

E17 What is the output of the following code?
```java
public class Test {
  public static void main(String[] args) {
    A a1 = new A();
    A a2 = new A();
    System.out.println(a1.equals(a2));
  }
}
```

```
}

class A {
  int x;
  public boolean equals(A a) {
    return this.x == a.x;
  }
}
```

E18 What is the output of the following code?
```
public class Test {
  public static void main(String[] args) {
    Object a1 = new A();
    Object a2 = new A();
    System.out.println(((A)a1).equals((A)a2));
  }
}
class A {
  int x;
  public boolean equals(A a) {
    return this.x == a.x;
  }
}
```

E19 What is the effect of executing the following set of statements?

```
class A { }
class B extends A { }
class C extends B { }
class D extends A { }
A[] arr1 = {new A(), new B(), new C()};
```

IOIOIOIOIOIOIOIOIOIOIOIOIOIOIOIOIOIOIOIOIOIOIOIOIOI

F. Exception Handling

True/False Questions

F1 An exception is a method. _____

F2 Java provides predefined exception classes. _____

F. Exception Handling

F3   Java provides some default exception handlers. _____

F4   A method must declare all exceptions that it can possibly throw. _____

F5   Unchecked exceptions can be thrown by any method. _____

F6   An unchecked exception must be caught in a **catch** block. _____

F7   An unchecked exception need not be declared in a **throws** clause. _____

F8   User programs cannot define their own exception classes. _____

F9   In case of system error, the user program can handle it by defining an exception handler. _____

F10 The exceptions can be caught and handled by your program. _____

F11 A method may declare to throw multiple exceptions. _____

F12 Exception handling can resolve exceptions. _____

F13 Exceptions can be thrown by calls from a try block to other methods. _____

F14 The try block must be followed by at least one catch block. _____

F15 You cannot have a try block without a catch block. _____

F16 A single try block cannot have multiple catch blocks associated with it. _____

F17 A finally block is placed after the last catch block. _____

F18 If a checked exception occurs in a method, it must be either caught or declared to be thrown from the method. _____

F19 A class that extends **Error** should not be declared, since **Error** raises a fatal error that terminates the program. _____

F20 An exception cannot be declared in the main method. _____

F21 In case of system error, the user is notified and the program is attempted to terminate gracefully. _____

F22 The errors caused by user program and external circumstance can be caught and handled by user program. _____

F23 Java does not throw any exception for floating point operations. _____

F24 The division 0 / 0 results in an exception. _____

F25 The division 0.0 / 0.0 results in an exception. _____

F26 Java does not throw integer overflow exceptions. _____

F27 An instance of **NumberFormatException** is an unchecked exception. _____

F28 An instance of **Throwable** is an unchecked exception. _____

F29 A method must declare **throw** for checked exceptions. _____

F30 A method must declare **throw** for unchecked exceptions. _____

F31 A method must declare **throw** for **RuntimeException**. _____

F32 A method may not have declarations to throw multiple exceptions. _____

F33 Declaration of an exception cannot be done in the main method. _____

F34 Upon an exception of type **Error**, the program terminates. _____

F35 A **try** block can throw only one exception. _____

F36 A **catch** block can catch exception of only one type. _____

F. Exception Handling

F37 A method that does not declare exceptions cannot be invoked inside a try block. _____

F38 When an exception is thrown, the code in the remainder of the try block could still be executed. _____

F39 The catch block is not a method definition. _____

F40 A catch block applies to any any preceding try blocks. _____

F41 After execution of the catch-block code, control returns to the try-block (from where it entered the catch-block). _____

F42 When no exception is thrown, none of the code in any of the catch blocks get executed. _____

F43 A try-block can contain any number of throw statements (either explicit or invoked in method calls). _____

F44 Unchecked exceptions are descendants of class **RuntimeException**. _____

F45 Checked exceptions are descendants of class **RuntimeException**. _____

F46 **IOException** is a checked exception. _____

F47 Some of the statements in a try{} block may never throw an exception. _____

F48 The statements in a try{} block may throw different types of exception. _____

F49 The statements in a try{} block cannot include a loop. _____

F50 The catch{} block for a child exception class must follow that of a parent execption class. _____

F51 There must be only one catch{} block in a try/catch structure. _____

F52 Every 'try' block must have a matching 'catch' block. _____

Java Quiz Book

F53   There must be a finally{} block in a try/catch structure. _____

F54   There can be more than one finally{} block in a try/catch structure. _____

F55   The finally {} block (if one exists) must be after the last catch{} block. _____

F56   A try{}/catch{} cannot be nested inside an outer try{} block. _____

IOIOIOIOIOIOIOIOIOIOIOIOIOIOIOIOIOIOIOIOIOIOIOIOI

Fill-in the-blanks Questions

F1   The two categories of exception are _____ and _____

F2   When an exception occurs it is said to have been _____

F3   The _____ serves as the argument to the catch block.

F4   An exception that must be caught in a catch block or declared in a throws clause, is known as _____ exception.

F5   If a _____ exception occurs in a method, it must be either caught or declared to be thrown from the method.

F6   The method **getMessage** that returns the descriptive string stored in an exception is provided by the class _____

F7   To catch an exception the code that might throw, the exception must be enclosed in a _____ block.

F8   The _____ block should contain statements that may throw an exception.

F9   The keyword that is used to throw an exception is _____

F. Exception Handling

F10 The keyword that is used to declare exceptions in the method heading is _____

F11 The keyword used to declare exceptions in the method heading is _____

F12 The keyword used to throw an exception is _____

F13 When an exception is thrown, the code in the _____ block begins execution.

F14 All exceptions are objects of classes that are descendants of the _____ class.

F15 The super class of all exceptions is the _____ class.

F16 The two predefined exception classes, the subclasses of **Throwable**, are _____ and _____

F17 Errors that are thrown by the run-time system are associated with the _____ exception class and its descendants.

F18 The keywords related to exception handling are _____, _____, _____, _____ and _____

F19 The statements that may throw exceptions are in the _____ block.

F20 The keyword for declaring an exception is _____

F21 The keyword for (manually) throwing an exception is _____

F22 If an exception occurs, it is caught and handled (processed) by the _____ block.

F23 All Java exceptions are instances of class _____

F24 A Java system error is an instance of class _____

F25 Upon an exception of type _____, the user program would terminate.

F26 Errors caused by both user programs and external circumstances are instances of class _____

F27 **NumberFormatException** is a subclass of _____

F28 The exception caused by division by 0 is _____

F29 The exception caused by trying to access elements beyond the array bounds is _____

F30 The exception caused by trying to access elements beyond the length of a string is _____

F31 The exception type thrown by the following code segment is _____

```
Object obj = new Object();
String str = (String)obj;
```

F32 The exception type thrown by the following code segment is _____

```
Object o1 = null;
System.out.println(o1.toString());
```

F33 The exception type thrown by the following code segment is _____

```
String s = "3.14";
Integer.parseInt(s);
```

F34 An instance of _____ class describes programming errors, such as bad casting, accessing an out-of-bounds array, and numeric errors.

F35 The method of an 'Exception' object that prints a list of methods that were called before the exception was thrown, is _____

F36 The method of an Exception object returns a message string, is _____

F37 The only type of exception that is not checked, is _____

Essay-type Questions

F1 Describe the structure and function of a **catch** block in Java.

F2 Describe the exception handling constructs in Java.

F3 In Java, which part of code gets executed whether exception is caught or not?

F4 In Java, what do `final`, `finally`, and `finalize()` do?

F5 What is the output of the following code segment?

```
try {
  int x = 0;
  int y = 1 / x;
}
catch (RuntimeException excep) {
  System.out.println("Division by 0");
}
try {
  String s = "3.14";
  Integer.parseInt(s);
}
catch (NumberFormatException excep) {
  System.out.println
      ("NumberFormatException");
}
```

F6 What is the output of the following code segment?

```
public static void main(String[] args) {
  try {
    testMethod();
    System.out.println("After testMethod");
  }
  catch (RuntimeException excep) {
    System.out.println("RuntimeException");
```

```java
    }
    catch (Exception excep) {
      System.out.println("Exception");
    }
  }

  static void testMethod() throws Exception {
    try {
      String s = "3.14";
      Integer.parseInt(s);
      int x = 0;
      int y = 1 / x;
      System.out.println("After division");
    }
    catch (RuntimeException excep) {
      System.out.println("RuntimeException");
    }
    catch (Exception excep) {
      System.out.println("Exception");
    }
  }
```

F7   What is the output of the following code segment?

```java
int x = 0;
int y = 1 / x;
System.out.println(y);
System.out.println("After division");
```

F8   What is the output of the following code segment?

```java
int x = 0;
double y = 1.0 / x;
System.out.println(y);
System.out.println("After division");
```

F9   What is the output of the following code segment?

```java
try {
  System.out.println("Java is fun");
}
finally {
  System.out.println("In finally clause");
```

}

F10 What is the output of the following code segment?

```
try {
  System.out.println("Java is fun");
  return;
}
finally {
  System.out.println("In finally clause");
}
```

F11 What is the output of the following code segment?

```
try {
  System.out.println("1: Java is fun");
  int x = 0;
  int y = 1/x;
  System.out.println("2: Java is fun");
}
catch (RuntimeException excep) {
  System.out.println("catch: Exception caught");
}
finally {
  System.out.println("finally: End of block");
}
```

F12 What is the output of the following code segment?

```
try {
  System.out.println("1: Java is fun");
  int x = 0;
  int y = 1/x;
  System.out.println("2: After div. by 0");
}
catch (RuntimeException excep) {
  System.out.println("catch: div. by 0");
}
finally {
  System.out.println("finally block");
}
System.out.println("End of block");
```

F13 What is the output of the following program?

```java
public class Test {
  public static void main(String[] args) {
    try {
      testMethod();
      System.out.println("After method call");
    }
    catch (RuntimeException ex) {
      System.out.println("RuntimeException");
    }
    catch (Exception ex) {
      System.out.println("Exception");
    }
  }

  static void testMethod() throws Exception {
    try {
      String s = "3.14";
      Integer.parseInt(s);

      int x = 0;
      int y = 1 / x;
      System.out.println("After division");
    }
    catch (NumberFormatException excep) {
      System.out.println
          ("NumberFormatException");
      throw excep;
    }
    catch (RuntimeException excep) {
      System.out.println("RuntimeException");
    }
  }
}
```

IOIOIOIOIOIOIOIOIOIOIOIOIOIOIOIOIOIOIOIOIOIOIOIOI

G. Files and I/O

True/False Questions

G1 Data can flow through a given stream in both directions. _____

G2 A stream could act as a data source for another stream. _____

G3 A **File** object is not an actual file. _____

G4 A file cannot exist without a **File** object. _____

G5 A **File** object can exist without a file. _____

G6 An instance of the File class can be used to determine whether the file exists. _____

G7 The properties of the file cannot be determined from an instance of the File class. _____

G8 An instance of the File class can be used to rename the file. _____

G9 An instance of the File class cannot be used to delete the file. _____

G10 The **Reader** and **Writer** are abstract classes. _____

G11 The **OutputStream** and **OutputStream** are abstract classes. _____

G12 Any file type can be read (meaningfully) with FileReader. _____

G13 A binary file is generally much smaller than a text file containing an equivalent amount of data. _____

G14 Input/Output with binary files is slower than with character-oriented files. _____

G15 It is not possible to make a copy of a file without knowing the format of the data it contains. _____

G16 Constructing a **File** object automatically creates a disk file. _____

G17 The use of **fileWriter** constructor with the name of an existing file replaces the file with an empty one. _____

G18 The method **getname** of the class **File** returns the path name of the file. _____

G19 Different types (ex. int, double, String) can be written to the same binary file. _____

G20 The method **readUTF** should be used only to read a string from a binary file. _____

G21 A number written to a file using **writeInt** can be read using **readLong** without error. _____

G22 The **fileInputStream** class has the **readInt** method. _____

G23 The **println()** method never throws exceptions. _____

G24 A 'null' is returned when **readLine()** encounters an error. _____

G25 The value returned by **readLine()** upon encountering end-of-file, is an empty string. _____

G26 Compressed text files can be read using a **FileReader** stream. _____

IOIOIOIOIOIOIOIOIOIOIOIOIOIOIOIOIOIOIOIOIOIOIOIOIOIOI

Fill-in the-blanks Questions

G1 The connection between a program and a data source or destination is known as _____

G2 The character data format used internally by Java programs is _____

G. Files and I/O

G3 The format of the characters used in text files written by Java programs is _____

G4 The type of the value returned by the method **next** of class **Scanner** is _____

G5 The type of the value returned by the method **nextLine** of class **Scanner** is _____

G6 The class containing the method for checking if a file exists is _____

G7 _____ returns the path separator character.

G8 The class that is used to write data into a text file is _____

G9 The class that is used to read data from a text file is _____

G10 The method that is used to write data is _____

G11 The method that is used to read a whole line from a file is _____

G12 The method that is used to create an input object for file named 'sales1.dat' is _____

G13 The package that holds the File class is _____

G14 The output displaying byte-by-byte contents of a binary file is known as _____

G15 The failure to open a file for reading results in _____ exception.

G16 The ancestor of all character-oriented input streams is _____

G17 The ancestor of all character-oriented output streams is _____

G18 The ancestor of all byte-oriented output streams is _____

G19 The ancestor of all byte-oriented input streams is _____

G20 Convenient methods for output of primitive data types is provided in the class _____

G21 The method of a stream which ensures that all pending output operations are completed is _____

G22 The method that reads 'int' values from a stream is _____

G23 The method that writes double precision values to a stream is _____

G24 The method that gives the number of bytes written to a stream so far is _____

G25 The method that is used to test if a file or directory exists is _____

G26 The class that is used for input of character data from a disk file is _____

G27 The class that is used for output of character data to a disk file is _____

G28 The parent class of **FileWriter** is _____

G29 The **readLine()** is a method belonging to the class _____

G30 The return type of **readLine()** is _____

G31 The value returned by **readLine()** return upon encountering end-of-file is _____

G32 The method to create a new disk directory is _____

G33 The method to remove a file is _____

G34 The exception that is thrown when the end of a file is reached, is _____

G. Files and I/O

H. Programming Problems

H1 Write a program to compute the average of three numbers which are read from the terminal.

H2 Write a program to compute the volume of a cone whose base radius and height are read from the terminal.

H3 Write the code segment to compute the largest of three numbers which are in variables num1, num2, and num3 of type double.

H4 Write the code segment to compute the largest of three numbers which are in variables num1, num2, and num3, using the ternary operator ('?', ':').

H5 Write a program to print the following based on age read from the terminal: (a) less than 3 years → Infant; (b) ≥ 3 and < 13 years → Child; (c) ≥ 13 and < 20 years → Teenager; (d) ≥ 20 and < 30 years → Youth; (e) ≥ 30 and < 65 years → Adult; (f) > 65 years → Senior Citizen.

H6 Write a program to determine the least number of coins using quarters, dimes, nickels, pennies to be given as change.

H7 Given two intervals (a_1, b_1) and (a_2, b_2) on the real number line, write a method **overlap** to determine if they overlap or not. For example, (2.7, 5.3) and (4.8, 12.2) overlap, (3.4, 6.6) and (6.6, 7.3) do not overlap, and (2.7, 5.3) and (7.1, 9.5) do not overlap. Each interval is represented by an array of two real numbers, and the method returns a Boolean.

H8 Write a method which takes as arguments three real numbers representing the sides of a triangle, and determines and returns true or false, based on whether it is a valid triangle or not. **Note:** In a valid triangle, the sum of the lengths of any two sides is greater than the length of the third side. For example, if the given side lengths are 10.7, 5.6, and 2.9, it should return false.

H9 Write a program to print the sequence: 1 2 4 7 11 … .The length of the sequence is read from the terminal.

H. Programming Problems

H10 Write a method which takes two integers 'num' and 'pos' as arguments, and returns the digit at position 'pos' of the number 'num'. Note that pos = 1 denotes the unit's position. For example, Input: (6753, 3), Output: 7; Input: (372514, 4), Output: 2. Assume that the value of 'pos' is > 0.

H11 Write a method which reads an integer limit and determines and prints out all 'Armstrong numbers' within the limit. An Armstrong number is one which equals the sum of the cubes of its digits. A sample output is shown below.

```
Enter limit: 1000
1 153 370 371 407
```

H12 Write a program that calculates and prints the sequence, as shown below.

```
        9
       89
      789
     6789
      ::
      ::
123456789
```

H13 Write a method to calculate and print all the well-ordered numbers of a given number of digits. It should take as input the number of digits, and return the number of well-ordered numbers of that many digits. A well-ordered number is one whose digits strictly increase from left to right. A sample output is given below.

```
Type the number of digits [1-9]: 2
12 13 14 15 16 17 18 19 23 24
25 26 27 28 29 34 35 36 37 38
39 45 46 47 48 49 56 57 58 59
67 68 69 78 79 89
Number of well ordered numbers of 2 digits = 36
```

H14 Write a method which takes a sorted array of integers, and an integer 'num', and determines and prints out the 'num' elements of the array which are closest to the median.
Note: Given two numbers a and b, a is closer to the median m if $|a - m| < |b - m|$

H15 Write a program that computes the square root 'r' of a number 'x' using Newton's method, and compare it with the value given by the library function. An example output is given below.

```
Type the number: 57
Square root of 57.000000 using Newton's method is
7.549835
The number of iterations required was 6
Square root computed by library function = 7.549834
```

Newton's method: Start with r = 1. If 'r' is an approximation to the square root of 'x', then a better approximation to the square root is given by: (x/r + r)/2 . This is iterated till the error converges (*i.e.* keep itearating until error becomes less than a small number ε, say 0.001.

H16 Write a method which takes as argument a number *N* (integer), and returns the sum of the sequence: 1/2 + 2/3 + 3/4 + ... + *N*/(*N*+1). Note that the sequence sum is a real number. For example, if *N* = 6, it should output 4.4071428 ...

H17 Write the code segment to determine if a given 'year' is leap year or not. Note that a year is leap year if it is divisible by 4 or if it is a century boundaries, it must be divisible by 400. For example, for an input of 1976, the output should be "1976 is a leap year"; for 1982, it should be "1982 is not a leap year"; for 1900, it should be "1900 is not a leap year"; for 2000, it should be "2000 is a leap year".

H18 Write a program to determine the value of *N* when the sum of the sequence: 1/2 + 2/3 + 3/4 + ... + *N*/(*N*+1) exceeds the value 42.7.

H19 Write a program to read a number *N* (integer) from the terminal, and compute π using the first N terms of the approximation given below.

$$\pi = 4\left(1 - \frac{1}{3} + \frac{1}{5} - \frac{1}{7} + \frac{1}{9} - \frac{1}{11} + \cdots + \frac{(-1)^{N+1}}{2N-1}\right)$$

H20 Write a program to read a number *N* (integer) from the terminal, and compute *e*, the base of the natural logarithm, using the first N terms of the approximation given below.

$$e = 1 + \frac{1}{1!} + \frac{1}{2!} + \frac{1}{3!} + \cdots + \frac{1}{N!}$$

H21 Write a program prints the first "N" numbers of the Padovan series. "N" is read from the keyboard. The Padovan series is 1,1,1,2,2,3,4,5,7,9,12,16,21,28,37,... Each number is obtained by skipping the previous one and adding the two before that. Have the program also print the ratio of two successive Padovan numbers.

H22 Write a program which generates a random integer between 1 and 1,000 and have the user guess the number. Based on the input, it should notify the user whether the guess was lower/higher than the generated number. There should be a maximum of 10 guesses allowed.

H23 Write a method which takes as input an Integer N, and prints out N down to 1 in the first row, (N – 1) down to 1 in the second row, etc., and 1 in the last row. For example, if the input value of N is 5, the output should be:

```
5 4 3 2 1
4 3 2 1
3 2 1
2 1
1
```

H24 Write a method which takes as argument two numbers (rows and columns), and prints a rectangle of '*'s.

H25 Write a method which takes an integer argument which specifies the height of a triangle and prints it using '*'s and spaces.

Examples:

height 1:   *

height 2:   *
                        ***

height 3:   *
                        ***
                       *****

H26 Write a program to read a number (integer) *N* from the terminal, and print an arrow of '*'s of a given height.

Examples:

height 1:
```
*
```

height 2:
```
 *
**
*
```

height 3:
```
  *
 **
***
 **
  *
```

H27 Write a method which takes two integer arguments (rows and columns), and prints a "hollow" rectangle of '*'s. (The boundary consists of single '*'s)

H28 Write a method to print an "X" shape of '*'s of a given height.

h=1
```
*
```

h=2
```
* *
 *
* *
```

h=3
```
*   *
 * *
  *
 * *
*   *
```

H29 Write a method to print an "Z" shape of '*'s of a given height.

h=2
```
**
**
```

h=3
```
* *
 *
* *
```

```
****
  *
```

```
h=4             *
              ****
```

H30 Write a method to print an "N" shape of '*'s of a given height.

```
h=2            **
               **

               *  *
h=3            ***
               *  *

               *    *
h=4            ** *
               *  **
               *    *
```

H31 Write a method to print an "M" shape of '*'s of a given height.

```
h=2            * *
               ***

               *   *
h=3            ** **
               * * *

               *     *
h=4            **   **
               * * * *
               *  *  *
```

H32 Write a method to print an "V" shape of '*'s of a given height.

```
h=1            *

h=2            * *
                *

               *   *
h=3             * *
                 *

               *     *
h=4            *     *
```

H33 Write a method to print an "K" shape of '*'s of a given height.

```
h=1              * *
                  *

                 * *
h=2              * *
                 * *

                 *   *
                 * *
h=3              * *
                 * *
                 *   *
```

H34 Write a program to compute the amounts after compounding of interest quarterly, monthly, and daily, over a range of years.

A sample output is given below.

```
Type in the principal: 10000
Type in the Interest rate (%): 6.5
Type in the term range (ex. 5 10): 6 12
Yield on 10000.0 at 6.5%

            Quarterly      Monthly        Daily

 6 Years    14,723.58      14,754.27      14,769.30
 7 Years    15,704.19      15,742.39      15,761.10
 8 Years    16,750.12      16,796.69      16,819.50
 9 Years    17,865.70      17,921.60      17,948.97
10 Years    19,055.59      19,121.84      19,154.30
11 Years    20,324.72      20,402.46      20,440.57
12 Years    21,678.38      21,768.85      21,813.21
```

H35 The formula for the future value of an Annuity is given below:

$$A = \frac{R\left[\left(1+\frac{r}{n}\right)^{nt} - 1\right]}{\frac{r}{n}}$$

Where A is the future value of the annuity, R is the regular periodic payment, r is the annual interest rate, n is the number of payments made per year, t is the term of the annuity in years.

Write a program which reads the values of A, r, and printout a table which gives the monthly payment required to reach the target with the given interest rate over 5, 10, 15, 20, 25, and 30 years.

A sample output is given below.

```
Type in the target amount: 35000
Type in the interest rate (%): 7.5

Years    Monthly Payment
-----------------------
  5         482.58
 10         196.71
 15         105.70
 20          63.21
 25          39.90
 30          25.98
```

H36 Write a program which determines the first common element, if any, in three sorted lists and prints that element and the indices of the three arrays where it occurs. Otherwise, it prints a "Not Found" message. (For simplicity you may use arrays initialized at declaration)

H37 Write a program to check if a given point is (a) inside, (b) on a border, or (c) outside of a given rectangle.

H38 Write a program to compute the solutions of the quadratic equation `ax^2 + bx + c`, given a, b, and c.

H39 Write a program to simulate the tossing of a fair coin for different number of tosses, which is read from the keyboard. A sample output is shown below:

```
Enter the no. of trials: 1000
Number of Tails: 496
Number of Heads: 504
```

H40 Write a program to simulate the tossing of a fair coin for different number of tosses, N: 100, 1,000, 10,000, 100,000. Display the number of outcomes of exactly 3 and exactly 5 consecutive heads coming up.

H41 Write a program to simulate the tossing of a fair coin and determine the minimum number of trials required for exactly 3 consecutive heads coming up. Also determine the number of tails and heads. Have the program to run a certain number of runs as specified by an input. A sample output for 2 runs is shown below.

```
Enter the no. of runs: 2
Run number: 1
T T T H H T T H H H H T H T H T T H H H H T H H H T
Number of Trials: 26
Number of Tails: 11
Number of Heads: 15
Run number: 2
H T H H H T
Number of Trials: 6
Number of Tails: 2
Number of Heads: 4
```

H42 Simulate and determine the number of throws of a single die until all faces have come up. A sample output is shown below. Note that the theoretical expected number of throws: $6/6+6/5+6/4+6/3+6/2+6/1 \approx 14.7$

```
2 5 2 1 3 4 2 3 4 4 2 4 3 5 6
Number of trials required for all faces to come up was
    15
```

H43 Write a program to count the number of times each of the faces of a die has come up in a given number of trials. A sample output is shown below.

```
Enter the no. of trials: 10000
Number of trials = 10000
Face   No. of times
1      1635
2      1714
3      1680
4      1653
5      1675
6      1643
```

H. Programming Problems

H44 Write a method to method to determine if an integer array has duplicates. It takes an array as argument and returns a Boolean.

H45 Write a program to determine if the elements of an array of integers are distinct or not (*i.e.* check if there are duplicates), and print out the index of the first element which has duplicate(s).

H46 Write a method which takes an array of integers as argument, and prints out the elements such that repeating (duplicate) elements are printed just once. For example, if the input is:
5,2,7,2,4,7,8,12,3,2,3,2,9,2,4 the output should be:
5,2,7,4,8,12,3,9

H47 Write a method to determine and return the maximum element in an array.

H48 Write a program to determine and print out the elements of an array of integers that are repeated, along with the indices of the first occurrence and the repetitions. For example, if the input array is:

```
17 7 18 2 3 18 18 16 3 18 17 4 10 19 3 11 10 8 16 8
```

the output should be:

```
17 at [0]  repeated at indices:  10
18 at [2]  repeated at indices:  5 6 9
3  at [4]  repeated at indices:  8 14
16 at [7]  repeated at indices:  18
10 at [12] repeated at indices:  16
8  at [17] repeated at indices:  19
```

H49 Write a method to print 'histogram' based on values in an array. A sample output for array of {5, 3, 2, 7, 4} is shown below.

```
      *
      *
*     *
*    **
**   **
*****
*****
```

H50 Write a method to partition an array into ODD and EVEN integers. After partition, the array will have all odd elements followed by all even elements. It takes an array as an argument and partitions it in-place.

H51 Write a method to print common elements in two sorted arrays, each having distinct values

H52 Write a program to find the longest plateau in a given array of numbers. For example, if array A[10] = [5, 3, 3, 1, 4, 4, 4, 2, 6, 6] the longest plateau is 4, 4, 4 starting at A[4] and of length 3. The output should be:

```
Longest plateau starts at A[4]
Length of the plateau: 3
```
For simplicity, you may assume the plateau lengths to be unique.

H53 Mathematically, a matrix *A* is said to be symmetric if *A(i, j)* = *A(j, i)* for all valid *i, j*. Write a method which takes a 2D array as an argument and returns true/false based on whether the matrix is symmetric or not.

H54 Write a code segment to initialize a square matrix represented by an array 'arr' to an Identity matrix. Note that in the Identity matrix all diagonal elements are 1's and all the remaining elements are 0's.

H55 Write a method which takes a string as argument and determines if it is a palindrome or not.

H56 Write a method which takes a 2D array as argument, and determines the minimum and maximum elements, and returns them in an array of two elements.

H57 Write a method to check if a given matrix is a unit matrix. An N x N unit matrix is a matrix of N rows and N columns where all the diagonal elements are '1's and all the remaining elements are '0's. The method should take a 2D array of integers as argument and return a Boolean which is true/false depending on whether the matrix corresponding to the 2D array is a unit matrix or not.

H58 A Magic Square is *N* x *N* matrix of integers such that the sum of every row, column, and diagonal is the same. Write a method which takes a 2D array as an argument and returns true/false depending on whether the array is a magic square or not.

H. Programming Problems

H59 Write a method which takes an integer 'N' (≥ 1) as argument, and generates the 'Pascal triangle' of height 'N', and returns it. 'Pascal triangle' is a triangular array of binomial coefficients. An example with N = 5 is shown below.

```
1
1 1
1 2 1
1 3 3 1
1 4 6 4 1
```

H60 Write a program which determines the maximum distance between two cities, based on the pair-wise distances between 'N' cities given in a triangular array, as shown below. It should printout the pair of cities with the largest distance and their distance. An example of pair-wise distance of 10 cities, and the expected output is given below. (Note: The C's marked in red are not part of the array).

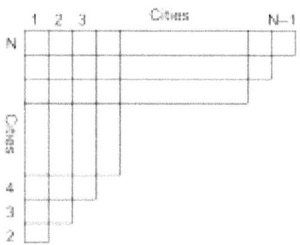

```
         C1      C2      C3      C4      C5      C6      C7      C8      C9
C10   202.26  164.96  134.24  181.28  205.76   77.31   10.87  103.76  240.65
C9     98.01  167.79   28.84   38.30   41.42  196.61  120.22   83.76
C8    212.39   86.70  195.99  210.22  227.05   91.37   93.19
C7    210.84  194.46  153.12   39.87   10.73   59.35
C6    119.70   51.58  188.96  248.81  124.86
C5    237.66  239.67   23.41  125.51
C4    110.72  161.45  103.84
C3    182.53   39.73
C2     16.43
```

Max distance is 248.81 between cities 6 and 4

IOIOIOIOIOIOIOIOIOIOIOIOIOIOIOIOIOIOIOIOIOIOIOIOIOIOIOI

Java Quiz Book

Answers

A. Java Basics

True/False Questions

A1   A `.class` file is not created if compilation of a class has no errors, but there are warnings. ***False***
[The `.class` file is not created if there are any errors. In other cases, warnings or not, the file is created]

A2   Java is dynamically typed. ***False***
[Java is statically typed. Variables have definite types, and the type of a declared variable cannot be changed at runtime]

A3   All the letters in a Java keyword is in lowercase. ***True***
[All Java reserved keywords consist entirely of lowercase letters (e.g., int, while, class, true, null)]

A4   Java keywords may be used as variable names. ***False***
[Java reserved keywords are off-limits as identifiers; using them causes a compile-time error]

A5 $amount is a valid identifier. ***True***
[Java identifiers may start with a letter, underscore, or dollar sign; subsequent characters may be letters, digits, underscores, or dollar signs]

A6 $6,379 is a valid identifier. ***False***
[The ',' (comma) symbol is not permitted]

A7   52_83 is a valid integer. ***True***
[Java 7 introduced the ability to use underscores as digit separators within integer literals, such as 52_83]

A8   3.1_4 is a valid real number. ***True***
[Underscores may appear between digits of a floating-point literal in Java 7+; they are stripped before the value is parsed]

A9   _738 is a valid integer. ***False***

[Integer literals cannot begin with an underscore; _738 would be treated as a (valid) identifier, not an integer literal]

A10   `class` is a valid identifier. ***False***
[`class` is a keyword]

A11   `74Points` is a valid identifier. ***False***
[Cannot start with a numeral]

A12   `total-count` is a valid identifier. ***False***
[The '–' symbol is not permitted]

A13   `current_sum` is a valid identifier. ***True***
[Current_sum contains only letters, digits, and underscores and starts with a letter, so it satisfies all Java identifier rules]

A14   The "_" (underscore character) can be used as digit separator for intergers or floating point numbers. ***True***
[Since Java 7, an underscore may be used as a digit group separator within numeric literals for readability]

A15   The following assignment statements are not equivalent. ***False***
[Both forms assign the value 1 to i, j, and k; they are completely equivalent in effect]

    a.   `i = j = k = 1;`

    b.   `i = 1; j = 1; k = 1;`

A16   The value of $1 - 0.1 - 0.1 - 0.1 - 0.1 - 0.1 - 0.1 - 0.1 - 0.1$ may not exactly be 0.2. ***True***
[There is no guarantee that it's value is exactly 0.2, due to the nature of floating point representation and floating point arithmetic. On the system tested, the value was 0.20000000000000015. This could vary slightly based on machine/compiler]

A17   Floating point arithmetic does not cause overflow. ***False***
[Floating-point values have a finite exponent range; exceeding it produces positive or negative infinity (overflow is possible)]

A18   Integer computations do not cause rounding errors. ***True***
[Integer arithmetic in Java operates on exact binary representations and never introduces rounding; overflow simply wraps (for int/long)]

A. Java Basics

A19 Arithmetic overflow causes a run-time error. *False*
[Upon arithmetic overflow, the execution continues. However, the condition can be caught and handled suitably by an exception handler]

A20 A Java character takes up 2 bytes of space. *True*
[Java characters use Unicode encoding which takes 2 bytes]

A21 Local variables must be initialized before their values are used in an expression. *True*
[The Java compiler requires local variables to be definitely assigned before they are read; using an uninitialized local is a compile error]

A22 Java requires all variables to have a type before they can be used in a program. *True*
[Java is statically typed; every variable must be declared with a specific type, which cannot change during execution]

A23 In Java, string is a primitive type. *False*
[String in Java is a class (java.lang.String), not a primitive type; the eight primitive types are boolean, byte, short, int, long, float, double, char]

A24 In Java, a string is treated as an array of characters. *False*
[In Java, strings are instances of the 'String' class. Methods of that class are used for various operations on strings]

A25 Nothing can be added or deleted from a string. *True*
[In Java, strings are constants. Characters cannot be added, deleted, or changed in a string. The methods (ex 'replace', etc.) which seem to change a string will actually not change anything 'in-place' in the string. Rather, they return a copy of a string, which has the changes made to the given string]

A26 A 'double' to 'float' promotion of primitive type is allowed to occur. *False*
[Converting double to float is a narrowing (lossy) conversion; it requires an explicit cast and is not a promotion]

A27 The operands of an operator are always evaluated from left to right. *False*
[Java does not specify a mandatory left-to-right evaluation order for all operator operands in general expressions]

A28   A Package is a group of related classes and interfaces. ***True***
[A package in Java groups related classes, interfaces, and sub-packages under a common namespace]

A29   Java does not allow overloading of primitive (ex. '+', '*') operators. ***True***
[Java deliberately omits operator overloading for user-defined types; only the built-in string + is a special case]

A30   An **enum** constructor cannot be overloaded. ***False***
[An enum in Java can have multiple constructors distinguished by their parameter lists (i.e., constructors can be overloaded)]

A31   Recursion is often more efficient than iteration. ***False***
[Recursion typically incurs more overhead than iteration because each call requires allocating and initialising a new stack frame]

A32   Recursion often is preferable to iteration because it models the problem more logically. ***True***
[Recursive solutions often map directly onto recursive mathematical definitions or naturally recursive data structures, making them easier to understand]

A33   Java compiler is a multipass compiler. ***True***
[The Java compiler makes multiple passes over the source to resolve forward references, perform type checks, and generate bytecode]

A34   In Java, a 'subpackage' is always contained within its 'parent' package. ***False***
[For example, java.awt.color is not part of java.awt. They are two separate entities]

A35   Java does not support the pointer type. ***True***
[Java has no pointer type; memory addresses are hidden and managed internally by the JVM]

A36   The 'int' datatype has different variations in Java. ***True***
[Java's int is one of several integer types; others include byte, short, and long]

A37   In Java, there are no operators or methods for explicit deallocation of objects. ***True***
[Memory is managed by the 'garbage collection' mechanism]

A38   An array may contain only primitive types. ***False***

A. Java Basics

[In Java, an array may contain both primitive and object types]

A39 The sub-expressions are executed from left to right. ***True***
[Java evaluates sub-expressions and operands from left to right, unlike C/C++ where this is implementation-defined]

A40 Java does not have built-in exponentiation operator. ***True***
[The operation is supported via library function]

A41 Java guarantees left–to–right evaluation of operands. ***True***
[The Java Language Specification guarantees that the left operand of a binary operator is fully evaluated before the right operand]

A42 Java is a type-safe language. ***True***
[Java enforces strong type rules at compile time and runtime, preventing unsafe type operations]

A43 Java bytecode can only be compiled, and not interpreted, into native code at run time. ***False***
[JVM implementations may use a JIT (Just-In-Time) compiler to compile bytecode to native machine code at runtime; interpretation is also common]

A44 Java does not have array-bounds checks. ***False***
[Java always checks array indices at runtime and throws ArrayIndexOutOfBoundsException if an index is out of bounds]

A45 Java does not have a pre-processor. ***True***
[Java has no preprocessor; there are no #include or #define directives]

A46 Java does not support macros. ***True***
[Java does not support macros; the preprocessor directives that provide macros in C/C++ do not exist in Java]

A47 Java has no pointer data type. ***True***
[Java has no pointer data type; references exist but their underlying addresses are hidden from the programmer]

A48 In Java, whenever a variable of non-primitive type is declared, a block of memory of the required size is allocated. ***False***
[When a non-primitive variable is declared, only a reference slot is created; no object is allocated until new is called]

A49 Java byte code does not hide machine-specific details. ***False***
[Java bytecode is designed to be platform-independent; it abstracts away machine-specific details]

A50 In Java, call-by-value is not used. ***False***
[Java uses call-by-value for all argument passing; for objects, the value passed is a copy of the reference]

A51 A garbage collection mechanism is supported by the Java Virtual Machine (JVM). ***True***
[The JVM's garbage collector automatically frees memory occupied by objects that are no longer reachable]

A52 The default value for data field of a boolean type is ***false***. ***True***
[Instance variables of boolean type are automatically initialised to false; this applies to class fields, not local variables]

A53 The default value for data field of a numeric type is 0. ***True***
[Instance variables of numeric types (byte, short, int, long, float, double) are automatically initialised to 0]

A54 The default value for object type is ***null***. ***True***
[Instance variables of reference (object) types are automatically initialised to null]

A55 Local variables do not have default values. ***True***
[Local variables in Java have no default value; they must be explicitly initialised before use or the compiler rejects the code]

A56 Local variables are initialized with default values when they are declared. ***False***
[Local variables are NOT default-initialised; the compiler enforces definite assignment before any read]

A57 A reference type does not store an object. ***True***
[A variable of a reference type contains only a reference (starting address) to where an object is stored in the memory]

A58 An `int` value can be assigned to a reference variable. ***False***
[An int is a primitive; a reference variable holds a reference to an object, not a primitive value]

A. Java Basics

A59 Use of an uninitialized variable in statement does not give compilation error. ***False***
[Using an uninitialized local variable is detected by the Java compiler as a definite-assignment error, preventing compilation]

A60 Java requires declaration of variables before use. ***True***
[Java requires every variable to be declared with a type before it is used]

A61 Variables declarations can be anywhere a statement can be. ***True***
[In Java, a variable declaration can appear anywhere a statement is allowed, not just at the start of a block]

A62 A variable in a nested block can have the same name as a variable in the enclosing block. ***False***
[Java prohibits a local variable in an inner block from shadowing a local variable of the same name in an enclosing block]

A63 Java supports multiple-selection statement. ***True***
[The switch statement provides multiple-selection based on an integer, string, or enum value]

A64 Arrays are not initialized at the time of allocation. ***False***
[When an array is created in Java, all elements are automatically initialised to 0, false, or null depending on the element type]

A65 Array index range checks are not done in Java. ***False***
[Java always checks array subscripts; out-of-bounds access throws ArrayIndexOutOfBoundsException]

A66 String is a primitive type in Java. ***False***
[String is a class in the java.lang package; it is not one of the eight Java primitive types]

A67 Java does not support enumeration types. ***False***
[Java has an enum type since Java 5; enum constants are objects of a special class]

A68 Java supports concurrency. ***True***
[Concurrency is supported via threads]

A69 Java has built-in garbage collection. ***True***
[Java supports only widening implicit conversions (e.g., int to long, float to double) in assignment coercions]

A70   Java supports only widening assignment coercions. ***True***

A71   Java does not have implicit type conversions (coercions). ***False***
[Java performs implicit widening conversions automatically; narrowing conversions require an explicit cast]

A72   Java does not support explicit type conversions (casts). ***False***
[Java supports explicit type casts, e.g., (int) 3.7 or (double) n; both widening and narrowing casts exist]

A73   Java supports short circuit evaluation of Boolean expressions. ***True***
[Java's && and || operators short-circuit: the right operand is only evaluated if necessary]

A74   Short circuit evaluation of Boolean expressions cannot be overridden in Java. ***False***
[The && and || are short circuit operators, while & and | are non-short circuit operators — they force the evaluation of all subexpressions]

A75   Java does not have the `goto` control structure. ***True***
[Java has "label" control structure to get the effect of a "goto"]

A76   Java has predefined overloaded subprograms. ***True***
[For example, System.out.println is predefined to accept many different argument types (method overloading)]

A77   In Java, the control expression must be Boolean. ***True***
[Unlike C/C++, the condition in Java's if, while, and for statements must be of boolean type; integer conditions are not allowed]

A78   Java does not allow mixed-mode expressions. ***False***
[Java allows mixed-mode arithmetic; widening conversions (e.g., int to double) are performed automatically]

A79   Java supports parameterized ADTs. ***True***
[Java generics (e.g., ArrayList<T>) provide parameterized abstract data types]

A80   Java has built-in support for exception handling. ***True***
[Java has built-in try/catch/finally and throw/throws syntax for exception handling]

A. Java Basics

A81 Local variables must be initialized before their values are used in an expression. **_True_**
[Local variables must be definitely assigned before use; the compiler enforces this at compile time]

A82 Java requires all variables to have a type before they can be used in a program. **_True_**
[Java's static type system requires every identifier to be declared with a type before it can be used]

A83 In Java, `string` is a primitive type. **_False_**
[String in Java is a class (java.lang.String). It is not a primitive type. the primitives are boolean, byte, short, int, long, float, double, and char]

A84 An expression cannot be an argument to a method. **_False_**
[Any expression that evaluates to the correct type can be passed as a method argument]

A85 The ++ and -- operators can be applied to a 'char' variable. **_True_**
[char is an integer type in Java, so ++ and -- increment or decrement the underlying Unicode code-unit value]

A86 The ++ and -- operators are binary operators. **_False_**
[They are unary operators. They have only one operand]

A87 A string variable is a primitive variable. **_False_**
[String is a reference type (a class), not a primitive type]

A88 The '%' operator is not valid on floating point numbers. **_False_**
[Java's % operator is defined for both integer and floating-point operands; e.g., 5.5 % 2.0 is valid]

A89 Relational operators are (generally) used for primitive types. **_True_**
[Relational operators (<, >, <=, >=) are primarily used with primitive numeric types; using them on objects compares references, not values]

A90 There is no value of x for which the expression `(x < 10) && (x > 10)` would be true. **_True_**
[No real number can be simultaneously less than 10 and greater than 10; the conjunction is always false]

A91   There is no value of x for which the expression **(x < 10) ||
(x > 10)** would be false. ***False***
[The compound expression would be false for x = 10, since both x < 10 and x > 10 would be false]

A92   The value of the expression **(x <= y ^ x >= y)** would always be true. ***False***
[When x equals y, both **x <= y** and **x >= y** are true, and therefore, the expression would be false]

A93   The value of the expression **(x < y ^ x > y)** would always be true. ***False***
[When x equals y, both **x < y** and **x > y** are false, and therefore, the expression would be false]

A94   The value of the expression **((x%y == 0) ^ (y%x == 0))** would always be true. ***False***
[For x = 4 and y = 7, x % y is 4 and y % x is 3, and thus the expression is false]

A95   For integers x and y, the value of the expression **(x/y == 0 ^ y/x == 0)** would always be true. ***False***
[When x = y, each of the conditions is false, and the expression is false]

A96   For integers x and y, the value of the expression **(x/y == 1 ^ y/x == 1)** could never be false. ***False***
[When x = y, each of the conditions is true, and the expression is false]

A97   For integers x and y, the value of the expression **(x/y == 0 ^ x/y != 0)** is always true. ***True***
[x/y==0 and x/y!=0 are logical complements; exactly one is always true, so their XOR is always true]

A98   The value of **(x < y || x > y)** is always true. ***False***
[The value of the expression is false when x equals y]

A99   The value of **(x <= y && x >= y)** is always true. ***False***
[The expression (x<=y && x>=y) is true only when x equals y; when x does not equal y, one of the conditions is false, making the conjunction false]

A100   The value of **(x < y && x > y)** is always false. ***True***

A. Java Basics

[A value cannot be simultaneously less than and greater than another; the conjunction is always false]

A101   The value of **(x == y || x != y)** is always true. ***True***
[x==y and x!=y are mutual complements; exactly one holds for any x,y, so their OR is always true]

A102   The value of **(x == y && x != y)** is always false. ***True***
[x==y and x!=y cannot both be true simultaneously; their AND is always false]

A103   The value of **(x == y ^ x != y)** is always true. ***True***
[x==y and x!=y are complements; exactly one is true, so their XOR is always true]

A104   The value of **(x % y == y % x)** is always false. ***False***
[When x = y, the LHS and RHS are both equal to 0]

A105   For integer values of x and y, the expression **(x/y == y/x)** would never be true. ***False***
[When x and y are equal, then x/y = y/x = 1]

A106   In Java, arithmetic overflow does not result in run-time error. ***True***
[Java integer overflow does not throw an exception; it silently wraps around using 2's-complement arithmetic]

A107   When x ≠ y, it is never the case that **x % y** is 0. ***False***
[When x is evenly divisible by y, then x % y is 0]

A108   For integers (positive or negative) x, y, when x < y, it is always the case that **x / y** is 0. ***False***
[For positive integers with x < y, integer division gives 0. But for negative values (e.g., x = –3, y = 2) x/y = –1, not 0]

A109   For integers (positive or negative) x, y, when x < y and x ≠ 0, it is never the case that **x % y** is 0. ***False***
[Counterexample: x = –6, y = –3; x < y and x ≠ 0, yet x % y = 0]

A110   For integers (positive or negative) x, y, when x ≥ y, it is never the case that **x / y** is 0. ***False***
[Counterexample: x = 0, y = –1; 0 ≥ –1 is true, yet 0/(–1) = 0]

A111 When x ≠ y, it is never the case that **x % y** and **x / y** are equal. *False*
[For x = 12 and y = 5, x % y is 2 and x/y is 2]

A112 **(x != y)** is equivalent to **! (x == y)**. *True*
[x!=y is defined as the negation of x==y; the two expressions are logically equivalent]

A113 **! (x < y)** is equivalent to **(x >= y)**. *True*
[By the complement rule, !(x<y) is true when x is not less than y, i.e., when x>=y]

A114 **(x > y || x < y)** is equivalent to **(x == y)**. *False*
[This is equivalent to x ≠ y]

A115 The value of the expression **(x < y ^ x > y)** would always be true. *False*
[When x = y, each part of the expression is false, and the value of the expression is false]

A116 Integer arithmetic is always gives the correct result. *False*
[Integer arithmetic can overflow, producing incorrect results when values exceed the type's range]

A117 All integer values in the range supported are accurately represented. *True*
[Every integer value within the range of a Java integer type is stored exactly in binary]

A118 Floating point arithmetic is always accurate. *False*
[Floating-point arithmetic introduces rounding errors because most real numbers cannot be represented exactly in binary]

A119 If 's' and 'i' are vaiables of type string and integer, respectively, then **s = i;** will automatically perform type conversion of the sequence of digits to a string. *False*
[s=i is a type mismatch in Java; there is no automatic int-to-string conversion by assignment]

A120 If 's' and 'i' are vaiables of type string and integer, respectively, then **s = i + "";** will automatically perform type conversion of the sequence of digits to a string. *True*
[Concatenating an integer with an empty string invokes integer-to-string conversion, producing the string representation]

A. Java Basics

A121 For any two strings s1 and s2, the value of the expression **s1.equalsIgnoreCase(s2) == s2.equals(s1)** is always true. *False*
[equalsIgnoreCase is case-insensitive while equals is case-sensitive; for s1="Hello" and s2="hello" the values differ]

A122 For any strings s1 and s2, the value of **s1.contains(s2) && s2.contains(s1)** is never true. *False*
[This is true when s1 equals s2]

A123 An Integer instance can be cast to a Double instance. *False*
[Note that these are not primitive types such as 'int' and 'double']

A124 **Integer i = 4.5** is a valid assignment. *False*
[4.5 is a double literal; it cannot be autoboxed to Integer, which holds only int values]

A125 **Double i = 4.5** is a valid assignment. *True*
[4.5 is a double literal; autoboxing converts it to a Double object, which is then assigned to the Double reference]

A126 **Object i = 4.5** is a not valid assignment. *False*
[Object i = 4.5 IS valid; 4.5 is autoboxed to Double, and Double is a subtype of Object, so the assignment is legal]

A127 **Number i = 4.5** is a not valid assignment. *False*
[Number i = 4.5 IS valid; 4.5 autoboxes to Double, and Double extends Number, so the assignment is legal]

A128 The String class implements Comparable method. *True*
[java.lang.String implements Comparable<String>, providing lexicographic ordering via compareTo()]

A129 The Double class does not implement Comparable method. *False*
[java.lang.Double implements Comparable<Double>, allowing Doubles to be compared and sorted]

A130 Even if two Random objects have the same seed, the sequence of the random numbers obtained from these two objects may not be identical. *False*
[Two Random objects initialised with the same seed produce identical pseudo-random sequences, which is deterministic]

A131   What are the values of the following expressions?

```
int a = 2, b = 3, c = 5;

a > b || c > b                     True

b < a + 2 && c <= a + b    True

(b > c - a) || (a < c / b + 1) False

b == b % c || a + b > c    True

(b <= c) && (b + c % a == 0) False
```

IOIOIOIOIOIOIOIOIOIOIOIOIOIOIOIOIOIOIOIOIOIOIOIOI

Fill-in the-blanks Questions

A1   The high-level language code / program written by the programmer is known as ***source*** code.
[The human-readable code written by the programmer is called source code; it must be translated into machine code before it can run]

A2   The code / program executed by the computer is known as ***machine*** code.
[The CPU executes machine code (binary instructions); all high-level languages must be compiled or interpreted into machine code first]

A3   The software which translates high-level language program into machine language program is known as ***compiler***.
[A compiler reads an entire high-level language program and translates it into an equivalent machine language (or bytecode) program]

A4   The software which manages various resources and activities in a computer is known as the ***operating system***.
[The operating system manages the CPU, memory, storage devices, input/output, and running programs]

A. Java Basics

A5   A(n) ***Integrated Development Environment (IDE)*** provides facilities such as editing, compiling, running, and debugging during program development.
[An IDE combines a source editor, compiler, debugger, and run environment into a single application to streamline program development]

A6   A program which does not compile is said to have ***syntax*** error(s).
[A syntax error is a violation of the grammar rules of the programming language; the compiler detects it and refuses to produce output]

A7   A program which compiles without error(s) but terminates abnormally when run is said to have ***runtime*** error.
[A runtime error occurs during execution, causing abnormal termination; examples include division by zero or a null-pointer dereference]

A8   A program which compiles without error(s) but produces incorrect result(s) is said to have ***logic*** (***logical***) error.
[A logic error produces the wrong output but does not crash; the code runs to completion with an incorrect result]

A9   The extension of a Java source code file is `.java`
[Every Java source file must have the extension .java; the file name must match the public class name]

A10   The extension of a Java bytecode file is `.class`
[The Java compiler produces platform-independent bytecode stored in a .class file, one per compiled class]

A11   A Java class `public class Test { ... }` must be defined in a file named ***Test.java***.
[Java requires that a file containing a public class named Test be saved as Test.java]

A12   A block is enclosed between ***braces***.
[A block (compound statement) in Java is enclosed by a matching pair of curly braces { }]

A13   In Java, the Boolean literals are `true` and `false`.
[Java has exactly two Boolean literals: true and false (both lowercase)]

A14   A set of separate programs for developing and testing Java programs, is collectively known as ***JDK*** (***Java Development Kit***).

[The JDK (Java Development Kit) is a bundle of tools -- compiler, debugger, javadoc, etc. -- used to develop Java programs]

A15 The software that interprets Java bytecode is known as ***Java virtual machine (JVM)***.
[The JVM (Java Virtual Machine) interprets Java bytecode and executes it on the host platform]

A16 ***Java API (Applications Programmer Interface)*** contains predefined classes and interfaces for developing Java programs.
[The Java API provides a large library of predefined classes and interfaces (I/O, data structures, networking, GUI, etc.) for building Java programs]

A17 Java compiler translates Java source code into ***Java bytecode***.
[javac compiles .java source files into .class bytecode files that can be executed by any JVM]

A18 The signed integer types supported by Java are, **byte**, **short**, **int**, and **long**.
[Java's four signed integer types are byte (1 byte), short (2 bytes), int (4 bytes), and long (8 bytes)]

A19 In Java, whenever a variable of non-primitive type is declared, a(n) ***reference*** is allocated.
[Space for a reference variable is allocated, not for the object itself]

A20 In Java, a ***package*** is a collection of classes.
[A Java package groups related classes and interfaces under a common namespace to avoid naming conflicts]

A21 After compilation of an interface without errors, a **.class** file is created for the interface.
[Compiling an interface produces a .class bytecode file just like compiling a class]

A22 Every statement in a Java program must end with a ***semicolon***.
[Every statement in Java must be terminated by a semicolon; missing it is a syntax error]

A23 The starting character of an identifier could only be ***letter***, ***underscore*** ('_'), or ***dollar sign ('$')***.

A. Java Basics

[An identifier must begin with a letter (a-z, A-Z), an underscore (_), or a dollar sign ($); digits are not allowed as the first character]

A24 The "_" (***underscore character***) can be used as digit separator for intergers or floating point numbers.
[Since Java 7, underscores may be placed between digits in numeric literals to improve readability (e.g., 1_000_000)]

A25 The declaration of a constant ARR_SIZE inside a method with value 100, is `final int ARR SIZE = 100;`
[A local constant is declared with the final keyword followed by the type, name, and initial value]

A26 The result of 4 / 5 is **0**
[4 / 5 uses integer division; both operands are int, so the fractional part is truncated, giving 0]

A27 The result of (double) (4 / 5) is **0.0**
[(double)(4/5): the integer division 4/5 = 0 is computed first, then cast to double, giving 0.0]

A28 The result of (double) 4 / 5 is **0.8**
[(double)4 / 5: the cast promotes 4 to 4.0 before the division, producing floating-point division 4.0/5 = 0.8]

A29 The result of 4 / (double) 5 is **0.8**
[4 / (double)5: the cast promotes 5 to 5.0, making the division 4/5.0 = 0.8]

A30 The result of 4.0 / 5 is **0.8**
[4.0 / 5: the presence of a double literal forces floating-point division, giving 0.8]

A31 The result of 4 / 5.0 is **0.8**
[4 / 5.0: the double literal 5.0 promotes 4 to 4.0, resulting in floating-point division 0.8]

A32 The result of 19 / 5 is **3** [integer division]

A33 The result of 19 / 5.0 is **3.8** [floating point division]

A34 The result of (double)19 / 5 is **3.8** [floating point division]

Java Quiz Book

A35 For **x % n** to be 0 for all values of **x**, the value of **n**, should be **1**.
     [Note that **x % n** gives the remainder of dividing **x** by **n**. Any number divided by 1 has a remainder of 0. Therefore **n** is 1]

A36 The result of 5 % 1 is **0**.
     [5 % 1 = 0 because any integer divided by 1 has remainder 0]

A37 The result of 17 % 3 is **2**.
     [17 = 5 x 3 + 2, so 17 % 3 = 2]

A38 The result of 3 % 17 is **3**.
     [3 < 17, so 3 = 0 x 17 + 3; the remainder is 3]

A39 The result of 25 % 5 is **0**.
     [25 = 5 x 5 + 0, so 25 % 5 = 0]

A40 The result of 5 % 1 is **0**.
     [5 % 1 = 0 (same as Q36); any number mod 1 is always 0]

A41 The result of 5.2 % 3.7 is **1.5**.
     [5.2 % 3.7: Java's % works on floating-point too; 5.2 - 3.7 = 1.5]

A42 The result of 3.7 % 5.2 is **3.7**.
     [3.7 % 5.2: since 3.7 < 5.2, the quotient is 0 and the remainder equals 3.7]

A43 The result of (int)(12.345 * 100) / 100.0 is **12.34**.
     [(int)(12.345*100)/100.0 = (int)(1234.5)/100.0 = 1234/100.0 = 12.34]

A44 The result of (int)(12.345 * 100 / 100) is **12**.
     [(int)(12.345*100/100) = (int)(12.345) = 12 (truncation)]

A45 The result of (int)(12.345) * 100 / 100.0 is **12.0**.
     [(int)(12.345)*100/100.0 = 12*100/100.0 = 1200/100.0 = 12.0]

A46 The value of (double)(7/3) is **2.0**
     [(double)(7/3): integer division 7/3 = 2 first, then cast to double gives 2.0]

A47 The value of x for which the expression **(x <= 10) && (x >= 10)** would be true is **10**.
     [Both x<=10 and x>=10 are satisfied simultaneously only when x equals exactly 10]

A. Java Basics

A48   The value of x for which the expression **(x < 10) || (x > 10)** would be false is **10**.
[(x<10)||(x>10) is false when both operands are false; that happens only when x == 10]

A49   Given x = 5, the value of **(x << 5)** would be **160**.

[The '<<' operator does a left shift of the bits of the left operand by the specified times. One left shift is equivalent to multiplication by 2. Left shift by 5 is equivalent to multiplication by $2^5 = 32$ times, which, in the example would be 5 x 32 = 160]

A50   Given x = 84, the value of **(x >> 3)** would be **10**.
[The '>>' operator does a right shift of the bits of the left operand by the specified times. One right shift is equivalent to division by 2. In this example, it is equivalent to 84 / 2^3 = 84 / 8 = 10. Note that it is integet divison]

A51   The value of **(x == y && x != y)** is always **false**.
[x==y and x!=y are always contradictory; their AND is always false]

A52   The value of **(x == y || x != y)** is always **true**.
[x==y and x!=y are complements; their OR covers all cases and is always true]

A53   When x ≠ y, the value of the expression **(x <= y && x >= y)** would always be **false**.
[When x≠y, x<=y implies x<y and x>=y implies x>y; they cannot both hold, so the AND is false]

A54   The value of **(x <= y || x >= y)** is always **true**.
[For any x and y, either x<=y or x>=y (or both) is true, so the OR is always true]

A55   The value of **(x == y || x != y)** is always **true**.
[(x==y || x!=y): since x==y and x!=y are exhaustive complements, their OR is always true]

A56   The value of **(x == y ^ x != y)** is always **true**.
[x==y and x!=y are complements; exactly one is true, so their XOR is always true]

A57   When x ≠ y, the value of the expression **(x < y ^ x > y)** would always be **true**.
[When x≠y, exactly one of x<y and x>y is true, so their XOR is true]

Java Quiz Book

A58 The value of **(x == y && x != y)** is always **false**.
[x==y and x!=y are contradictory; their AND is always false]

A59 The value of **(x <= y && x >= y)** is true only under the condition **x == y**.
[(x<=y && x>=y) requires both x<=y and x>=y simultaneously, which is only possible when x==y]

A60 The value of **(x < y ^ x > y)** is false only under the condition **x == y**.
[(x<y ^ x>y): when x==y both operands are false, giving XOR=false; for all other cases exactly one is true giving XOR=true]

A61 The value of **(x >= 0) || (x < 0)** is always **true**.
[Every real number is either >=0 or <0; the disjunction is always true]

A62 The value of **(x < y && x > y)** is always **false**.
[(x<y && x>y) requires x to be simultaneously less than and greater than y, which is impossible]

A63 The value of **(x == y ^ x != y)** is always **true**.
[x==y and x!=y are complements; exactly one is always true, so XOR is always true]

A64 For integer values of x and y, the expression **(x/y == y/x)** would be true only under the condition **x equals y**.
[For positive integers with x==y, x/y=1 and y/x=1; otherwise the integer division values differ]

A65 **(true) && (false)** evaluates to **false**.
[true AND false evaluates to false by the AND truth table]

A66 **(true) || (false)** evaluates to **true**.
[true OR false evaluates to true by the OR truth table]

A67 The value of **(x > 0) || (x < 0)** is always **true** except when x is **0**.
[(x>0)||(x<0) is false only when x is 0; for all other integer values it is true]

A68 The value of **(x > 0) && (x < 0)** is always **false**.

134

A. Java Basics

[(x>0)&&(x<0) requires x to be both positive and negative simultaneously, which is impossible]

A69   The value of **! (x > 0) && (x > 0)** is always <u>**false**</u>.
[!(x>0) is true when x<=0; (x>0) is true when x>0; these two conditions are mutually exclusive, so AND is always false]

A70   The value of **(x != 0) || (x == 0)** is always <u>**true**</u>.
[(x!=0)||(x==0): exactly one of the two conditions holds for any x, so the OR is always true]

A71   The expression to check if the value of **age** is at least 18 is <u>**(age >= 18)**</u>
[(age>=18) is true when age is 18 or older; it is false when age is less than 18]

A72   The expression to check if the value of **age** is between 18 and 65 (inclusive) is <u>**(age >= 18 && age <= 65)**</u>
[Both bounds must hold simultaneously: age>=18 ensures the lower bound and age<=65 ensures the upper bound]

A73   The expression to check if the value of x is at least 3 and at most 10 is <u>**(x >= 3 && x <= 10)**</u>
[x must be at least 3 (x>=3) AND at most 10 (x<=10)]

A74   The expression to ckeck if x is evenly divisible by 3 and 7 is <u>**(x % 3 == 0 && x % 7 == 0)**</u>
[x is divisible by 3 if x%3==0, and by 7 if x%7==0; both must hold simultaneously]

A75   The expression to check if the value of **count** is not in the range 25 to 35 (inclusive) is <u>**(count < 25 || count > 35)**</u>
[count is outside [25,35] when it is either below 25 (count<25) or above 35 (count>35)]

A76   The value of **Math.round(1.49)** is <u>**1**</u>.
[Math.round(1.49): the argument is less than 1.5, so it rounds down to the nearest long, which is 1]

A77   The value of **Math.round(1.5)** is <u>**2**</u>.
[Math.round(1.5): the argument is exactly at the half-way point; Math.round uses round-half-up, giving 2]

A78 The value of **Math.rint(1.49)** is **1.0**.
[Math.rint(1.49): rounds to the nearest integer (1.0) using round-half-even]

A79 The value of **Math.rint(1.5)** is **2.0**.
[Math.rint(1.5): rounds to the nearest even integer; both 1 and 2 are equidistant, and 2 is even, so the result is 2.0]

A80 The value of **Math.ceil(1.01)** is **2.0**.
[Math.ceil(1.01): returns the smallest double that is >= the argument and is an integer; that is 2.0]

A81 The value of **Math.ceil(1.99)** is **2.0**.
[Math.ceil(1.99): the smallest integer >= 1.99 is 2.0]

A82 The value of **Math.floor(1.99)** is **1.0**.
[Math.floor(1.99): the largest integer <= 1.99 is 1.0]

A83 The value of **Math.floor(1.01)** is **1.0**.
[Math.floor(1.01): the largest integer <= 1.01 is 1.0]

A84 Given i=12, j=3, k=9, the value of **Math.min(i, Math.min(j,k))** is **3**.
[Math.min(12, Math.min(3,9)) = Math.min(12,3) = 3]

A85 Given i=12, j=3, k=9, the value of **Math.min(i, Math.max(j,k))** is **9**.
[Math.min(12, Math.max(3,9)) = Math.min(12,9) = 9]

A86 Given i=12, j=3, k=9, the value of **Math.abs(j-k-i)** is **18**.
[Math.abs(j-k-i) = Math.abs(3-9-12) = Math.abs(-18) = 18]

A87 Given x = 3 and y = 7, the value of y after evaluating the expression **(x >= 3) && (y-- > 5)**, is **6**.
[x>=3 is true; y-- uses the current value of y (7) then decrements it: 7>5 is true, so y becomes 6]

A88 Given x = 3 and y = 7, the value of y after evaluating the expression **(x > 3) && (y-- > 5)**, is **7**.

A. Java Basics

[Note that **(x > 3)** evaluates to **false**, and since the value of the entire expression would be false irrespective of the second term, the evaluation of the second term is 'short-circuited' (is not evaluated)]

A89 Given x = 3 and y = 7, the value of y after evaluating the expression **(x > 3) & (y-- > 5)**, is **6**.
[The '&' operator is non-short-circuit operator. Therefore, even when its left term is false, the right term is evaluated, which decrements y]

A90 Given x = 5 and y = 9, the value of y after evaluating the expression **(x > 5) || (y++ >= 12)**, is **10**.
[x>5 is false (5>5); y++ evaluates: 9>=12 is false, y becomes 10; false||false = false]

A91 Given x = 5 and y = 9, the value of y after evaluating the expression **(x >= 5) || (y++ >= 12)**, is **9**.
[Note that **(x >= 5)** evaluates to **true**, and since the value of the entire expression would be true irrespective of the second term, its evaluation of the second term is 'short-circuited' (is not evaluated)]

A92 Given x = 5 and y = 9, the value of y after evaluating the expression **(x >= 5) | (y++ >= 12)**, is **10**.
[The '|' operator is non-short-circuit operator. Therefore, even when its left term is true, the right term is evaluated, which increments y]

A93 Given x = 3 and y = 7, the value of the expression **(x >= 3) && (y-- <= 6)**, is **false**.
[x>=3 is true; y-- uses 7 then decrements to 6: 7<=6 is false; true&&false = false]

A94 Given x = 3 and y = 7, the value of the expression **(x >= 3) && (y-- == 6)**, is **false**.
[x>=3 is true; y-- uses 7 then decrements to 6: 7==6 is false; true&&false = false]

A95 Given x = 3 and y = 7, the value of the expression **(x >= 3) && (y-- >= 7)**, is **true**.
[x>=3 is true; y-- uses 7 then decrements to 6: 7>=7 is true; true&&true = true]

A96 Given x = 3 and y = 7, the value of the expression **(x >= 3) && (y-- == 7)**, is **true**.
[x>=3 is true; y-- uses 7 then decrements to 6: 7==7 is true; true&&true = true]

A97 Given x = 3 and y = 7, the value of the expression **(x >= 3) && (--y <= 6)**, is **true**.
[x>=3 is true; --y decrements y to 6 then uses 6: 6<=6 is true; true&&true = true]

A98 Given x = 3 and y = 7, the value of the expression **(x++ == 3) && (y-- == 7)**, is **true**.
[x++ uses 3 then increments to 4: 3==3 is true; y-- uses 7 then decrements to 6: 7==7 is true; true&&true = true]

A99 Given x = 3 and y = 7, the value of the expression **(++x >= 4) && (--y == 6)**, is **true**.
[++x increments x to 4 then uses 4: 4>=4 is true; --y decrements y to 6 then uses 6: 6==6 is true; true&&true = true]

A100 Given x = 3 and y = 7, the value of the expression **(x++ > 3) && (y-- == 7)**, is **false**.
[x++ uses 3 then increments to 4: 3>3 is false; short-circuit skips y--; result is false]

A101 Given x = 5 and y = 9, the value of the expression **(x > 5) || (y++ > 9)**, is **false**.
[x>5 is false (5>5); y++ evaluates: uses 9, y becomes 10: 9>9 is false; false||false = false]

A102 Given x = 5 and y = 9, the value of the expression **(x > 5) || (++y > 9)**, is **true**.
[x>5 is false; ++y increments y to 10 then uses 10: 10>9 is true; false||true = true]

A103 Given x = 3 and y = 7, the value of the expression **(x > 3) && (--y <= 6)**, is **false**.
[(x > 3) evaluates to (3 > 3) = false. Short-circuit evaluation skips the next sub-expression. false && anything = false]

A104 The ***boolean*** primitive type is never promoted to another type.
[The boolean type represents true/false values; it has no wider numeric type to be promoted to]

A105 To improve readability and maintainability, you should declare ***constants*** instead of using literal values such as 3.14159.

A. Java Basics

[Using named constants instead of magic numbers makes code self-documenting and easier to update]

A106 The size in bytes of the data type long is **8**, short is **2**, byte is **1**, and int is **4**.
[long is 8 bytes, short is 2 bytes, byte is 1 byte, int is 4 bytes in Java]

A107 The default initial value of a String instance variable is **null**.
[A String instance variable that has not been initialised defaults to null]

A108 The default value of a reference is **null**.
[All reference variables in Java default to null when declared but not assigned an object]

A109 The number of parameters of a default constructor is **0**.
[A default constructor takes no arguments; its parameter list is empty (0 parameters)]

A110 The expression to increment element of array **numlist** at index i is **numlist[i]++**
[numlist[i]++ applies the post-increment operator to the array element at index i]

A111 The declaration of a constant PI inside a method with value 3.14159265358979, is **final double PI = 3.14159265358979;**
[A local constant is declared with final, then the type, name, and initial value; double is the appropriate type for PI]

A112 When a literal which is too large to be stored in a Byte is assigned to a variable which has the size of a Byte causes ***compilation*** error.
[Assigning a value too large for a byte (outside -128 to 127) to a byte variable is detected at compile time]

A113 The Java statement to compute $3.2^{4.5}$ is **Math.pow (3.2, 4.5)**.
[Math.pow(base, exponent) returns base raised to the power exponent as a double]

A114 **Math.pow(3,4)** evaluates to **81.0**.
[**Math.pow** returns a double value]

A115 **Math.pow(9,1/2)** evaluates to **1.0**.
[Note that 1/2 is 0, and $9^0 = 9^0 = 1.0$]

Java Quiz Book

A116   **Math.pow(9,1.0/2)** evaluates to **3.0**.
       [1.0/2 = 0.5 (double division); Math.pow(9, 0.5) = sqrt(9) = 3.0]

A117   **Math.pow(25, 1/2.0)** evaluates to **5.0**.
       [1/2.0 = 0.5 (double division); Math.pow(25, 0.5) = sqrt(25) = 5.0]

A118   The **Math.pow (a, b)** method evaluates to a^b.
       [Math.pow(a, b) computes a raised to the power b and returns the result as a double]

A119   The statement to assign a variable **d** of type double to a float variable **f**, is **f = (float)d;**
       [This requires use an explicit type cast]

A120   A Java character is stored in *two* bytes [Java characters use Unicode encoding]
       [Java uses the Unicode character set, encoding each char as a 16-bit (2-byte) value]

A121   **(int)(Math.random() * (100))** returns a random number between **0** and **99**.
       [Math.random() returns a value x where 0.0 <= x < 1.0; multiplying by 100 gives 0.0 <= x < 100.0; casting to int truncates to the range 0-99]

A122   **(int)(Math.random() + 0.5)** generates random integer **0** or **1**.
       [Math.random() gives 0.0 <= x < 1.0; adding 0.5 shifts it to 0.5 <= x < 1.5; casting to int gives 0 when x < 0.5 and 1 when x >= 0.5 (after the shift, 0.5 added)]

A123   Write a statement that generates random integers in the range 18 to 65. **(int) (Math.random()*(48)) + 18**
       [The range 18 to 65 has 48 values (65 - 18 + 1 = 48); (int)(Math.random()*48) gives 0-47; adding 18 shifts the range to 18-65]

A124   **(char)('a' + Math.random() * ('z' - 'a' + 1))** returns a random character between **'a' and 'z'**.
       [The expression 'a' + Math.random() * 26 produces a random floating-point value in ['a', 'z'+1); casting to char yields a random lowercase letter]

A125   Unary arithmetic operators are **+, -, ++, --**

A. Java Basics

[The four unary arithmetic operators are + (identity), - (negation), ++ (increment), and -- (decrement)]

A126   Unary logical operator is **!**
[! is the only unary logical operator in Java; it negates a boolean value]

A127   The just one statement to assign to x the larger of the values of x and y, is **x = (x > y) ? x : y;**
[The conditional (ternary) operator evaluates the condition and returns the larger of x and y in a single expression]

A128   A collection of classes that have been grouped together into a folder is known as a ***package***.
[A package is a folder that groups related classes; it provides a namespace to avoid name conflicts]

A129   The datatype of the result of adding an int, a byte, a long, and a double, is ***double***.
[When operands of different numeric types are combined, Java promotes all to the widest type; double is the widest here]

A130   The method in the Random class which returns the next random int value is **nextInt()**.
[nextInt() returns the next uniformly distributed pseudorandom int from the Random object]

A131   The method in the Random class which returns the next random double value is **nextDouble()**.
[nextDouble() returns the next uniformly distributed pseudorandom double in [0.0, 1.0) from the Random object]

A132   The statement to declare a constant ARR_SIZE of value 25 as a class member, is **final static int ARR_SIZE = 25;**
[The **final** keyword prevents the value from being modified once assigned, effectively making it a constant]

A133   In the statement **System.out.println(num)**, **System** refers to ***class name***, **out** refers to ***static (class) variable***, **println** refers to ***instance method***, refers to a ***variable***.

[System is the class; out is a static field of type PrintStream; println is an instance method of PrintStream called on the out object]

A134 Methods and variables that are not declared as **static** are known as **_instance_** methods and **_instance_** variables.
[Members not declared static belong to individual objects; they are called instance methods and instance variables]

A135 Java's **_public class_ (or _public static_)** variables act as global variables.
[Java has no true globals; public static fields of a public class serve as the closest equivalent since they are accessible everywhere]

A136 The value returned by **(int)Math.random()** is **0**.
[The value x returned by Math.random() is such that $0 \leq x < 1.0$. When x is cast into integer by (int), it's value becomes 0]

A137 The possible range of values returned by **(int)(Math.random() * 10)** is between **0** and **9**.
[Math.random() * 10 gives 0.0 <= x < 10.0; casting to int gives the integers 0, 1, 2, ..., 9]

A138 The method which immediately terminates a program is **System.exit(0)**.
[System.exit(0) immediately terminates the JVM; the argument 0 conventionally signals normal termination]

A139 The short-circuit operators are **&&** and **||**.
[&& and || short-circuit: they skip evaluating the right operand when the result is determined by the left operand]

A140 The difference between the computed value in a program and the exact mathematical value is known as **_round-off_ (or _rounding_)** error.
[Finite-precision floating-point arithmetic cannot represent all real numbers exactly; the discrepancy is the round-off (rounding) error]

A141 In Java, the variables declared in methods are, by default, of type **_stack dynamic_**.
[Variables declared inside a method are created on the call stack when the method is invoked and destroyed when it returns — this is stack-dynamic storage]

A. Java Basics

A142 The keyword used for method declaration to indicate that the method cannot be overridden by subclasses is, **`final`**.
[Declaring a method final prevents any subclass from overriding it]

A143 A class that cannot be subclassed must be declared **`final`**.
[Declaring a class final prevents it from being extended (subclassed)]

A144 Only ***primitive scalar (Boolean, character, numeric)*** types are not objects.
[The eight primitive types (boolean, byte, short, int, long, float, double, char) are not objects; all other Java values are objects]

A145 The statement to display the character whose Unicode is stored in variable **x** is **`System.out.println((char)x);`**
[Casting an integer x to char reinterprets it as a Unicode code point; println then displays the corresponding character]

A146 The output of **`System.out.println(5)`** is $\underline{5}$
[println(5) prints the integer 5 followed by a newline]

A147 The output of **`System.out.println('5')`** is $\underline{5}$
[println('5') prints the character '5' (not the integer 53) because the argument type is char]

A148 The output of **`System.out.println('A')`** is $\underline{A}$
[println('A') prints the character A because the argument type is char]

A149 The output of **`System.out.println((int)'A')`** is $\underline{65}$
[Casting char to int yields its Unicode/ASCII code point; 'A' has code point 65]

A150 The output of **`System.out.println('Z'-'A'+1)`** is $\underline{26}$
['Z'=90, 'A'=65; 90-65+1=26, which is the number of uppercase letters in the English alphabet]

A151 The output of **`System.out.println('A'+7)`** is $\underline{72}$
[When an operand is a character in an arithmetic expression, the character is cast to an 'int' value]

A152 The output of **`System.out.println((char)'A'+7)`** is $\underline{72}$

[(char)'A' casts 'A' to char (still 65), then +7 promotes to int 72; println(int) prints 72, not the character H]

A153 The output of `System.out.println((char)('A'+7))` is **H**
['A'+7=72; (char)72='H'; println(char) prints the character H]

A154 The output of `System.out.println((int)('H'))` is **72**
[(int)'H' converts char 'H' to its code point 72]

A155 The output of `System.out.print ('1');` is **1**
[print('1') prints the character '1'; no newline is appended]

A156 The output of `System.out.print ('1' + 1);` is **50**
['1' has ASCII value 49; 49+1=50; print(int) prints the integer 50]

A157 The output of `System.out.print ((char)('1' + 16));` is **A**
['1'=49; 49+16=65; (char)65='A'; print prints the character A]

A158 The output of `System.out.print ((char)('1' + 1));` is **2**
['1'=49; 49+1=50; (char)50='2'; print prints the character 2]

A159 Given a sring s1 to be "Example", the value of `s1.length()` is **7**.
["Example" has 7 characters (E-x-a-m-p-l-e); length() returns the count]

A160 Given a sring s1 to be "Example", the value of `s1.charAt(2)` is **a**.
[Zero-based indexing: E(0) x(1) a(2) m(3) p(4) l(5) e(6); charAt(2) returns 'a']

A161 Given a sring s1 to be "In" and s2 to be "habit", the value of `s1.concat(s2)` is **"Inhabit"**.
[concat appends s2 to s1: "In" + "habit" = "Inhabit"]

A162 Given a sring s1 to be "Example" and s2 to be "example", the value of `s1.equals(s2)` is **false**.
[equals() is case-sensitive; "Example" and "example" differ in the first character, so the result is false]

A. Java Basics

A163 Given a sring s1 to be "Example" and s2 to be "EXAMPLE", the value of **s1.equalsIgnoreCase(s2)** is **true**.
[equalsIgnoreCase() ignores case differences; "Example" and "EXAMPLE" are equal ignoring case]

A164 Given a sring s1 to be "antelope" and s2 to be "zebra", the value of **s1.compareTo(s2)** is −25
[compareTo compares the first differing characters; 'a'=97, 'z'=122; 97-122 = -25]

A165 Given a sring s1 to be "Antelope" and s2 to be "Zebra", the value of **s1.compareTo(s2)** is −25
[First characters: 'A'=65, 'Z'=90; 65-90 = -25]

A166 Given a sring s1 to be "Antelope" and s2 to be "ZEBRA", the value of **s1.compareTo(s2)** is −25
[First characters: 'A'=65, 'Z'=90; 65-90 = -25 (uppercase 'Z' and 'Z' in ZEBRA are the same value)]

A167 Given a sring s1 to be "antelope" and s2 to be "ZEBRA", the value of **s1.compareTo(s2)** is 7
[First characters: 'a'=97, 'Z'=90 (uppercase letters have smaller ASCII values than lowercase); 97-90 = 7]

A168 Given a sring s1 to be "antelope" and s2 to be "Zebra", the value of **s1.compareTo(s2)** is 7
[First characters: 'a'=97, 'Z'=90; 97-90 = 7]

A169 Given a sring s1 to be "Antelope" and s2 to be "zebra", the value of **s1.compareTo(s2)** is −57
[First characters: 'A'=65, 'z'=122; 65-122 = -57]

A170 Given a sring s1 to be "zebra" and s2 to be "ZEBRA", the value of **s1.compareToIgnoreCase(s2)** is 0.
[compareToIgnoreCase treats both strings as equal regardless of case differences between 'z'/'Z', 'e'/'E', etc.]

A171 For any string s1, the value of **s1.compareTo(s1)** is 0.
[compareTo(s1) compares s1 to itself; every character is identical, so the result is 0]

Java Quiz Book

A172 Given a sring s1 to be "venture", the value of **s1.startsWith("vent")** is **true**.
["venture" begins with the substring "vent", so startsWith("vent") returns true]

A173 Given a sring s1 to be "Inhabit", the value of **s1.endsWith("habit")** is **true**.
["Inhabit" ends with the substring "habit", so endsWith("habit") returns true]

A174 For any string s1, the value of **s1.startsWith(s1)** is **true**.
[Every string s1 starts with itself as a prefix, so startsWith(s1) is always true]

A175 For any string s1, the value of **s1.startsWith(s1) && s1.endsWith(s1)** is **true**.
[Both startsWith(s1) and endsWith(s1) are true for any string s1 with itself as argument, so the conjunction is true]

A176 For any string s1, the value of **s1.contains(s1)** is always **true**.
[Every string contains itself, so contains(s1) is always true]

A177 For any strings s1 and s2, the value of **s1.concat(s2).contains(s1)** is always **true**.
[s1.concat(s2) places s1 at the start; the resulting string always contains s1, so contains(s1) is always true]

A178 Given a sring s1 to be "Inhabit", the value of **s1.substring(0)** is **"Inhabit"**.
[substring(0) returns the whole string from index 0 to the end]

A179 Given a sring s1 to be "Inhabit", the value of **s1.substring(2)** is **"habit"**.
[I(0) n(1) h(2) a(3) b(4) i(5) t(6); substring(2) starts at index 2 and returns "habit"]

A180 Given a sring s1 to be "Transportation", the statement using **substring** which returns "sport" is **s1.substring(4,9)**.
[T(0)r(1)a(2)n(3)s(4)p(5)o(6)r(7)t(8)a(9)t(10)i(11)...; substring(4,9) extracts indices 4-8: "sport"]

A181 Given a string s to be "Java Programming", the statement to return "Program" is **s.substring(5, 12)**.

146

A. Java Basics

[J(0)a(1)v(2)a(3) (4)P(5)r(6)o(7)g(8)r(9)a(10)m(11)m(12)...; substring(5,12) extracts indices 5-11: "Program"]

A182   The value of **"HABITAT".substring(0, 5)** is **"HABIT"**
[H(0)A(1)B(2)I(3)T(4)A(5)T(6); substring(0,5) extracts indices 0-4: "HABIT"]

A183   The value of **"HABITAT".substring(4, 4)** is *empty string*.
[substring(i, i) with equal begin and end indices returns an empty string (zero-length range)]

A184   The value of **"HABITAT".substring(2, 5)** is **"BIT"**
[H(0)A(1)B(2)I(3)T(4)A(5)T(6); substring(2,5) extracts indices 2-4: "BIT"]

A185   The value of **"example".substring(2)** is **"ample"**
[e(0)x(1)a(2)m(3)p(4)l(5)e(6); substring(2) starts at 'a' and returns "ample"]

A186   The value of **"upper".toUpperCase()** is **UPPER**.
[toUpperCase() converts every lowercase letter to its uppercase equivalent]

A187   The value of **"uPpEr".toUpperCase()** is **UPPER**.
[toUpperCase() converts all characters to uppercase, regardless of the original mix]

A188   The value of **"UPPER".toUpperCase()** is **UPPER**.
["UPPER" is already all uppercase; toUpperCase() returns it unchanged]

A189   The value of **"lower".toLowerCase()** is **lower**.
[toLowerCase() converts every uppercase letter to its lowercase equivalent]

A190   The value of **"LoWeR".toLowerCase()** is **lower**.
[toLowerCase() converts the entire mixed-case string to all lowercase]

A191   The value of **"LOWER".toLowerCase()** is **lower**.
["LOWER" is already all lowercase; toLowerCase() returns it unchanged]

A192   For any two strings s1 and s2, the value of the expression **s1.equals(s2) == s2.equals(s1)** is always **true**.
[equals() is symmetric: s1.equals(s2) always returns the same boolean as s2.equals(s1), so == is always true]

Java Quiz Book

A193 For any two non-null strings s1 and s2, the value of the expression
s1.equals(s2) != s2.equals(s1) is always **false**.
[equals() is symmetric, so s1.equals(s2) and s2.equals(s1) always return the same value. Their != is therefore always false]

A194 The expression **"Desire"+2+"Learn"** evaluates to ***Desire2Learn***.
["Desire"+2 concatenates to "Desire2" (number is converted to string); then +"Learn" gives "Desire2Learn"]

A195 The statement to access the last character a string **str** is **str.charAt(str.length()-1)**.
[str.length()-1 is the index of the last character; charAt retrieves the character at that position]

A196 Given a string s to be "Java Programming", the value of **s.startsWith("Java")** is **true**.
["Java Programming" begins with "Java", so startsWith returns true]

A197 Given a string s to be "Java Programming", the value of **s.endsWith("ing")** is **true**.
["Java Programming" ends with "ing", so endsWith returns true]

A198 Given a string s to be "Java Programming", the value of **s.indexOf("Java")** is **0**.
["Java" is at the beginning of the string; indexOf returns the index of the first occurrence, which is 0]

A199 Given a string s to be "Java Programming", the value of **s.lastIndexOf("gram")** is **8**.
[J(0)a(1)v(2)a(3) (4)P(5)r(6)o(7)g(8)r(9)a(10)m(11)m(12)i(13)n(14)g(15); "gram" starts at index 8]

A200 Given a string s to be "Java Programming", the value of **s.charAt(9)** is **'r'**.
[Index 9: J(0)a(1)v(2)a(3) (4)P(5)r(6)o(7)g(8)r(9); charAt(9) = 'r']

A201 Given a string s to be "Java Programming", the value of **str.indexOf('m')** is **11**.

148

[The first 'm' in "Java Programming" is at index 11 (P=5,r=6,o=7,g=8,r=9,a=10,m=11)]

A202 Given a string s to be "Java Programming", the value of **str.lastIndexOf('m')** is <u>12</u>.
[The last 'm' in "Java Programming" is at index 12 (the second 'm' in 'mm')]

A203 For any string s, the value of **s.startsWith(s)** is <u>true</u>.
[Every string uses itself as its own prefix, so startsWith(s) with s as argument always returns true]

A204 Given **String str = "Java C++ Python Ruby"**, the value of **str.matches("Python")** is <u>false</u>.
[matches() requires the entire string to match the regex; "Python" alone does not equal the full string]

A205 Given **String str = "Java C++ Python Ruby"**, the value of **str.matches(".*Python.*")** is <u>true</u>.
[.*Python.* matches any string that contains "Python" anywhere; the string does contain "Python"]

A206 Given **String str = "Java C++ Python Ruby"**, the value of **str.replaceAll(" ", ", ")** is <u>Java, C++, Python, Ruby</u>
[Each space is replaced by ", "; four spaces become four ", " separators giving the comma-separated result]

A207 Given **String str = "Java, C++, Python; Ruby;"**, the value of **str.replaceAll("[,;]", "")** is <u>Java C++ Python Ruby</u>
[[,;] is a character class matching comma or semicolon; replacing all matches with empty string removes them]

A208 Given char[] chArr = {'c','h','a','r','a','r','r','a','y'}, the statement to return a string from the content of charr is **new String(chArr)**
[The String(char[]) constructor creates a new String from the character array content]

A209 Given s is "Example", the statement to convert the string to an array of characters is **s.toCharArray()**.

149

[toCharArray() returns a new char[] array containing each character of the string in order]

A210 Given s is " example   ", the statement to remove leading and trailing spaces and return a new string "abc" is **s.trim()**.
[trim() removes all leading and trailing whitespace and returns the trimmed string]

A211 Given s1 is "Example", **s1.replace("Ex", "S")** returns **"Sample"**.
[replace("Ex", "S") substitutes the first matching substring; "Example" becomes "Sample"]

A212 Given s1 is "Sample", **s1.replace('a', 'i')** returns **"Simple"**.
[replace('a', 'i') replaces every 'a' with 'i'; "Sample" becomes "Simple"]

A213 Given s1 is "Example", **s1.replace("Ex", "S").replace('a', 'i')** returns **"Simple"**.
[First replace("Ex","S") turns "Example" into "Sample"; then replace('a','i') turns "Sample" into "Simple"]

A214 **String.valueOf(12.34).replace('.',   '\'')** returns **12'34**
[String.valueOf(12.34) = "12.34"; replace('.','\'') replaces the dot with an apostrophe, giving "12'34"]

A215 Given the following declarations,
[s2 = s1 makes both variables point to the same String object; == compares references, which are identical, so true]

```
String s1 = "Java is fun";
String s2 = s1;
```

The value of **(s1 == s2)** is **true**.

[s1 and s2 reference the same String object]

A216 Given the following declarations,
[new String(...) creates two separate objects; == compares references, which are different, so false]

150

A. Java Basics

```
String s1 = new String("Java is fun");
String s2 = new String("Java is fun");
```

The value of **(s1 == s2)** is **false**.
[s1 and s2 reference different String objects]

A217   Given the following declarations,
[equals() compares the content of the strings; both contain "Java is fun", so the result is true]

```
String s1 = new String("Java is fun");
String s2 = new String("Java is fun");
```

The value of **(s1.equals(s2))** is **true**.
[s1 and s2 refer to strings with the same content]

A218   The output of **System.out.print ("1" + 1);** is **11**
["1"+1 uses string concatenation because the left operand is a String; the int 1 is converted to "1", giving "11"]

A219   The output of **System.out.print ("1" + 1 + 1);** is **111**
["1"+1 = "11" (string concatenation); "11"+1 = "111" (left operand is still a String)]

A220   The output of **System.out.print ("1" + (1+1));** is **12**
[Parentheses force arithmetic addition first: (1+1)=2; then "1"+2 = "12" via string concatenation]

A221   Given int i = 3, j = 5, The output of **System.out.println("i + j is " + i + j)** is **i + j is 35**
[The + operators after the 'quoted' expression "i + j is " are treated as string concatenation operators]

A222   Given int i = 3, j = 5, The output of **System.out.println("i + j is " + (i + j))** is **i + j is 8**
[(i+j) is evaluated first as arithmetic addition: 3+5=8; then the result 8 is concatenated to the string]

A223 The output of `System.out.printf("%.2f", 1234.567)` is **1234.57**.
[The `%.2f` specifies up to 2 decimal places]

A224 The output of `System.out.printf("%.3e", 1234.56)` is **1.235e+03**
[The `%.3e` specifies up to 3 decimal places and scientific notation]

A225 The output of `System.out.printf("%3d", 123456)` is **123456**
[The `%3d` specifies an integer with display width 3. The width is automatically expanded if the number of digits is more than the specified width]

A226 The method to parse a string `s` to an int value is `Integer.parseInt(s)`.
[Integer.parseInt(s) converts a decimal string to an int; it throws NumberFormatException if s is not a valid integer]

A227 The method to parse a string `s` to a double value is `Double.parseDouble(s)`.
[Double.parseDouble(s) converts a string representation of a floating-point number to a double]

A228 The (decimal) value of `Integer.parseInt("1001", 2)` is **9**.
["1001" in base 2: 1×8 + 0×4 + 0×2 + 1×1 = 9]

A229 The (decimal) value of `Integer.parseInt("1001", 10)` is **1001**.
["1001" parsed as base 10 is simply one thousand and one: 1001]

A230 The (decimal) value of `Integer.parseInt("1A", 16)` is **26**.
["1A" in base 16: 1×16 + A(10) = 26]

A231 The (decimal) value of `Integer.parseInt("359")` is **359**.
[Integer.parseInt("359") with no radix defaults to base 10, giving 359]

IOIOIOIOIOIOIOIOIOIOIOIOIOIOIOIOIOIOIOIOIOIOIOIOIOI

Essay-type Questions

A1 Give examples of syntax errors.
a) Missing semicolon at the end of a statement
b) Missing closing quotation mark on a string.
c) Use of misspelt keywords (ex. 'brake' in place of 'break')
d) Using keywords with capitalization (ex. "While" in place of "while")
e) Missing corresponding closing brace (}) for an opening brace ({)
f) Putting spaces between some relational operators ("!=", "<=", ">=", "==")
g) Using the modulus operator, %, with non-integer operands.
h) Missing return statement in a method that is defined to return a value.

A2 Give examples of run-time errors.
a) Division by 0.
b) Termination due to excessive memory use (Memory leak).
c) Caught in an infinite loop

A3 Give examples of logical errors
a) Use of '=' where an equality check ('==') is intended.
b) Having an 'else' for an unintended 'if'.
c) Using "<=" in place of ">=" (and vice versa)
d) Mixing variables of different types (ex. integer and double types) in expressions without explicit cast.
e) Omitting the **break** clause from **switch** statements.

A4 What is the role of Java package?

In Java, a package broadly refers to a collection of related classes and interfaces. It facilitates organization of large programs into logical and manageable units.

A5 What are Java's primitive types?

Java's primitive types are: boolean, char, byte, short, int, long, float, double.

A6 What was the first application for Java?

Java was developed with the software for embedded consumer electronics systems in mind. However, it became extremely popular for Web programming and in graphical browsers.

A7 Analyze the following code segment:

```
boolean a, b, c;
a = (5 < 7); b = (5 == 6);
c = (a < b);
```

Gives a compilation error: bad operand types for binary operator '<'

A8 What is the output of the following code segment:

```
boolean a, b, c;
a = (5 < 7); b = (5 == 6);
c = (a == b);
System.out.format("%b %b %b\n", a, b, c);
```

true false false

A9 What is the output of the following code segment?

```
int n = 09;
System.out.println("n = " + n);
```

It gives a compilation error, since **09** is not a literal. Any number with the prefix 0 is treated as an octal number.

A10 What is the output of the following code segment?

```
int n = 99;
System.out.println("n = " + n);
```

It prints **99**.

A11 What is displayed by the following code segment?

```
int j = 0;
int i = ++j + j * 5;
```

A. Java Basics

```
System.out.println("i = " + i);
```

```
i = 6
```

Operands are evaluated from left to right in Java. The left-hand operand of a binary operator is evaluated before any part of the right-hand operand is evaluated. Therefore, ++j is evaluated first, and j is now 1. Then j * 5 is evaluated, returns 5. So, i is 6.

A12 What is displayed by the following code segment?

```
int j = 0;
int i = j++ + j * 5;
System.out.println("i = " + i);
```

```
i = 5
```

Operands are evaluated from left to right in Java. The left-hand operand of a binary operator is evaluated before any part of the right-hand operand is evaluated. Therefore, j++ is evaluated first. j is now 1. Since j++ is postincrement, the old value of j is returned for j++. So j++ + j * 5 equals 0 + 1 * 5. So, the result is 5.

A13 What is displayed by the following code segment?

```
int x = 1;
int y = x++ + x;
System.out.println("y is " + y);
```

```
y is 3
```

When evaluating x++ + x, x++ is evaluated first, which does two things: 1. returns 1 since it is post-increment. x becomes 2. Therefore y is 1 + 2.**

A14 What is displayed by the following code segment?

```
int x = 1;
int y = ++x + x;
System.out.println("y is " + y);
```

```
y is 4
```

A15   What is displayed by the following code segment?

```
int x = 1;
int y = x + x++;
System.out.println("y is " + y);
```

y is 2

When evaluating x + x++, x is evaluated first, which is 1. x++ returns 1 since it is post-increment. Therefore y is 1 + 1.

A16   Give examples of two operators that are not associative.

Subtraction (–) and division (/) are not associative.

9 – 3 – 1: when left associative would be (9 – 3) – 1 = 5;
when right associative would be 9 – (3 – 1) = 7
8 / 4 / 2: when left associative would be (8 / 4) / 2 = 1
when right associative would be 8 / (4 / 2) = 4

A17   What are the values of **a** and **n** after the execution of the following statements?

```
a = 2; n = a++; a = n++; n = a++;
```

n = a++; → n is assigned 2, and a is then incremented to 3, since it is post-increment.
a = n++; → a is assigned 2, and n is then incremented to 3, since it is post-increment.
n = a++; → n is assigned 2, and a is then incremented to 3, since it is post-increment.

Therefore, the values are: a = 3 and n = 2

A18   What are the values of **a** and **n** after the execution of the following statements?

```
a = 2; n = a++; a = ++n; n = a++;
```

n = a++; → n is assigned 2, and a is then incremented to 3, since it is post-increment.

A. Java Basics

      a = ++n; → n is incremented to 3, since it is pre-increment, and then a is assigned 3.
      n = a++; → n is assigned 3, and a is then incremented to 4, since it is post-increment.

      Therefore, the values are: **a = 4** and **n = 3**

A19 What are the values of **a** and **n** after the execution of the following statements?

      `a = 2; n = ++a; a = n++; n = ++a;`

      n = ++a; → a is incremented to 3, since it is pre-increment, and then n is assigned 3.
      a = n++; → a is assigned 3, and n is then incremented to 4, since it is post-increment.
      n = ++a; → a is incremented to 4, since it is pre-increment, and then n is assigned 4.

      Therefore, the values are: **a = 4** and **n = 4**

A20 What are the values of **a** and **n** after the execution of the following statements?

      `a = 2; n = ++a; a = ++n; n = ++a;`

      n = ++a; → a is incremented to 3, since it is pre-increment, and then n is assigned 3.
      a = ++n; → n is incremented to 4, since it is pre-increment, and then a is assigned 4.
      n = ++a; → a is incremented to 5, since it is pre-increment, and then n is assigned 5.

      Therefore, the values are: **a = 5** and **n = 5**

A21 What is the difference between coercion and cast?

      Coercion is implicit type conversion which is automatically done by the compiler. Cast is explicit type conversion done by the programmer.

Java Quiz Book

A22 What is an overloaded operator?

An overloaded operator has the same form, but has different actions based on the data types. For example, the '+' (addition) operator has totally different underlying operations when the operands are integers, floating-point numbers, strings, or matrices.

A23 What is short-circuit evaluation?

In the case of compound expressions made up of sub-expressions, the value of the expression may be determined without evaluation all of the component sub-expressions, based on rules of Logic. This is known as short-circuit evaluation.

A24 What is the output of the following code segment?
```
int n = 1000 * 1000 * 2000;
System.out.println("n = " + n);
```

n = 2000000000

A25 What is the output of the following code segment?
```
int n = 1000 * 1000 * 3000;
System.out.println("n = " + n);
```

n = -1294967296

The result of 1000 * 1000 * 3000 is too large to be stored in the int variable n. This causes an overflow and gives erroneous results. However, the program continues to run because Java does not report overflow errors.

A26 What is the output of the following code segment?
```
int n = 1000 * 1000 * 5000;
System.out.println("n = " + n);
```

n = 705032704

The result of 1000 * 1000 * 5000 is too large to be stored in the int variable n. This causes an overflow and gives erroneous results. However, the program continues to run because Java does not report overflow errors.

A. Java Basics

B. Control Structures

True/False Questions

B1 The 'for' loop is more powerful (in terms of controlling the flow of statement executions) than a 'while' loop. *False*
[All three loop constructs (for, while, do-while) have equivalent expressive power and can simulate each other]

B2 The **for** statement can be rewritten as a **while** loop. *True*
[A for loop can always be rewritten as a while loop by moving initialization before the loop and update to the end of the body]

B3 The **for**, **while**, and **do-while** loops do not have equivalent expressive power. *False*
[The for, while, and do-while loops are all equivalent in expressive power; any one can be transformed into another]

B4 Any of the **for**, **while**, and **do-while** loops can be transformed to the other having the same effect. *True*
[All three loop constructs are equivalent – each can be transformed into either of the other two with the same behavior]

B5 The **do-while** loop always executes at least once. *True*
[In a do-while loop, the body is executed first, then the condition is tested; so the body always runs at least once]

B6 The **while** loop always executes at least once. *False*
[A while loop tests its condition before execution; if the condition is initially false, the body never executes]

B7 The **for** loop always executes at least once. *False*
[A for loop also tests its condition before the first iteration; if exp2 is initially false, the body never executes]

B8 The index variable of a **for** loop cannot be of type double. *False*
[The index (loop control) variable of a for loop can be of any numeric type, including double]

B. Control Structures

B9   **for (; ;);** is equivalent to **for (; true;);** *True*
[An empty for condition is treated as always true, making for(;;) equivalent to for(;true;) — both are infinite loops]

B10   The **switch** statement cannot be rewritten by using multiple **if-else** statements. *False*
[Any switch statement can be rewritten using a chain of if-else-if statements]

B11   The **break** statement inside an inner loop of a nested loop will pass control out of the all the nested loops to the statement outside of the outermost loop. *False*
[The **break** statement passes control to the first statement outside of the (innermost) loop where it is executed]

B12   The **break** statement inside a loop of a nested loop will pass control out of the entire loop. *False*
[The **break** statement will pass control out of the loop at that level and to the enclosing loop, if any]

B13   Assignment statements always produce side effects. *True*
[An assignment statement changes the state of memory (produces a side effect) every time it executes]

B14   An Iterator is a method. *False*
[An Iterator is an object]

B15   An Iterator can be used to loop through an array. *False*
[An Iterator is an object that can be used to loop through collections like ArrayList]

B16   All the three expressions of the 'for' statement are optional. *True*
[All three expressions in a for statement (initialization, condition, update) are optional; omitting the condition makes it infinite]

B17   The **exp1** in **for (exp1; exp2; exp3)** can be executed more than once. *False*
[The initialization expression (exp1) in a for loop executes exactly once, before the first iteration]

B18 The **exp1** in **for (exp1; exp2; exp3)** cannot consist of multiple statements. *False*
[Multiple statements separated by commas is valid]

B19 The **exp3** in **for (exp1; exp2; exp3)** can consist of multiple statements. *True*
[Multiple statements separated by commas is valid]

B20 The **continue** control statement transfers control to the the outermost loop. *False*
[The **continue** statement transfers control to the update expression (exp3) of the current loop, not to any outer loop]

B21 The **continue** control statement transfers control to the start of the loop, ignoring further statements after the **continue**. *True*
[The **continue** statement skips the remaining statements in the current iteration and restarts the loop from the condition check]

IOIOIOIOIOIOIOIOIOIOIOIOIOIOIOIOIOIOIOIOIOIOIOIOI

Fill-in the-blanks Questions

B1 Statement that is used to modify the order of execution is known as *control* statement.
[A control statement is any statement that changes the default sequential execution flow of a program]

B2 A control statement together with its associated block of statements is known as *control structure*.
[A control structure combines a control statement with the block of statements whose execution it governs]

B3 A loop whose number of iterations is determined by the numeric value of a variable is known as *counter-controlled* loop.
[A counter-controlled loop uses a numeric variable (counter) to track and limit the number of iterations]

B. Control Structures

B4 A loop whose number of iterations is determined by the Boolean condition of an expression is known as ***condition-controlled*** loop.
[A condition-controlled loop repeats as long as a Boolean expression evaluates to true; the iteration count is not fixed in advance]

B5 In a ***post-test*** (***do-while***) loop control structure, the loop body is executed at least once.
[Because the condition is tested after the loop body executes, the do-while loop guarantees at least one execution of the body]

B6 It is more natural to use the **for** loop when the number of iterations is known *a priori* (before hand).
[When the number of iterations is known before the loop begins, the for loop is the natural choice because it groups the initialisation, condition, and update together]

B7 The statement block in a ***post–test*** (or ***do–while***) control structure is executed at least once.
[Because the condition is evaluated at the end of the loop body, a post-test (do-while) construct always executes the block at least once]

B8 The ***multiple–selection* (switch-case)** construct allows the selection of one of a number of statements or statement groups.
[The switch-case (multiple-selection) statement evaluates a single expression and branches to one of several labeled statement groups]

B9 ***Pre–test loop* (ex. *while loop*)** causes a (compound) statement to be executed zero or more times.
[A pre-test loop checks its condition before each iteration; if the condition is initially false the body is never executed (zero executions)]

B10 The **break** control statement transfers control out of the smallest enclosing loop.
[break immediately terminates the innermost enclosing loop (or switch), transferring control to the first statement after that construct]

B11 The **continue** control statement transfers control to the control mechanism of the smallest enclosing loop.
[continue skips the rest of the current iteration and transfers control to the update expression (for loop) or the condition test (while/do-while) of the innermost enclosing loop]

B12 An optional **else** clause in an **if–then** [–**else**] statement resulting in nested conditionals being ambiguous is known as *dangling-else* problem.
[The dangling-else problem arises when an else clause is ambiguous because it could be associated with more than one preceding if; Java resolves it by always pairing else with the nearest preceding if]

B13 The effect of the statement **for (; ;)**; is *an infinite loop*.
[With all three for-loop expressions omitted (for(;;)), the condition is treated as always true, creating an infinite loop]

B14 The numbet of times the **STATEMENT BLOCK** is executed in the following loop is **25**.
[i runs from 23 through 47 inclusive; count = 47 - 23 + 1 = 25 iterations]

```
for (int i=23; i <= 47; i++) {
    STATEMENT BLOCK
}
```

B15 The numbet of times the **STATEMENT BLOCK** is executed in the following loop is **15**.
[i runs from 51 down to 37 (while i > 36); count = 51 - 37 + 1 = 15 iterations]

```
for (int i=51; i > 36; i--) {
    STATEMENT BLOCK
}
```

IOIOIOIOIOIOIOIOIOIOIOIOIOIOIOIOIOIOIOIOIOIOIOIOIOI

Essay-type Questions

B1 Do the **while**, **do-while**, and **for** loops have different expressive powers?
The above three forms have equivalent powers in the sense that any loop type can be transformed to any of the other loop types, while achieving the same effect.

B2 What is the difference between **break** and **continue** statements (of C-family) of languages?
When a **break** statement is encountered, it transfers control out of the innermost loop to the statement right after the end of that loop.

The net effect is the termination of the innermost loop immediately when the **break** is seen. When a **continue** statement is encountered, the control stays within the loop, but the remainder of the statements after the **continue** statement are skipped. The net effect is starting the next loop iteration immediately.

B3 What are the two broad categories of control statements?
Control statements facilitate the altering of the sequential order of statement executions. The two broad categories are, (a) conditional selections (two–way or multi–way) and (b) loops.

B4 Briefly describe the two categories of loops.
The two loop categories are:
1. Counter–controlled loops, where the number of iterations is determined by a counter, a variable keeping a count.
2. Logically–controlled loops, where the number of iterations is determined by a condition which is specified by a Boolean expression.

B5 When is it beneficial have the **if** and multiple **else if** statements in a certain order?

Suppose the code segment has the following structure (where **statement** represents a block):
```
if (cond1)
   statement1
else if (cond2)
   statement2
else if (cond3)
   statement3
   : : : : :
else
   statementN
```

Suppose the average number of times each of the conditions if true is known. Then, it is beneficial to order the statements in decreasing order of the probabilities of the conditions being true. For example, if Probability (cond1) > Probability (cond2) > Probability (cond3) > ..., then using this order, the average number of condition checks is minimized. **cond1** is true most number of times on average, and the further **else if** statements will not be done, and so on.

B6 The following loop was intended to compute 1/2 + 2/3 + 3/4 + ... + 99/100. What is the error and what is a fix?.

```
double sum = 0;
for (int i = 1; i <= 99; i++) {
   sum += i / (i + 1);
}
```

In each iteration, the division in `i / (i + 1)` is performed on integers, and each of them results in a 0. Thus, sum remains 0.0. Each of the following code segments shows a fix.

```
double sum = 0;
for (int i = 1; i <= 99; i++) {
   sum += (double)i / (i + 1);
}

double sum = 0;
for (int i = 1; i <= 99; i++) {
   sum += i / (i + 1.0);
}

double sum = 0;
for (int i = 1; i <= 99; i++) {
   sum += 1.0 * i / (i + 1);
}
```

B7 Do the following loops result in the same value of sum?

```
for (int i = 1; i <= 10; ++i) {
   sum += i;
}

for (int i = 1; i <= 10; i++) {
   sum += i;
}
```

Here, ++i and i++ are used standalone with no side-effect. So, they are equivalent.

B8 What is flaw with the following segment? How could it be overcome?

```
double sum = 0;
double n = 0;
while (n != 10.0) {
   n += 0.1;
   sum += n;
}
```

There is no guarantee that the value of n will be exactly 10.0 because real numbers are represented using approximation in computers. Thus, the code could get caught in an infinite loop.

The important point to note is not to compare floating point numbes for "equality/non-equality" whose values are based on a sequence of computations. One way is to see if they are arbitrarily "close to each other" by using ABS $(x - y) < \varepsilon$ (for some ε, say 0.001).

```
double sum = 0;
double n = 0;
while (Math.abs(n - 10.0) > 0.001) {
   n += 0.1;
   sum += n;
}
```

B9 The following code which was intended to print 1, 2, ... 10 has a flaw. What does it print? What is the correction required?

```
int i;
for (i = 1; i <= 10; i++);
   System.out.println(i);
```

The program prints 11. Note that there is a ";" after the **for** statement. Thus, there is no body of statements in the **for** loop. After the loop exits, the value of i is 11, which is printed. The corrected code is shown below.

```
int i;
for (i = 1; i <= 10; i++)
   System.out.println(i);
```

B10 How many times does the **while** loop execute in the following code segment?

```
int x = 0;
while (x < 5)
   x++;
```

5 times.

B11 How many times does the **while** loop execute in the following code segment?

```
int x = 10;
while (x < 5)
   x++;
```

0 times.

B12 How many times does the **while** loop execute, and what will be the value of **sum** after the loop has finished?

```
double n = 0, sum = 0;
while (n <= 1.0) {
   n += 0.1;
   sum += n;
}
```

The loop executes 11 times. The value of **sum** after the loop has finished is 6.6.

B13 Does the following code segment result in an infinite loop?

```
int x = 0;
while (x >= 0)
   x++;
```

No. x keeps on incrementing, and after it reaches the maximum representable integers, further increment results in an overflow, which results in x becoming negative, at which time the condition becomes false, and the loop exits. Note that the largest representable positive integer (in 32 bits) is $2^{31} - 1 = 2147483647$, and the largest representable negative integer (in 32 bits) is $-2^{31} = -2147483648$. When the value of x reaches the largest representable value, and it is incremented, there will be an overflow.

B. Control Structures

B14   What is the output of the following code segment?

```
int i=0, x = 0;
while (x >= 0){
  x++;
  i++;
}
System.out.println("i=" + (i-1) + " x=" + x);
```

i = 2147483647 x = -2147483648

B15   What is the output of the following code segment?

```
int x = 0;
while (x < 5)
  x++;
System.out.println("x = " + x);
```

x = 5

B16 Rewrite the following code segment using a **for** loop with the same effect.

```
int x = 0;
while (x < 5)
  x++;
System.out.println("x = " + x);
```

There are several ways of doing it. A couple of ways are given below.

```
int x = 0;
for (int i=0; i < 5; i++)
  x++;
System.out.println("x = " + x);

int x = 0;
for (; x < 5; x++);
System.out.println("x = " + x);
```

B17   Convert the following 'for' loop to 'while' loop.

```
for (int i=low; i <= high; i++){
```

```
      STATEMENT BLOCK
    }

    int i=low;
    while (i <= high) {
      STATEMENT BLOCK
      i++;
    }
```

B18   Convert the following 'while' loop to 'do-while' loop, assuming low ≤ high.

```
    int i=low;
    while (i <= high) {
      STATEMENT BLOCK
      i++;
    }

    int i=low;
    do {
      STATEMENT BLOCK
      i++;
    } while(i <= high);
```

For arbitrary values of 'low' and 'high',

```
    int i=low;
    if (low <= high) {
      do {
        STATEMENT BLOCK
        i++;
      } while(i <= high);
    }
```

B19   What is the output of the following code segment?

```
    double sum = 0;
    while (sum != 10)
      sum += 0.1;
    System.out.println(sum);
```

It is likely that it gets caught in an infinite loop. Unlike integer arithmetic, due to the nature of floating point arithmetic, the result of adding 0.1 to the variable sum, may not result in an exact value of 10. Thus the value of sum may never equal to 10

B20   What is the output of the following code segment?

```
double sum = 0;
while (sum < 10)
   sum += 0.1;
System.out.println(sum);
```

It is likely prints out 10.09999 ...98.

B21   What is the output of the following code segment?

```
double sum = 0, incr = 0.01;
for (int i=1; i<=100; i++)
   sum += incr;
System.out.println(sum);
```

1.0000000000000007

Results may vary slightly based on the system on which it is run.

B22   What is the output of the following code segment?

```
double sum = 0, incr = 0;
for (int i=1; i<=100; i++){
   incr += 0.01;
   sum += incr;
}
System.out.println(sum);
```

50.50000000000003

Results may vary slightly based on the system on which it is run. Note that the loop has 100 iterations. incr is initially 0, and is incremented by 0.01 in every iteration before adding to sum, and it will be (close to) 1.0 in the last iteration. The (ideal) sum will be 0.01 + 0.02 + 0.03 + ... 1.0.

Java Quiz Book

B23 What is the output of the following code segment?

```
double sum = 0, decr = 1;
for (int i=1; i<=100; i++) {
  sum += decr;
  decr -= 0.01;
}
System.out.println(sum);

50.49999999999995
```

Results may vary slightly based on the system on which it is run. Note that the loop has 100 iterations. decr is initially 1, and is decremented by 0.01 in every iteration, and it will be (close to) 0.0 in the last iteration. The (ideal) sum will be 1.0 + 0.99 + 0.98 + ... 0.01.

B24 What is the output of the following code segment?

```
double sum = 0, incr = 0, decr = 1.0;
for (int i=1; i<=50; i++) {
  incr += 0.01;
  sum = sum + incr + decr;
  decr -= 0.01;
}
System.out.println(incr);
System.out.println(sum);

50.49999999999999
```

Results may vary slightly based on the system on which it is run.

B25 What error does the following code segment have?

```
int x;
double d = 1.5;

switch (d) {
  case 1.0: x = 1;
  case 1.5: x = 2;
  case 2.0: x = 3;
}
```

172

It results in a compilation error. The switch control variable cannot be 'double'.

B26   What error does the following code segment have?

```
int x;
double d = 1.5;

switch ((int)d) {
   case (int)1.0: x = 1;
   case (int)1.5: x = 2;
   case (int)2.0: x = 3;
}
```

It results in a compilation error due to duplicate 'case' values.

B27   What error does the following code segment have, if any?

```
int x;
double d = 1.5;

switch ((int)d) {
   case (int)1.5: x = 1;
   case (int)2.5: x = 2;
   case (int)3.5: x = 3;
}
```

There is no error.

B28   What is the output of the following program?

```
public class Main {

  public static void main(String[] args) {
    int i, j;
    for (i=1; i<=3; i++) {
      for (j=1; j<=3; j++) {
        if ((i+j) % 4 == 0) {
           System.out.println("\nIteration (" + i + "," + j
 + ") is not done");
           break;
        }
        else
           System.out.print("("+ i + ", " + j + ") is done
");
```

```
        }
        System.out.println();
      }
    }
}
```

```
        (1, 1) is done (1, 2) is done
        Iteration (1,3) is not done

        (2, 1) is done
        Iteration (2,2) is not done


        Iteration (3,1) is not done
```

B29   What is the output of the following program?

```
public class Main
{
  public static void main(String[] args) {
    int i, j;
    for (i=1; i<=3; i++) {
      for (j=1; j<=3; j++) {
        if ((i+j) % 4 == 0) {
           System.out.println("\nIteration (" + i + "," + j +
   ") is not done");
           continue;
        }
        else
          System.out.print("("+ i + ", " + j + ") is done ");
      }
      System.out.println();
    }
  }
}
```

```
        (1, 1) is done (1, 2) is done
        Iteration (1,3) is not done

        (2, 1) is done
        Iteration (2,2) is not done
        (2, 3) is done

        Iteration (3,1) is not done
        (3, 2) is done (3, 3) is done
```

B30   What is the output of the following program?

```
public class Main {
  public static void main(String[] args) {
```

B. Control Structures

```
for (int i = 0; i < 10; i++){
  for (int j = 0; j < 10; j++){
    if ((i+j) % 3 == 0)
      break;
    System.out.print("(" + i + "," + j + ") ");
  }
  System.out.println();
}
```

```
(1,0) (1,1)
(2,0)

(4,0) (4,1)
(5,0)

(7,0) (7,1)
(8,0)
```

IOIOIOIOIOIOIOIOIOIOIOIOIOIOIOIOIOIOIOIOIOIOIOIOIOIOI

C. Arrays and Arraylists

True/False Questions

C1 An array cannot be passed as argument to a method. ***False***
[Arrays can be passed as arguments to methods; the method receives a reference to the array, not a copy]

C2 When an array is passed to a method, the method receives a copy of the array. ***False***
[Arrays can be passed as argument to a method. The pass-by-reference is used for array arguments]

C3 The parameter passing mechanisms of arrays and array elements are the same. ***False***
[The parameter passing mechanism used for arrays is pass-by-reference, and that for array elements is pass-by-value]

C4 Arrays cannot be returned from methods. ***False***
[A method can return an array by returning a reference to it, just as it can return any reference type]

C5 Multidimensioal arrays cannot be returned from methods. ***False***
[A method can return a multidimensional array, just as it can return any reference type]

C6 The elements of an array of primitive type can be heterogeneous. ***False***
[All elements of an array of primitive type must be of the same type]

C7 The elements of an array for instances of a class should be instances of that same class. ***False***
[The elements an array for instances of a class could have instances of that class, as well as instances any its subclasses]

C8 When an array is created using the 'new' statement, the element values are automatically initialized to 0. ***True***
[When an array is created with 'new', numeric elements are initialized to 0, boolean to false, and object references to null]

C. Arrays and Arraylists

C9   The size of an array can be changed after it is created. *False*
[Once an array is created, its size is fixed and cannot be changed; use ArrayList for a resizable structure]

C10 The datatype of an array must be specified at the time of declaration. *True*
[The data type of an array must be declared, which determines the type of all elements it can hold]

C11 An array of a generic type can be declared. *False*
[At the time of declaration of an array, the datatype must be specified]

C12 The datatype of an array could be changed during run time. *False*
[Once declared, the data type of an array is fixed at compile time and cannot change during execution]

C13 An array is an instance of a class. *False*
[In Java, an array is a special built-in type; it is an object but not an instance of any user-defined class]

C14 An ArrayList is an instance of a class. *True*
[An ArrayList is an instance the ArrayList class which is provided by a Java Library]

C15 The size of an ArrayList can change (shrink/grow) after its creation. *True*
[ArrayList is a dynamic data structure; elements can be added or removed, causing it to grow or shrink automatically]

C16 Methods for common operations on ArrayList are available via APIs. *True*
[The Java Collections Framework provides a rich set of methods for ArrayList operations through its API]

C17 The elements of an ArrayList can be heterogeneous. *False*
[An ArrayList declared with a specific type parameter (e.g., ArrayList<Integer>) can only hold elements of that type]

C18 An ArrayList can contain elements of primitive (ex. int, double) types. *False*
[An ArrayList must contain objects, not primitive types]

C19   An ArrayList can be declared to be of 'generic' type. ***True***
[An ArrayList can be declared with a generic type parameter, e.g., ArrayList<E>, to specify the element type at instantiation]

C20   Given the declaration `int i1`, the value of `i1` is a reference to an integer. ***False***
['int' is a primitive type. A variable of a primitive type stores a value of that type]

C21   Given the declaration `Integer i2`, the value of `i2` is a an integer. ***False***
['Integer' is a class, and a variable of that class contains a reference (or address) to an object/instantiation of that class]

C22   Given the declaration `int[] i3`, the value of `i3` is `null`. ***True***
[i3 has been declared, but is not referecing any object, and has a value of null]

C23   Given the declaration `int[] i3 = new int[3]`, the value of `i3` is `null`. ***False***
[i3 is referencing a chunk of memory which has been allocated using 'new', and is not null]

C24   Given the declaration `int[] i4 = {1, 2, 3}`, the value of `i4` is not `null`. ***True***
[An array created with an initializer list is immediately allocated and populated, so its reference is not null]

IOIOIOIOIOIOIOIOIOIOIOIOIOIOIOIOIOIOIOIOIOIOIOIOIOI

Fill-in the-blanks Questions

C1   When an array is returned from a method, ***the reference of the array*** is returned.
[In Java, arrays are objects; returning an array from a method returns the reference (address) of the array object on the heap]

C2   When an array is passed to a method, the method receives ***the reference of the array***.

C. Arrays and Arraylists

[When an array is passed to a method, the reference to the array object is copied into the parameter; no copy of the array elements is made]

C3 The parameter passing mechanism used, when arrays are passed as arguments to methods, is ***pass-by-reference***.
[Because the reference to the array is passed, the method can modify the original array elements -- this is pass-by-reference semantics]

C4 The parameter passing mechanism used, when array elements are passed as arguments to methods, is ***pass-by-value***.
[Individual array elements of primitive type are copied into the method's parameter variable, so changes inside the method do not affect the original element]

C5 The parameter passing mechanism used, when primitive types are passed as arguments to methods, is ***pass-by- value***.
[Primitive-type arguments are copied into the method's local parameter; the caller's variable is unaffected by any changes]

C6 The parameter passing mechanism used, when objects are passed as arguments to methods, is ***pass-by- reference***.
[When an object is passed to a method, the reference (address) of the object is copied; the method can modify the object through that reference]

C7 In Java, arrays are always allocated on ***heap***.
[Java allocates all arrays on the heap; the array variable on the stack holds only a reference (pointer) to the heap array]

C8 Given int[] a = {12, 9, 5, 14, 25}, a.length is **5**.
[a.length for {12, 9, 5, 14, 25} is 5 because the array has five elements]

C9 Given int[] a = {12, 9, 5, 14, 25}, element 14 is accessed using **a[3]**.
[Indices are 0-based: a[0]=12, a[1]=9, a[2]=5, a[3]=14, a[4]=25; so a[3] gives 14]

C10 Given double[][] x = new double[4][5], x.length is **4**.
[The first dimension of a double[4][5] array has 4 rows; x.length returns 4]

C11 Given double[][] x = new double[4][5], x[2].length is **5**.
[Each row of a double[4][5] array has 5 columns; x[2].length returns 5]

C12 The number of objects created by the following code is **1**.
[The new keyword creates exactly one array object on the heap; b is assigned the same reference as a, so no additional object is created]

```
double[] a = new double[10];
double[] b;
b = a;
```
[An object (array of 10 'double') is created by the 'new' and 'a' is a reference to that object, while 'b' is a reference to the same object referenced by 'a']

C13 Given the following code segment, the number of elements of x is **6**.
[The ragged array has rows of length 1, 2, and 3; total elements = 1 + 2 + 3 = 6]
```
boolean[][] x = new boolean[3][];
x[0] = new boolean[1]; x[1] = new boolean[2];
x[2] = new boolean[3];
```

[x is a ragged array, with 1 element in the first row, 2 elements in the second row, and 3 elements in the third row]

C14 Given `int[][] x = {{1, 2}, {3, 4}, {5, 6}, {7, 8}}`, `x.length` is **4** and `x[0].length` is **2**.
[The 2-D array has 4 rows (x.length = 4) and each row has 2 elements (x[0].length = 2)]

C15 Given int[][] x = {{1}, {2, 3}, {4, 5, 6}}, the values of `x.length`, `x[0].length`, `x[1].length`, and `x[2].length` are **3**, **1**, **2**, and **3**.
[x has 3 rows (x.length = 3); x[0] has 1 element, x[1] has 2 elements, and x[2] has 3 elements]

C16 Given the declaration `int i1`, the data type of `i1` is ***integer***.
[The declaration int i1 creates a variable of the primitive type integer (int)]

C17 Given the declaration `int[] i2`, the data type of `i2` is ***reference to an array of integers***.
[int[] i2 declares a reference variable whose type is an array of integers; no array is yet created]

C18 Given the declaration `int[] i2`, the value of `i2` is **null**.
[An uninitialized array reference variable in Java holds the value null until it is assigned an array object]

C19 Given the declaration `int[] i3 = new int[3]`, the value of `i3` is ***address of start of an array of 3 integers***.

[new int[3] allocates an array of 3 integers on the heap; i3 holds the address (reference) of the first element]

C20 Given the declaration **int[] i3 = new int[3]**, the values of the elements of the array of 3 integers referenced by **i3** are **0s**.
[Java automatically initializes the elements of a newly allocated int[] array to 0]

C21 A statement to remove all elements in an ArrayList list is **list.clear()**.
[ArrayList.clear() removes all elements from the list, leaving an empty list]

C22 Assuming ArrayList pcolor of type String is [Red, Blue], a statement to make it [Red, Green, Blue] is **pcolor.add(1, "Green")**
[add(int index, E element) inserts the element at the specified index, shifting subsequent elements right; add(1, "Green") inserts at position 1]

C23 Assuming ArrayList pcolor of type String is [Red, Green, Cyan, Blue], a statement to make it [Red, Green, Blue] is **pcolor.remove(2)** or **pcolor.remove("Cyan")**
[remove(int index) removes by position; remove(Object o) removes the first occurrence by value; both correctly remove "Cyan" at index 2]

C24 A statement to return the last element in an ArrayList list is **list.get(list.size()-1)**.
[list.size()-1 is the index of the last element; get() returns the element at that index]

C25 Assuming ArrayList list of type Integer is [10, 11, 12], a statement to add 13 as the new element at the end of the list is **list.add(list.size(), 13)**.
[add(list.size(), 13) appends 13 at the end because size() equals the index one past the last element]

C26 Given an ArrayList list contains {"red", "green", "blue", "red", "yellow", "blue"}, the list after list.remove("red") would be **{"green", "blue", "red", "yellow", "blue"}**
[ArrayList.remove(Object) removes the first occurrence of the specified element; removing "red" from position 0 leaves the remaining elements in order]

IOIOIOIOIOIOIOIOIOIOIOIOIOIOIOIOIOIOIOIOIOIOIOIOIOIOIOI

Essay-type Questions

C1   What is the output of the following code segment?

```
int[] a = new int[5];
int i;
for (i = 0; i < a.length; i++)
   a[i] = i+1;
System.out.print(a[i] + " ");
```

It gives a runtime error. The value of i used in a[i] in the print statement is 5, which is beyond the bounds of 'a', and causes ArrayIndexOutOfBoundsException.

C2   What is the output of the following code segment?

```
int[] a = new int[5];
int i;
for (i = 0; i < a.length; i++) {
  a[i] = i+1;
  System.out.print(a[i] + " ");
}
```

1 2 3 4 5

C3   What is the output of the following code segment?

```
int[] list = {1, 2, 3, 4, 5};
for (int i = list.length - 2; i >= 0; i--) {
   list[i+1] = list[i];
}
for (int e: list)
   System.out.print(e + " ");
```

1 1 2 3 4

C4   What is the output of the following code segment?

```
int[] list = {1, 2, 3, 4, 5};
for (int i = list.length - 1; i > 0; i--) {
   list[i-1] = list[i];
}
```

C. Arrays and Arraylists

```
for (int e: list)
   System.out.print(e + " ");
```

5 5 5 5 5

C5 What is the output of the following code?

```
int[] list = {1, 2, 3, 4, 5};
for (int i = 1; i < list.length; i++) {
   list[i-1] = list[i];
}
for (int e: list)
   System.out.print(e + " ");
```

2 3 4 5 5

C6 What is output of the following code segment?

```
public class Base {
  public static void main(String[] args) {
    int x = 25, y = 025;
    System.out.println("x = " + x + " y = " + y);
  }
}
```

x = 25 y = 21.
025 is treated as an octal number. The prefix 0 indicates that a number is in octal. The decimal equivalent of 025 is 21.

C7 What is the output of the following code segment?

```
final int i=10;
i=12;
System.out.println (i);
```

It gives a compilation error, since a variable declared with 'final' keyword is immutable.

C8 What is the output of the following code segment?

```
final int[] a = {1, 2, 6, 4, 5};
System.out.println (a[2]);
a[2] = 3;
```

183

```
System.out.println (a[2]);
```

6
3

Note that 'a' which is a reference to an array is declared with the 'final' keyword. Therefore, the reference is immutable, in other words, it cannot be made to refer to a different object. However, the array elements can be assigned different values.

C9 What is the output of the following code segment?

```
int[] a = {1, 2, 3, 4, 5};
System.out.println (a[2]);
a = new int[5];
System.out.println (a[2]);
```

3
0

After the first 'println', 'a' is assigned reference to a new array with all elements being 0's.

C10 What is the output of the following code segment?

```
final int[] a = {1, 2, 3, 4, 5};
System.out.println (a[2]);
a = new int[5];
```

It gives a compilation error. Note that 'a' which is a reference to an array is declared with the 'final' keyword, and there is an attempt to make it to refer to a different object.

C11 What is the output of the following code segment?

```
int[] x = {1, 2, 3, 4, 5};
int[] y = x;
x = new int[]{5, 6, 7, 8, 9};
for (int i = 0; i < y.length; i++)
    System.out.print(y[i] + " ");
```

The program outputs **1 2 3 4 5**. Note that when 'y' was declared, it had reference to the array object with {1, 2, 3, 4, 5}. Subsequently, 'x' was made to refer to a new object, and y's reference was not changed.

C12 What is the output of the following code segment?

```
int[] x = {1, 2, 3, 4, 5};
int[] y = x;
x[0]=5; x[1]=6; x[2]=7; x[3]=8; x[4]=9;
for (int i = 0; i < y.length; i++)
   System.out.print(y[i] + " ");
```

The program outputs **5 6 7 8 9**. Note that when 'y' was declared, it had reference to the array object with {1, 2, 3, 4, 5}. Subsequently, the contents of the array referenced by 'x' was changed, and y's reference was not changed.

C13 What is the output of the following code segment?

```
int[] x = {1, 2, 3, 4, 5};
int[] y = x;
y[0]=5; y[1]=6; y[2]=7; y[3]=8; y[4]=9;
for (int i = 0; i < x.length; i++)
   System.out.print(x[i] + " ");
```

The program outputs **5 6 7 8 9**. Note that when 'y' was declared, it had the same reference as x to the array object. Subsequently, the contents of the array referenced by 'y' was changed. Since 'x' has the same reference as 'y' to the array object, it reflects the changes.

C14 What is the output of the following code segment?

```
int[] x = {1, 2, 3, 4, 5}, y = {6, 7, 8, 9};
int[] z = new int[9];
System.arraycopy(y, 0, z, 0, y.length);
System.arraycopy(x, 0, z, 4, x.length);
for (int i = 0; i < z.length; i++)
  System.out.print(z[i] + " ");
```

6 7 8 9 1 2 3 4 5

C15 What is the output of the following program?

```java
public class Test {
  public static void main(String[] args) {
    int[] x = {1, 2, 3, 4, 5};
    increment(x);
    int[] y = {1, 2, 3, 4, 5};
    increment(y[0]); increment(y[1]);
    increment(y[2]); increment(y[3]);
    increment(y[4]);

    for (int i=0; i<x.length; i++)
      System.out.print(x[i] + " ");
    System.out.println();
    for (int i=0; i<y.length; i++)
      System.out.print(y[i] + " ");
  }
  public static void increment(int[] a) {
    for (int i = 0; i < a.length; i++)
      a[i]++;
  }
  public static void increment(int a) {
    a++;
  }
}
```

    2 3 4 5 6
    1 2 3 4 5

The method 'increment' with array as parameter uses pass-by-reference, so the method has direct access to the locations and changes (increments) are made in the array elements. The method 'increment' with scalar integer as parameter uses pass-by-value, so only copies of the passed arguments are used, and the original values are unaffected.

C16 What is the output of the following code segment?

```java
ArrayList<String> list = new ArrayList<String>();
String s1 = new String("Example");
String s2 = new String("Example");
list.add(s1);
list.add(s2);
```

```
System.out.println(list.get(0) == list.get(1));
System.out.println (list.get(0).equals(list.get(1)));
```

> false
> true

C17 What is the output of the following code segment?

```
ArrayList<String>list =
    new ArrayList<String>();
list.add(0,"red");list.add(1,"green");
list.add(2,"blue");list.add(3,"red");
for (int i = 0; i < list.size(); i++)
   System.out.print(list.get(i) + " ");
list.remove("red");
for (int i = 0; i < list.size(); i++)
   System.out.print(list.get(i) + " ");
```

C18 What is the output of the following code segment?

```
ArrayList<Integer>list =
    new ArrayList<Integer >();
for (int i = 0; i < list.size(); i++)
  list.add(i);
System.out.println(list);
```

> []

> Note that initially **list.size()** would return 0, and the 'for' loop would not iterate, and nothing gets added to 'list'.

C19 Given an ArrayList **list** contains
[apple, pear, pear, banana, pear, pear, orange, pear, pear]
what is the list after executing the following code segment?

```
String fruit = "pear";
  for (int i = 0; i < list.size(); i++)
    if (list.get(i).equals(fruit))
       list.remove(fruit);
```

> [apple, banana, pear, orange, pear, pear]

C20 Given an ArrayList **list** contains
[apple, pear, pear, banana, pear, pear, orange, pear, pear]
what is the list after executing the following code segment?

```
String fruit = "pear";
  for (int i = 0; i < list.size(); i++)
    if (list.get(i).equals(fruit)) {
      list.remove(fruit);
      i--;
    }
```

[apple, banana, orange]

C21 Given an ArrayList **list** contains
[apple, pear, pear, banana, pear, pear, orange, pear, pear]
what is the list after executing the following code segment?

```
String fruit = "pear";
  for (int i = list.size()-1; i >= 0; i++)
    if (list.get(i).equals(fruit))
      list.remove(fruit);
```

[apple, banana, orange]

C22 What is the output from the following code segment?

```
ArrayList<String> list1 = new ArrayList<String>();
list1.add("C++");
list1.add("Java");
java.util.ArrayList<String> list2 = list1;
list2.add("Python");
list2.add("Ruby");
System.out.println(list1);
System.out.println(list2);
```

[C++, Java, Python, Ruby]
[C++, Java, Python, Ruby]

C23 What is the output of the following code?

```
class Test<E> {
  E obj;
  Test(E obj) { this.obj = obj; }
```

```
    public E getObject()    { return this.obj; }
}

class Main {
  public static void main (String[] args){
    Test <Integer> intObj = new Test<Integer>(25);
    System.out.println(intObj.getObject());
     Test <String> strObj = new Test<String>("Test of
   ArrayList");
    System.out.println(strObj.getObject());
  }
}

25
Test of ArrayList
```

C24 What is the output of the following code?

```
class Test {
  static <T> void genericDisplay (T element){
  System.out.println(element.getClass().getName() + "
  = " + element);
  }
  public static void main(String[] args) {
    genericDisplay(10);
    genericDisplay("Java is fun");
    genericDisplay(1.0);
  }
}

    java.lang.Integer = 10
    java.lang.String = Java is fun
    java.lang.Double = 1.0
```

C25 What is the output of the following program? What does the program do in general?

```
public class Test {
  public static void main(String[] args) {
    int[][] matrix = {{10, 4, 10, 18}, {12, 7, 2,
    11}};
    int x = matrix[0][0];
    for (int[] row : matrix)
      for (int e : row)
        if (x > e)
```

```
      x = e;
   System.out.print(x);
  }
}
```

1.
It prints out the minimum element in the matrix (2-D array).

C26 What is the output of the following program? What does the program do in general?

```
public class Test {
  public static void main(String[] args) {
    int[][] matrix = {{12, 7, 5, 10}, {9, 16, 14, 2}};
    for (int row = 0; row < matrix.length; row++)
    {
       System.out.print(max(matrix[row]) + " ");
    }
  }

  public static int max(int[] vec) {
    int e = vec[0];
    for (int i = 1; i < vec.length; i++)
      if (e < vec[i])
        e = vec[i];
    return e;
  }
}
```

12 16
It prints out the maximum element of each row of the matrix on a single line.

D. Classes, Objects, Methods

True/False Questions

D1 The variables declared within a method's body can be used outside of the method. *False*
[Local variables declared inside a method body exist only for the duration of the method call and cannot be accessed from outside it]

D2 Explicit use of **this** reference is made to access a field that is shadowed by a local variable. *True*
[The this reference is explicitly used to distinguish an instance variable from a local variable or parameter with the same name]

D3 The collection interfaces declare the operations that can be performed on each type of collection. *True*
[Collection interfaces (List, Set, Queue, Map, etc.) define operations that concrete collection classes must implement]

D4 A List is an ordered Collection. *True*
[A List maintains insertion order and allows positional access; ordering is one of its defining characteristics as a Collection subtype]

D5 In Java, there are no standalone methods (subprograms). *True*
[A method must belong to a class]

D6 If the method is declared 'final', static binding occurs. *True*
[Declaring a method final prevents overriding, so the compiler can resolve the call at compile time (static binding)]

D7 When an argument is passed by reference, the called method can access the argument's value in the caller directly and modify that data. *True*
[Pass-by-reference means the called method receives the caller's variable directly and can change its value as seen by the caller]

D8 An array element used as an argument to a method is treated as call by reference. *False*
[An array element passed as an argument is treated as pass-by-value: a copy of the element's value (or reference) is passed, not the element's slot in the array]

D9 The private members of a class are directly accessible to the client of a class. ***False***
[Private members of a class are accessible only within the class itself; no other class — even in the same package — can access them directly]

D10 An expression cannot be used as an argument to a method. ***False***
[Any valid expression that evaluates to a compatible type can be used as a method argument]

D11 The parameter list in the method header and the arguments in the method call must agree in number, order, and type. ***True***
[The number, order, and types of arguments at the call site must match the declared formal parameter list of the method]

D12 A method being called must appear after it its definition in the class. ***False***
[Java resolves method calls through the class file, not by textual order; a method may be called before its definition appears in the source file]

D13 A 'static' method can call only other 'static' methods of the same class directly. ***True***
[It cannot call non-static (instance) methods directly because static methods belong to the class itself, whereas non-static methods belong to a specific object instance that may not even exist when the static method is called]

D14 The generic parameters of Java can be primitive types. ***False***
[Java generics only work with reference types; primitive types (int, double, etc.) must be replaced by their wrapper classes (Integer, Double, etc.)]

D15 Objects are accessed through reference variables. ***True***
[In Java, an object can only be reached and manipulated through a reference variable that holds its memory address]

D16 All objects (class instances) are heap dynamic. ***True***
[Objects are created on the heap with new and persist independently of any method invocation; they are all heap-dynamic]

D17 Redeclaring a method parameter as a local variable in the method's body causes a compilation error. ***True***
[Redeclaring a formal parameter as a local variable in the same method body is a compile-time error because the names would conflict in the same scope]

D. Classes, Objects, Methods

D18 Absence of a return statement in a method that should return a value causes runtime error. ***False***
[Absence of a return statement in a method that returns a value causes compilation error]

D19 An overloaded method has the same name as another method, but different parameters (by number, types or order of the types). ***True***
[Method overloading means providing two or more methods with the same name in the same class, distinguished by their parameter lists]

D20 Method calls can be distinguished by return type. ***False***
[Method calls are distinguished by the number and type of arguments]

D21 When a method or variable has package access, no access specifier need be specified. ***True***
[Package-private (default) access is the access level when no modifier is specified; the member is accessible to all classes in the same package]

D22 Java supports nesting of classes. ***True***
[Java supports inner classes, static nested classes, local classes, and anonymous classes as forms of nested (nesting) classes]

D23 Java does not (directly) support multiple inheritance. ***True***
[Java classes can implement multiple interfaces but can extend only one class, which avoids the diamond problem of C++ multiple inheritance]

D24 All local variables in the methods of Java are stack-dynamic. ***True***
[Local variables and parameters are allocated on the call stack when the method is invoked and freed when it returns – classic stack-dynamic storage]

D25 The variables declared within a method's body can be used outside of the method. ***False***
[A variable declared inside a method body is a local variable; its scope is limited to the method (or the block containing it)]

D26 An instance method can access instance variables and instance methods directly. ***True***
[An instance method is associated with an object and has direct access to all instance variables and instance methods of its class]

D27 An instance method cannot access static variables and static methods directly. ***False***
[An instance method has access to all members of its class, both instance and static, without needing an explicit class name]

D28 A static method can access static variables and static methods directly. ***True***
[Static variables and methods belong to the class; a static method can access them directly using the class name or unqualified]

D29 A static method can call instance methods directly. ***False***
[Instance method can be called only via a reference to an object of a class]

D30 Each obect of a class has its own instance method in memory. ***False***
[There is just once instance method in memory irrespective of the number of the number of objects of a class]

D31 The private modifier is used to encapsulate data fields. ***True***
[Declaring instance variables private prevents direct access from outside the class, implementing the principle of data encapsulation]

D32 The current method executing is always the method whose activation record is at the top of the stack. ***True***
[The call stack is maintained so that the currently executing method's activation record is always at the top]

D33 The contents of an immutable object cannot be modified. ***True***
[An immutable object's state is set during construction and no methods exist to alter it afterward]

D34 All members of an immutable object must be private. ***True***
[Private fields prevent external code from directly modifying the object's state, which is required for immutability]

D35 All members of an immutable object must be of primitive types. ***False***
[An immutable object may contain reference fields (e.g., a final String), provided those referenced objects are themselves immutable or not exposed]

D36 An immutable object contains no mutator methods. ***True***

D. Classes, Objects, Methods

[A mutator method modifies the object's state; immutable objects must not provide any such methods]

D37 A constructor may be static. ***False***
[A constructor cannot be declared static because it is inherently tied to instance creation and requires an implicit object context]

D38 A constructor may never be private. ***False***
[A constructor can be declared private; this is a common pattern for Singleton classes and factory method patterns]

D39 A constructor may invoke a static method. ***True***
[A constructor can call any static method within the class since static methods are available without an object]

D40 A constructor may invoke an overloaded constructor. ***True***
[Using this() as the first statement in a constructor delegates to another constructor in the same class (constructor chaining)]

D41 A constructor which is private can be used to create (instances) objects of the class. ***False***
[A private constructor cannot be called from outside the class; only code within the same class can invoke it]

D42 To override a method, the method must be defined in the subclass using the same signature and compatible return type as in its superclass. ***True***
[Method overriding requires defining a method in the subclass with the same name, return type, and parameter list as the superclass method]

D43 Overloading a method is to provide more than one method with the same name but with different signatures to distinguish them. ***True***
[Overloading lets multiple methods share a name, distinguished by their parameter lists (number, type, or order of parameters)]

D44 Overloaded methods always have the same name. ***True***
[Overloaded methods by definition share the same name; what differentiates them is the method signature (parameter list)]

D45   It is a compile error if two methods differ only in return type in the same class. ***True***
[Two methods with the same name and parameter types but different return types produce a compile error because the call site would be ambiguous]

D46   A private method can be overridden. ***False***
[Private methods are not inherited by subclasses, so they cannot be overridden; a subclass can define a same-named method, but that is not overriding]

D47   A static method cannot be overridden. ***True***
[Static methods are bound to the class, not instances; subclasses can define a same-named static method (hiding), but that is not overriding]

D48   A method can be overloaded in the same class. ***True***
[A class can have multiple methods with the same name but different parameter lists – this is method overloading within the same class]

D49   A method can be overridden in the same class. ***False***
[Method overriding is done in a subclass of a class]

D50   Overloaded methods must have the same signature. ***False***
[The overloaded methods must differ in their signature]

D51   Overloaded methods must have different return types. ***False***
[Overloaded methods may have the same or different return types; the return type alone does not distinguish overloads]

D52   Overloaded methods must have the same return types. ***False***
[The return types of overloaded methods may be the same or different]

D53   If a method overrides another method, these two methods must have the same signature. ***True***
[Method overriding requires that the overriding method in the subclass has the identical signature as the overridden method in the superclass]

D54   If a method overrides another method, these two methods could have different types. ***False***
[An overriding method must have the exact same parameter list as the overridden method; different numbers of parameters would make it an overload, not an override]

D. Classes, Objects, Methods

D55 A method in a subclass can override *any* method in the superclass. ***False***
[A method in a subclass can override only the public or protected methods in its superclass]

D56 An instance of a subclass can be passed to a parameter of its superclass type. ***True***
[Java allows an instance of a subclass to be assigned to a superclass reference (widening/upcasting), including passing it as a superclass parameter]

D57 The matching method based on the type, number, and order of the parameters is determined at run time. ***False***
[The compiler finds the matching method based on the type, number, and order of the parameters]

D58 A method may not be implemented in several subclasses. ***False***
[Polymorphism allows a method to be implemented differently in each subclass; a method may be overridden in any number of subclasses]

D59 The Java Virtual Machine dynamically binds the implementation of the method at runtime. ***True***
[At runtime, the JVM uses the actual (dynamic) type of the object to determine which overriding version of a virtual method to invoke]

D60 Dynamic binding can apply to static methods. ***False***
[Static methods are resolved at compile time using the static type of the reference; dynamic binding (runtime dispatch) does not apply to them]

D61 Dynamic binding cannot apply to instance methods. ***False***
[Dynamic binding (late binding) is specifically designed for instance methods; the JVM dispatches instance method calls based on the object's runtime type]

D62 Static methods are bound at compile time. ***True***
[Static method calls are resolved at compile time because the method is tied to the class, not to any object instance]

D63 A class should always contain a no-arg constructor. ***False***
[A class does not need to provide a no-arg constructor; the compiler only inserts a default no-arg constructor if no constructor is defined at all]

D64 In Java's Math class, all methods are static. ***True***

[All methods in java.lang.Math (sin, cos, sqrt, pow, etc.) are static; you call them directly on the class name without creating a Math object]

D65   The constructors must always be public. ***False***
[A constructor may be declared private, however, it cannot be (directly) used to instatiate objects of the class]

D66   The constructors of a class may be protected. ***True***
[Abstract class constructors are typically declared protected so that subclasses can call them via super(), but they cannot be called externally]

D67   A reference variable is an object. ***False***
[It points to an object, it is not the object itself]

D68   A data field in a class can only be of a primitive type. ***False***
[A data field can be of any type: primitive, class type, interface type, or array type]

D69   A data field in a class can be of an object type. ***True***
[A data field can hold a reference to an object, making it of an object (reference) type]

D70   An abstract class will not have constructors. ***False***
[Abstract classes can and usually do have constructors, which are called by subclass constructors via super()]

D71   The constructors in an abstract class are of type 'protected'. ***True***
[Abstract class constructors are typically protected so that only subclasses (through super()) can invoke them, not external code]

D72   The constructors in an abstract class are private. ***False***
[Abstract class constructors are usually protected (not private) so that subclass constructors can call super(); a private constructor would block inheritance]

D73   A 'final' abstract class may be declared. ***False***
[Abstract classes are usually extended, and therefore cannot be 'final']

D74   An interface may contain constructors. ***False***
[Interfaces cannot have constructors because they cannot be instantiated directly; only classes that implement the interface can be instantiated]

D75   Actual data is stored in primitive variables. ***True***

D. Classes, Objects, Methods

[A primitive variable (int, double, etc.) directly contains its value in memory, not a reference to a separately allocated location]

D76 Primitive types are not reference types. ***True***
[The eight primitive types (int, double, boolean, etc.) hold values directly and are not objects; reference types hold addresses of heap objects]

D77 Array types are reference types. ***True***
[Arrays are objects in Java; an array variable holds a reference to an array allocated on the heap, making it a reference type]

D78 Actual data is sometimes stored in a reference variable. ***False***
[Actual data is never stored in a reference variable. It contains reference (address) of an object]

D79 A default constructor is automatically provided if no constructors are explicitly declared in the class. ***True***
[If a class has no constructor, the Java compiler inserts a default no-argument constructor that calls the superclass no-arg constructor]

D80 At least one constructor must always be defined explicitly for a class. ***False***
[If no constructor is defined, Java provides a default one automatically; explicit definition is not required]

D81 Every class provides a default constructor. ***False***
[Once a class defines any constructor, the compiler no longer provides a default no-arg constructor; the class may then have no no-arg constructor]

D82 The default constructor is a no-arg constructor. ***True***
[The default constructor generated by the compiler takes no arguments (no-arg) and initialises the object with default field values]

D83 Multiple constructors cannot be defined in a class. ***False***
[Multiple constructors can be defined in a class as long as they have different parameter lists (constructor overloading)]

D84 Constructors do not have a return type (including void). ***True***
[Constructors have no return type declaration (not even void); specifying a return type would make the compiler treat it as an ordinary method]

D85   Constructors must have the same name as the class itself. ***True***
[A constructor must have the exact same name as the class; this is how the compiler identifies it as a constructor]

D86   **final class A {   }** cannot be extended. ***True***
[A class declared final cannot be subclassed; any attempt to extend it causes a compile-time error]

D87   An instance of a subclass cannot be passed as a parameter of its superclass type. ***False***
[It can be passed. This is polymorphism]

D88   Cast is not required for widening conversion. ***True***
[Widening (upcasting) from a subclass type to a superclass type is always safe and requires no explicit cast]

D89   An object cannot be treated as a type of its superclass or of any ancestor class. ***False***
[Treating an object as a superclass type (upcasting) is done automatically by Java without any cast]

D90   Treating an object as a type of its subclass requires a cast. ***True***
[Treating a superclass reference as a subclass type (downcasting) is not guaranteed to be safe and requires an explicit cast operator]

D91   A method may be implemented in several subclasses. ***True***
[Polymorphism allows the same method name to be implemented differently in each subclass]

D92   Dynamic binding can apply to instance methods, ***True***
[Instance method calls are resolved at runtime based on the actual type of the object — this is dynamic (late) binding]

D93   When a method with an object argument is invoked, a copy of the object is passed. ***False***
[When an object is passed to a method, the reference (address) is copied, not a clone of the object; the method can modify the original object's state]

D94   When a method with an object argument is invoked, the content of the object is passed. ***False***

D. Classes, Objects, Methods

[In case of object being a formal parameter to a method, at method ivocation, the object reference is passed as argument]

D95   A public class can be accessed by a class in a different package. ***True***
[A public class is accessible from any package, not just the one in which it is defined]

D96   A protected method cannot be accessed by a subclass in a different package. ***False***
[A protected method is accessible within the defining class, within the same package, and in subclasses – including subclasses in different packages]

D97   A method with no visibility modifier cannot be accessed by a class in a different package. ***True***
[Package-private (default) access restricts visibility to classes in the same package; classes in other packages cannot access the member]

D98   The value of a private instance variable cannot be changed inside the class definition. ***False***
[A private instance variable can be modified by public (or other accessible) methods within the class, such as setter (mutator) methods]

D99   A private method cannot be accessed by a class in a different package. ***True***
[Private members are not accessible from any code outside the class – not even from subclasses in a different package]

D100   A private method cannot be invoked outside the class where it is defined. ***True***
[Private restricts method invocation to code within the same class; it cannot be called from any other class]

D101   A derived class can define a method that invokes a private method of its base class. ***False***
[Private methods of the superclass are not inherited by the derived class; the derived class cannot see or invoke them]

D102   A method in a derived class can use an inherited public method of its base class that invokes a private method of the base class. ***True***
[Public methods inherited from the superclass are part of the subclass's public interface and can be called directly within the subclass]

D103 If an interface compiles with warnings, a .class file is not created for the interface. ***False***
[Warnings in Java do not prevent the compiler from producing a .class file; only errors prevent file generation]

D104 If a class definition does not compile without errors, a .class file is not created for the class. ***True***
[Compile errors cause the compiler to abort without producing a .class file; the output file is only written when compilation succeeds]

D105 If a class definition compiles with warnings, a .class file is not created for the class. ***False***
[Warnings are informational messages; they do not prevent the compiler from generating the .class file]

D106 A local variable and a formal parameter in a method cannot have the same name. ***True***
[A formal parameter and a local variable in the same method occupy the same scope; redeclaring the parameter name as a local variable is a compile error]

D107 Two variables with the same name cannot be declared in different methods in a class. ***False***
[Variables with the same name can be declared in different nested blocks (inner scope shadows outer), which is legal in Java]

D108 A non-static method can be called from a static method. ***False***
[A non-static (instance) method requires an object instance and cannot be called directly from a static context without one]

D109 A static method can be accessed from a non-static method. ***True***
[Static methods belong to the class; they can be called from anywhere – including from instance methods – using the class name or directly]

D110 The static method exists even before an object of a defined class is created. ***True***
[Static members are loaded with the class definition; they exist before any instance of the class is created]

D111 More than one variable-length parameter may be specified in a method. ***False***

D. Classes, Objects, Methods

[Java allows at most one variable-length (varargs) parameter per method, and it must be the last parameter]

D112 The variable-length parameter specified in a method must be the last parameter. ***True***
[The varargs parameter must be the last parameter so the compiler can identify which arguments belong to it]

D113 The return type of a method could be a variable-length parameter. ***False***
[A return type is a type declaration, not a parameter; variable-length (varargs) syntax applies only to parameters, not return types]

D114 Local variables are not initialized. ***True***
[Local variables in Java have no default value; the compiler ensures they are explicitly initialised before use]

D115 Methods cannot be overloaded based on the return types. ***True***
[Java determines which overloaded method to call from the name and parameter list (signature); return type is not part of the resolution]

D116 Methods having the same signature cannot be overloaded. ***True***
[Two methods with the same signature (name + parameter types) in the same class are identical declarations, making overloading impossible]

D117 More than one variable-length parameter may be specified in a method. ***False***
[A method can specify at most one variable-length parameter]

D118 The variable-length parameter of a method must be the last parameter. ***True***
[The varargs parameter collects all remaining arguments, so it must be placed last in the parameter list]

D119 The return type of a method can be a variable-length parameter. ***False***
[A return type specifies what a method returns; varargs (T...) syntax is only valid for method parameters, not return types]

D120 The 'main' method is always a 'void' method. ***True***

[The main method signature is always: public static void main(String[] args); the void return type is required]

D121 A class cannot have a 'main' method if it is not run as a program. ***False***
[It may have a 'main' method, but is ignored if it is not run]

D122 There cannot be statements after the 'return' statement in a method. ***False***
[Statements can appear after a return statement; the compiler will warn they are unreachable, but the code is syntactically legal]

D123 Execution of the return statement ends a method's execution. ***True***
[Executing a return statement immediately transfers control back to the caller, ending the current method's execution]

D124 A 'void' method may or may not have a return statement. ***True***
[A void method may include return; to exit early, or have no return statement at all; both are legal]

D125 A method cannot return more than one value. ***True***
[Java's return statement supports only one value; to return multiple values you must wrap them in an array or object]

D126 The scope of a variable declared in a class can extend beyond the class definition. ***False***
[A class variable (field) is in scope throughout the entire class, including inside all instance and static methods]

D127 The names of the formal parameters in a method definition, and names of the arguments in the method invocation must be the same. ***False***
[Formal parameter names are local to the method and are independent of the names used at the call site; only the types and order must match]

D128 The types of the formal parameters in a method definition, and types of the arguments in the method invocation must be the same. ***True***
[The type of each argument in the call must be assignment-compatible with the corresponding formal parameter type]

D. Classes, Objects, Methods

D129 The arguments passed in a method invocation can only be variables. ***False***
[The arguments passed in a method invocation can be literals, variables, or expressions]

D130 Multiple values cannot be returned by a method. ***True***
[The language syntax permits at most one value to be returned from a method. However, multiple values can be returned in an indirect way by the use of reference parameters]

D131 A class can be instantiated when the 'public' modifier is used on the constructor. ***True***
[A class whose constructor has public access can be instantiated from any code that can reach the class]

D132 A class cannot be instantiated when the 'static' modifier is used on the constructor. ***False***
[Not using the static keyword on a class means instances can be created; static in Java is used for class-level members, not to prevent instantiation]

D133 All Java methods must be contained in some class. ***True***
[Java does not allow top-level (standalone) functions; every method must be declared inside a class]

D134 The `main` method is always static. ***True***
[The main method must be declared public static void main(String[] args); the static keyword is mandatory]

D135 A variable of type `double` can be assigned an `int` variable (or an expression returning `int`) without cast. ***True***
[This is known as widening primitive conversion or implicit casting]

D136 A variable of type `int` can be assigned a `double` variable (or an expression returning `double`) without cast. ***False***
[Assigning a double to an int is a narrowing conversion that can lose information; an explicit cast (int) is required]

D137 The cast of a floating point value (literal, variable, or expression) to an integer will round the value. ***False***
[It truncates the value]

D138 Static variables must be declared with the private access specifier. ***False***

[Static variables may have any access modifier (public, protected, package-private, or private)]

D139　The constructor method may have a return type. ***False***
[A constructor has no return type]

D140　The default constructor has no arguments. ***True***
[The default constructor Java generates takes no parameters and simply calls super()]

D141　A class definition must have a constructor definition. ***False***
[It is not mandatory for a class definition to have a constructor definition. Java automatically defines a default constructor if there is no constructor defined in a class]

D142　In the method calls (invocations), primitive types are passed by value. ***True***
[Primitive arguments are copied into the parameter; the called method cannot affect the caller's original variable]

D143　In the method calls (invocations), object references are passed by reference. ***False***
[Object references are passed by value, similar to primitive types]

D144　In case of overloaded methods, the methods need not belong to the same class. ***False***
[The overloaded methods must belong to the same class]

D145　The decision about the correct method to call among the overloaded methods is done at run time. ***False***
[Overload resolution (choosing which overloaded method to call) is done entirely at compile time, not at runtime]

D146　Two or more methods with the same signatures but different return types can be overloaded. ***False***
[Two methods with the same signature (same name and parameter types) cannot coexist in a class regardless of their return types]

D147　Two or more methods with different signatures but the same return types cannot be overloaded. ***True***
[Two methods with different signatures (different parameter lists) are overloaded regardless of whether they have the same or different return types]

D. Classes, Objects, Methods

D148 The default constructor could have arguments for initialization. *False*
[The default constructor does not have any parameters]

D149 Java automatically defines a default constructor when a class does not define any constructor methods. *True*
[Java automatically provides a no-arg default constructor only when the class defines no constructors at all]

D150 When none of the constructors defined in a class is a default constructor, Java automatically defines a default constructor. *False*
[Only when a class has no constructor definitions at all, Java automatically defines a default constructor]

D151 Constructor methods cannot be overloaded. *False*
[Constructors can be overloaded just like methods; a class can have multiple constructors with different parameter lists]

D152 A constructor cannot call another constructor. *False*
[One constructor can call another constructor in the same class using this() as the first statement]

D153 Instances can be created using the constructor of the abstract class. *False*
[Abstract classes cannot be instantiated; new AbstractClass() causes a compile-time error]

D154 An abstract class cannot be extended. *False*
[Abstract classes are designed to be extended; a subclass can implement the abstract methods and be instantiated]

D155 A subclass of a non-abstract superclass cannot be abstract. *False*
[A subclass of a concrete (non-abstract) class may itself be declared abstract, forcing its own subclasses to complete the implementation]

D156 A subclass can override a concrete method in a superclass to declare it abstract. *True*
[A subclass can provide its own implementation of any inherited concrete (non-abstract) method from the superclass]

D157 An abstract class cannot be used as a data type. *False*

[An abstract class can be used as a reference type (data type) for variables and parameters, even though it cannot be instantiated directly]

D158 A class that contains abstract methods must be abstract. ***True***
[Java requires that any class containing at least one abstract method be itself declared abstract]

D159 An abstract class need not contain abstract methods. ***True***
[A class may be declared abstract as a design decision even if it currently has no abstract methods]

D160 An abstract method cannot be contained in a non-abstract class. ***True***
[An abstract method declaration must appear inside an abstract class; placing it in a concrete class is a compile error]

D161 An abstract class must contain at least one abstract method. ***False***
[A class can be declared abstract even if it does not actually have any abstract methods]

D162 An abstract class cannot have non-abstract methods. ***False***
[An abstract class may have any combination of abstract and concrete (non-abstract) methods]

D163 A class containing at least one abstract method must be declared abstract. ***True***
[If a class has at least one abstract method, then the class must be declared abstract. However, an abstract class need not have any abstract methods and may contain only non-abstract methods]

D164 A data field may be declared abstract. ***False***
[Only classes and methods can be declared abstract]

D165 The subclass of an abstract class cannot itself be an abstract class. ***False***
[The subclass of an abstract class will itself be an abstract class if it does not implement all the abstract methods it inherits]

D166 Instances cannot be created for an abstract class. ***True***
[Abstract classes cannot be instantiated with new; they serve only as base types for concrete subclasses]

D. Classes, Objects, Methods

D167   A class declared to be final has no subclasses. ***True***
[A final class is sealed; no other class can extend (subclass) it]

D168   A 'final' class may contain any abstract methods. ***False***
[A class cannot be both final and abstract: final means it cannot be extended, but abstract requires extension for use]

D169   A class can be both 'abstract' and 'final'. ***False***
[Declaring a class both abstract and final is a compile error because the two modifiers contradict each other]

D170   A static method may reference an instance variable. ***False***
[A static method has no implicit object (no this reference) and therefore cannot directly access any instance variable]

D171   A static method can directly call another static method. ***True***
[Since static methods belong to the class itself rather than a specific object, they do not require an instance to be created before being invoked]

D172   A static method cannot be invoked within a non-static method. ***False***
[A static method can be invoked within a non-static method]

D173   A non-static method can never be invoked within a static method. ***False***
[A non-static method can be invoked within a static method if there is an object of the class that can be used in the invocation of the non-static method]

D174   A non-static method can reference any variable within its class. ***True***
[An instance method has access to all variables and methods of its class – both instance and static – through the implicit this reference]

D175   A class cannot contain both instance variables and static methods. ***False***
[A class may freely combine both instance variables and static (class) variables]

D176   A class can contain both static and non-static methods. ***True***
[A class is free to define any mix of static and non-static (instance) methods]

D177　A static variable can be referenced by name within the definition of a static method without class name and 'dot'. **_True_**
[A static variable belongs to the class and can be referenced by name from any method (static or instance) in the same class]

D178　An instance variable can be referenced by name within the definition of a static method. **_False_**
[A static method does not have a this reference and therefore cannot access instance variables by name; an explicit object reference is required]

D179　Instance variables cannot be defined within an enumeration. **_False_**
[An enum in Java is a special kind of class; it can have instance variables, just like a regular class]

D180　Constructors and methods cannot be defined within an enumeration. **_False_**
[An enumeration is actually a class. Thus, anything that is valid for a class is valid for enumeration]

D181　Given Car is a class and the declaration Car c1, c1 is an object of type Car. **_False_**
[c1 is a reference to an object of type Car]

D182　Given Car is a class and the declaration Car c1, the value of c1 is a reference to an object of type Car. **_False_**
[c1 is a reference to an object of type Car. In this case, since no new object has been created, the value of c1 is null]

D183　Given Car is a class, the declaration required to make the value of c1 to be a reference to an object of type Car is **`Car c1 = new Car()`** ; **_Car c1 = new Car();_**
[Car c1 = new Car(); declares a reference variable and assigns it a newly created Car object; c1 is now a reference to that object]

D184　A class need not have a parent class. **_False_**
[In Java, all classes are subclasses of a 'root' class called Object]

D185　Objects can be either stack dynamic or heap dynamic. **_False_**
[In Java, objects are heap dynamic]

D186　Method bindings can only be dynamic. **_False_**

D. Classes, Objects, Methods

[In Java, the method bindings can be either static or dynamic]

D187 The constructor methods must always be public. ***False***
[Constructors can have any access modifier (public, protected, package-private, or private)]

D188 The methods or data members declared as 'protected' are accessible within same package but not in sub classes in different package. ***False***
[Protected members are accessible within the same package as well as in any subclass, including those in different packages]

D189 The static method exists even before an object of a defined class is created. ***True***
[Static members are loaded with the class definition at class-loading time, before any instance is created]

D190 More than one variable-length parameter may be specified in a method. ***False***
[Java permits at most one varargs parameter per method, and it must be the last parameter in the list]

D191 A variable-length parameter specified in a method must be the last parameter. ***True***
[The varargs parameter must be last so the compiler can determine which arguments belong to it]

D192 The return type of a method could be a variable-length parameter. ***False***
[A return type cannot use varargs syntax; only parameters can be declared with variable length]

D193 A non-static method can be called from a static method. ***False***
[A non-static method cannot be called directly from a static context; an object reference is required]

D194 A static method can be accessed from a non-static method. ***True***
[Static methods and variables are accessible from instance methods directly, without any class name prefix]

D195 A static method may call an instance method. ***True***

[A static method can call an instance method, but it must do so through an explicit object reference]

D196   A static method may not access a private instance variable. ***True***
[Without an object reference, a static method has no access to any instance variable; instance variables require an object]

D197   Local variables are not initialized. ***True***
[Local variables in Java are not initialised to a default value; the compiler requires explicit initialisation before use]

D198   Two methods can have the same name but different parameter types. ***True***
[Two methods with the same name but different parameter lists are overloaded and can coexist in the same class]

D199   Only public methods are made use of in encapsulation. ***False***
[Encapsulation uses private data fields hidden from the outside and public accessor/mutator methods to control access]

D200   Given 'Car' is a class, after the declaration **Car c1**, **c1** is an object of type 'Car'. ***False***
[Car cl = new Car() creates a Car object and stores the reference in cl; cl is a reference variable, not the object itself]

D201   Given 'Car' is a class, after the declaration **Car c1**, **c1** is a valid reference to an object of type 'Car'. ***False***
[An object has not been instantiated. The value of cl will be null]

D202   Given 'Car' is a class, after the declaration **Car c1 = new Car()**, **c1** is an object of type 'Car'. ***False***
[Car cl = new Car() creates a Car object; cl stores a reference to that object – cl is the reference, not the object]

D203   Given 'Car' is a class, after the declaration **Car c1 = new Car()**, **c1** is a valid reference to an object of type 'Car'. ***True***
[After Car cl = new Car(), cl holds a reference to (the address of) the newly created Car object]

D204   Given a class Car and the declaration Car[] cars = new Car[1000], cars is an array of 1000 objects of type Car. ***False***

D. Classes, Objects, Methods

[new Car[10] creates the array and initialises each slot to null; no Car objects are created, only the array structure itself]

D205 Given a class Car and the declaration Car[] cars = new Car[1000], cars is reference to an array of 1000 objects of type Car. ***False***
[Car[] cars = new Car[10] creates the array object with 10 null slots; individual Car objects must be created separately with new Car()]

D206 Given a class Car and the declaration Car[] cars = new Car[1000], cars is reference to an array of 1000 references to objects of type Car. ***True***
[new Car[10] allocates and returns an array object containing 10 null Car references; the array object itself is created]

D207 A method parameter can be re-declared as a local variable in the method's body. ***False***
[No. It causes a compilation error]

D208 Missing return statement in a method that should return a value results in a compilation error. ***True***
[If the compiler cannot verify that every code path returns a value, it reports an error]

D209 Overloaded methods have the same name, but different parameters (by number, types or order of the types). ***True***
[Overloaded methods share the same name within a class but are distinguished by their parameter lists]

D210 Overloaded method calls can be distinguished by return type. ***False***
[Return type is not part of the method signature used for overload resolution; only name and parameter list are used]

D211 Arrays cannot be passed as arguments to methods – each array element must be passed to the method separately. ***False***
[An entire array can be passed to a method that has a compatible array parameter; the reference to the array is passed]

D212 Every Java application is composed of at least one public class declaration. ***True***
[A Java application must have at least one class with a public static void main(String[]) method as the entry point]

D213 Two variables with the same name can be declared in different methods in the same class. *__True__*
[Variables in different blocks or scopes may share a name; an inner scope variable shadows the outer one]

D214 A local variable of a method could have the same name as that of a formal parameter of the method. *__False__*
[local variable declared within the main body of a method cannot have the same name as one of its formal parameters]

D215 Two variables with the same name cannot be declared in a block. *__True__*
[Two variables cannot share a name within the same block scope; this would be a duplicate local variable declaration]

D216 The class Integer is not immutable. *__False__*
[Integer is an immutable class; once an Integer object is created, its value cannot be changed]

D217 The class BigInteger is immutable. *__True__*
[BigInteger is immutable; all arithmetic operations return new BigInteger objects rather than modifying the existing one]

D218 The class BigDecimal is immutable. *__True__*
[BigDecimal is immutable; operations on BigDecimal values always produce new objects]

D219 Objects of String class are immutable. *__True__*
[Methods in the String class will not change a string. They return a value which may be assigned to another string variable]

D220 Given two reference variables s1 and s2, if s1 == s2 is true, s1.equals(s2) may not be true. *__False__*
[If s1 == s2 is true, then s1 and s2 reference the same memory location, and therefore the content referenced by s1 and s2 is the same object]

D221 Given two reference variables s1 and s2, if s1.equals(s2) is true, s1 == s2 may not be true. *__True__*
[equals() is content equality and == is reference equality. equals() compares the content (state) of two objects. E.g., Two distinct String objects with the same characters will be equal under equals(), but not equal under ==]

D. Classes, Objects, Methods

D222 Given the following declarations, the value of s1 == s2 is ***True***
[String literals are interned by the JVM; 'Apple' appears once in the string pool, so s1 and s2 refer to the same object]

```
String s1 = "Apple";
String s2 = "Apple";
```

D223 Given the following declarations, the value of s1 == s2 is ***False***
[new String('Apple') creates a new object in the heap distinct from the interned literal; == compares references, which differ]

```
String s1 = "Apple";
String s2 = new String ("Apple");
```

D224 Given the following declarations, the value of s1.equals (s2) is ***True***
[equals() for String compares character sequences; both contain 'Apple', so s1.equals(s2) is true regardless of how each was created]

```
String s1 = "Apple";
String s2 = new String ("Apple");
```

D225 An abstract method can be defined in a non-abstract class. ***False***
[An abstract method cannot be declared in a concrete (non-abstract) class; the class must also be abstract]

D226 An abstract class cannot define both abstract methods and non-abstract methods. ***False***
[An abstract class may freely mix abstract and concrete (non-abstract) methods]

D227 The derived class of an abstract base class must be an abstract class. ***False***

[The derived class of an abstract base class can either be abstract or non-abstract]

D228 The child of an abstract parent class that does not override all of the parent's abstract methods must be declared to be abstract. ***True***
[If a concrete subclass does not implement all inherited abstract methods, it must itself be declared abstract; otherwise it is a compile error]

D229 A child class can extend a parent or implement an interface, but cannot do both. ***False***
[A child class can extend just one parent and can implement zero or more interfaces]

D230 An interface cannot contain a method that returns a value. ***False***
[Interface methods can have any return type, including primitive types, object types, or void]

D231 An interface cannot extend another interface. ***False***
[An interface can extend one or more other interfaces using the extends keyword]

D232 An interface can have the 'private' access modifier. ***False***
[Since Java 9, interfaces can have private methods (used as helpers for default methods); earlier Java versions did not allow this]

D233 There is no limit on the number of objects created in a program. ***True***
[It is only limited by the system resource/user memory]

D234 One object named 'a' is created by the statement `Object a;` ***False***
[It only creates an object reference. Object is created by the 'new' operator]

D235 Only one object is created by the following statements. ***True***
[Object b = a copies the reference; both a and b point to the same single object — only one object was ever created]

```
Object a = new Object;
Object b = a;
```

[It creates an object using the 'new' operator and 'a' refers to that object. 'b' is a reference to the same object referenced by 'a']

D236 The access modifier must always be specified for class members. ***False***
[If no access modifier is specified, the member gets package-private (default) access; the modifier is optional, not mandatory]

D237 The return value of a method must be exactly the same type as the return type. ***False***

[The return value type could be the same as return type or of a type that can be converted to return type without loss of information]

D238 Private methods are final. ***True***
[Private methods cannot be overridden (they are not inherited), so the compiler always knows exactly which implementation to call — they are effectively final]

D239 Protected methods are final. ***False***
[A protected method can be overridden in a subclass; protected does not imply final]

D240 Class members must be assigned a value to before they are accessed. ***False***
[Instance variables (fields) are automatically initialised to default values (0, false, null, etc.); explicit assignment before use is not required]

D241 Accessing an uninitialized local variable of a method results in compile error. ***True***
[The compiler performs definite-assignment analysis for local variables; using an uninitialized local variable is a compile-time error]

IOIOIOIOIOIOIOIOIOIOIOIOIOIOIOIOIOIOIOIOIOIOIOIOIOI

Fill-in the-blanks Questions

D1 The signature of a method consists of ***method name*** and ***parameter list***.
[A method's signature uniquely identifies it within its class by the combination of its name and its parameter list (types and order)]

D2 All Java applications must have a method named **main** where the execution starts.
[Every Java application must define a main method with the signature public static void main(String[] args); execution starts there]

D3 A class instance creation is done using the **new** keyword.
[The new keyword allocates memory on the heap for a new object and invokes the class's constructor to initialise it]

D4   More than one reference variable referring to the same object, is known as ***aliasing***.
[Aliasing means two or more reference variables point to the same object; changes through one alias are visible through all others]

D5   The general order of declarations/descriptions in a class definition are ***instance variables***, ***constructors***, and ***methods***.
[The conventional ordering in a class body is: instance variable declarations, constructors, then methods]

D6   When the access modifier is not specified for a class member, it would have ***default*** modifier.
[A class member without an explicit access modifier has default (package-private) access; it is accessible within the same package only]

D7   Calling a method of another object requires the ***dot (.)*** separator.
[The dot operator separates an object reference from the method or field being accessed on that object]

D8   The values the method call passes to the method for the parameters are called ***arguments***.
[Arguments are the actual values or expressions supplied by the caller at the point of the method invocation]

D9   Attributes of a class are also known as ***fields***.
[The data members (variables) that describe the state of an object are called fields (or instance variables)]

D10 An instance of a class is known as ***object***.
[An object is a runtime instance of a class; it has its own copy of the class's instance variables]

D11 An object is created by invoking a special method known as ***constructor***.
[A constructor is a special method (with no return type, not even void) that is called to initialise a newly created object]

D12 When an object is created, constructors are invoked using the **new** operator.
[The new operator allocates heap memory for the object and then invokes the appropriate constructor]

D. Classes, Objects, Methods

D13 The access specifiers keywords are **private**, **protected**, and **public**.
[Java defines three explicit access specifiers: private (most restrictive), protected, and public (least restrictive)]

D14 A member of a class with ***private*** specifiers is accessible only within the class itself.
[A private member is accessible only within the class body in which it is declared]

D15 A member of a class with ***public*** specifiers is accessible anywhere the containing class is accessible.
[A public member is accessible from any code that can reach the class itself]

D16 A member of a class with ***protected*** specifiers is not accessible to another class in a different package, but is accessible to any of its subclass in any package.
[A protected member is accessible within its own class, within the same package, and within any subclass (even in a different package)]

D17 A member of a class with ***default*** access is accessible to code within all classes that are defined in the same package, but inaccessible outside of the package.
[A member not declared with 'private', 'protected', or 'public' modifiers is said have default access]

D18 The modifiers in order of increasing visibility are ***private***, ***none*** (***no modifier used***), ***protected***, and ***public***.
[From most restrictive to least: private (class only), no modifier (package), protected (package + subclasses), public (everywhere)]

D19 An instance variable with access specifier ***private*** is not accessible outside of the class definition.
[Declaring an instance variable private prevents direct access from outside the class, enforcing encapsulation]

D20 In Java, instance variables that are visible only in the class where they are defined are called ***private***.
[Private instance variables can be read and modified only within the class that declares them]

D21 In Java, instance variables that are visible everywhere are specified with access qualifier ***public***.

219

[Public instance variables (though generally discouraged) are accessible from any class that can see the containing class]

D22 Instance variables that are visible in the class where they are defined and in all of the subclasses are specified with access qualifier ***protected***.
[Protected instance variables are accessible within the defining class, within the same package, and in subclasses]

D23 A method that is associated with a specific class is known as ***static*** method.
[A static method belongs to the class itself rather than to any instance; it is invoked via the class name]

D24 A method that is associated with an object of a class is known as ***non-static*** or ***instance*** method.
[A non-static (instance) method operates on a specific object and has access to the object's instance variables via 'this']

D25 A simple but incomplete version of a method used while testing, is known as a ***stub***.
[A stub is a minimal placeholder implementation of a method; it has the correct signature but little or no logic, used during incremental development]

D26 The methods that allow a client of a class to assign values to a private instance variable, are known as ***mutator* (or *setter*)** methods.
[These methods are a key part of encapsulation. They provide a controlled way to modify an object's internal state]

D27 The number of *parameters* of a default constructor is ***zero***.
[A default constructor takes no arguments; the parameter count is zero]

D28 The ***static*** class variables are shared by all objects of a class.
[Static (class) variables reside in a single memory location shared by every instance of the class]

D29 The ***private*** members cannot be accessed outside of the class.
[Private members are inaccessible to code outside the class; they can only be used inside the class body itself]

D30 The classes and interfaces which comprise the collections framework are members of package ***java.util***.

D. Classes, Objects, Methods

[The Java Collections Framework classes and interfaces (ArrayList, LinkedList, HashMap, etc.) are in the java.util package]

D31 A method should use the class's *set* and *get* methods to access the class's ***private*** data.
[Accessing private instance data through the class's own accessor (get) and mutator (set) methods maintains encapsulation]

D32 A variable defined inside a method is referred to as ***local variable***.
[A variable declared inside a method body is a local variable; it exists only during that method's execution]

D33 A class cannot be instantiated when the ***private*** modifier is used on the constructor.
[Making a constructor private prevents external code from calling new ClassName(), effectively preventing direct instantiation]

D34 The decision about the correct method to call, among the overloaded methods, is done by examining the method's ***signature***.
[Overload resolution is done by comparing the method's signature (name + parameter types) against the call; the best match is selected]

D35 The decision about the correct method to call among the overloaded methods is done at ***compile*** time.
[Overload resolution is performed by the compiler at compile time, based on the static types of the arguments]

D36 ***Static*** variables are shared by all objects of a class.
[Static variables belong to the class, not to any instance; all objects share the same static variable]

D37 A ***static*** method is invoked using a class name instead of an object name.
[Because a static method belongs to the class rather than to an object, it is called using the class name (e.g., ClassName.method())]

D38 Variables that are shared by every instances of a class are known as ***class variables***.
[Class variables (static variables) are stored once per class and are shared among all instances]

D39 All Java objects (class instances) are allocated on the ***heap***.

[Java allocates all objects on the heap via new; the heap persists for the lifetime of the program]

D40 A method that is associated with an individual object is known as *instance method*.
[An instance method is associated with a particular object; it can access and modify the object's instance variables]

D41 The keyword used for referring to the current object in a method or constructor is **this**.
[The this keyword inside an instance method or constructor refers to the object on which the method was invoked]

D42 A constructor invokes its *superclass no-arg* constructor by default, if a constructor does not invoke an overloaded constructor or its superclass's constructor.
[If a constructor does not explicitly call this(...) or super(...), Java automatically inserts a call to the superclass's no-argument constructor]

D43 A method that is defined to be **final** cannot be overridden in any descendant class.
[Declaring a method final prevents it from being overridden in any subclass]

D44 When a method with an object argument is invoked, *the reference of the object* is passed.
[When an object is passed to a method, the reference (address) of the object is copied; this gives the method access to the original object]

D45 The keyword **class** is required to declare a class.
[The keyword class begins every class declaration in Java]

D46 Static methods are bound at *compile* time.
[Static method binding is resolved at compile time because the method belongs to the class and is not subject to dynamic dispatch]

D47 A matching method based on parameter type, number of parameters, and order of the parameters is found at *compile* time.
[Method overload resolution -- matching a call to the correct overloaded method -- is done entirely at compile time by the Java compiler]

D. Classes, Objects, Methods

D48 The arguments passed in a method invocation must match the formal parameters in the method definition in their ***number***, ***order***, and ***type***.
[Java requires that the arguments at a method call match the declared formal parameters in number, order, and compatible types]

D49 A method that is associated with a specific class is known as ***static*** method.
[A static method is tied to the class, not to any instance, and is invoked via the class name]

D50 A method that is associated with an object of a class is known as ***non-static*** (or ***instance***) method.
[A non-static (instance) method is invoked on a specific object and can access that object's instance state]

D51 The method name and parameter list, together are known as, the method's ***signature***.
[A method signature is the combination of the method name and its parameter list; return type is not part of the signature in Java]

D52 In a method's parameter list, a data type followed by a(n) ***ellipses (...)*** indicates that the method receives a variable number of arguments of that data type.
[An ellipsis (...) after a type in the parameter list declares a varargs parameter; the method can then receive zero or more arguments of that type]

D53 Array passed as argument to a method uses the ***pass-by-reference*** parameter passing mechanism.
[Passing an array passes its reference; the called method can read and modify the original array elements]

D54 An array element passed as argument to a method uses the ***pass-by-value*** parameter passing mechanism.
[An individual array element of primitive type is copied into the method's parameter, so changes inside the method do not affect the original]

D55 Using the ***pass-by-reference*** parameter passing, the called method can access the argument's value and can modify it.
[Pass-by-reference means the called method receives a reference to the caller's variable, allowing it to both read and change the original value]

D56 The operator to create an object, which is a class instance, is **`new`**.
[The new operator allocates heap memory and calls the constructor; it is used to create every object in Java]

D57 Calling a method of another object requires the ***dot separator***.
[The dot (.) operator is the member-access separator: objectRef.methodName() or objectRef.fieldName]

D58 At the time of method invocation (call), the variables/expressions used in place of the formal parameters of the method definition are known as ***arguments***.
[Arguments are the concrete values, variables, or expressions that appear in a method call; they become the actual data passed to the formal parameters]

D59 The attributes of a class are known as ***fields***.
[The data members of a class are referred to as fields; they represent the state (attributes) of an object]

D60 The method that does not return any value has return type **`void`**.
[A method declared with return type void performs an action but does not return a value to the caller]

D61 The signature of a method consists of ***method name*** and ***parameter list***.
[A method's signature is its name combined with its parameter list; two methods in the same class may not share the same signature]

D62 All Java programs must have a method named **`main`**.
[Every Java application must contain a method named main; the JVM calls it to begin program execution]

D63 The local variables and arguments of a method are stored the area of memory called ***stack***.
[Local variables and formal parameters of a method are stored on the call stack and are created when the method is called and destroyed when it returns]

D64 A variable whose value is shared by all instances of a class is known as ***static*** variable.
[A static variable is a class-level variable; its single copy is shared by all instances of the class]

D. Classes, Objects, Methods

D65 Methods with **_public_** modifier are usable outside of the class where they are defined.
[Methods declared public are accessible from any class that can access the class that contains them]

D66 Methods with **_static_** modifier will not access objects of a class.
[Static methods belong to the class, not to any instance; they have no implicit 'this' reference and therefore cannot access instance fields or methods directly]

D67 **_Constructor_** is a method which creates an object of a class.
[A constructor has the same name as the class, no return type (not even void), and is called by new to initialise the object]

D68 The method that has no return type, including **void**, is the **_constructor_**.
[A constructor has no return type -- not even void; this distinguishes it syntactically from ordinary methods]

D69 A method which accesses values (of instance variables) in an object without altering the object is known as **_accessor_** method.
[Also called 'getter' method]

D70 A method which modifies the state of an object is known as **_mutator_** method.
[Also called 'setter' method]

D71 A method that performs operations for the whole class is known as **_static_** (or **_class_**) method.
[A static (class) method is associated with the class itself rather than with any particular instance]

D72 A method that performs operations for the individual objects of a class is known as **_instance_** method.
[An instance method is associated with an individual object and operates on that object's data]

D73 Given 'Car' is a class, after the declaration **Car c1**, the value of c1 is **null**.
[After Car c1; without any new call, c1 holds null because no Car object has been created yet]

D74 A **_static_** variable is shared by all objects of a class.

225

[A static variable exists once per class; every object of that class shares the same static variable]

D75 A class version of a primitive data type is known as a ***wrapper*** class.
[Java provides wrapper classes (Integer, Double, Boolean, etc.) that encapsulate each primitive type as an object]

D76 Conversion of a primitive data type value to its wrapper object is facilitated by ***auto boxing***.
[Autoboxing automatically converts a primitive value to an instance of its corresponding wrapper class when needed]

D77 Conversion of a wrapper object to its primitive type value is facilitated by ***auto unboxing***.
[Auto-unboxing automatically extracts the primitive value from a wrapper object when a primitive is expected]

D78 The program component that contains (only) the headings of several public methods is known as a(n) ***interface***.
[An interface in Java declares public method signatures (and optionally constants) without providing implementations; classes that implement the interface supply the method bodies]

D79 The ***number***, ***type***, and ***order*** of the arguments at method invocation should match those of the formal parameters in the method definition.
[The arguments in a method call must correspond to the formal parameters in number, type (compatible), and order]

IOIOIOIOIOIOIOIOIOIOIOIOIOIOIOIOIOIOIOIOIOIOIOIOIOI

Essay-type Questions

D1 Given that the following methods are in the same class, what is the output of the following code segment?

```
public static double max(int x, double y){
  System.out.println("max(int, double) called");
  return (x > y) ? x : y;
}
public static double max(double x, int y){
```

```
    System.out.println("max(double, int) called");
    return (x > y) ? x : y;
  }
  public static void main(String[] args){
    System.out.println(max(2, 5));
  }
```

The compiler cannot determine which max method should be invoked and gives the error:
reference to max is ambiguous

D2 What is the output, if in the 'main' method of problem D1, the statement is `System.out.println(max(2.0, 5));` ?

```
max(double, int) called
5.0
```

D3 What is the output, if in the 'main' method of problem D1, the statement is `System.out.println(max(2, 5.0));` ?

```
max(int, double) called
5.0
```

D4 What is the output, if in the 'main' method of problem D1, the statement is `System.out.println(max(2.0, 5.0));` ?

The compiler gives an error:
**no suitable method found for
    max(double,double)**

D5 Given that the following methods are in the same class, what is the output of the following code segment?

```
public static int test (int x) {
  System.out.println("test(int) called");
  return x;
}
public static double test (double x) {
  System.out.println("test(double) called");
  return x;
}
public static void main(String[] args)  {
  System.out.println(test(5.0));
```

}

```
    test(double) called
    5.0
```

D6 What is the output, if in the 'main' method of the above problem, the statement is `System.out.println(test(5));` ?

```
    test(int) called
    5
```

D7 What is the output of the following code segment?

```
    String s1 = new String("Java");
    String s2 = s1;
    System.out.println(s1 == s2);
    s1 += "Programming";
    System.out.println(s1 == s2);

    true
    false
```

D8 What is the output the following code segment?

```
    String str = "Java C++ Python Ruby";
    String[] words = str.split(" ");
    for (int i = 0; i < words.length; i++)
      System.out.println(words[i] + " ");

    Java
    C++
    Python
    Ruby
```

D9 What is the output of the following program?

```
public class Example {
  int i;
  static int s;

  public static void main(String[] args) {
    Example ex = new Example();
```

```
    System.out.println ("i: " + ex.i + " s: " +
ex.s);
    ex = new Example ();
    System.out.println ("i: " + ex.i + " s: " +
ex.s);
    ex = new Example ();
    System.out.println("i: " + ex.i + " s: " +
ex.s);
  }

  public Example () {
    i++; s++;
  }
}
```

```
    i: 1 s: 1
    i: 1 s: 2
    i: 1 s: 3
```

[Note that 's' is a static or class variable, and 'i' is the instance variable. Upon each instatiation of an object the values of 'i' and 's' are incremented in the constructor **Example ()**. However, 'i' starts with an initial value of is 0 each time, while the value of 's' is retained in the 'class']

D10   What is the output of the following code?

```
public class Example {
  private int a = 5;
  public static void main(String[] args) {
    System.out.println (a);
  }
}
```

It gives a compilation error. The variable 'a' is non-static and it cannot be referenced in a static context in the 'main' method.

D11   What is the output of the following code?

```
public class Example {
  private int a = 5;
  public static void main(String[] args) {
```

```
        Example ex = new Example ();
        System.out.println (ex.a);
    }
}
```

    5

[The non-static (instance) variable 'a' can be accessed via the object 'ex']

D12 What is the output of the following program?

```
public class Example {
  static int i = 0, j = 0, k = 0;

  public static void main(String[] args) {
    int i = 2;
    {
      int j = 3;
      System.out.println ("i: " + i + " j: " + j + " k: " + k);
    }
    System.out.println ("i: " + i + " j: " + j + " k: " + k);
  }
}
```

    i: 2 j: 3 k: 0
    i: 2 j: 0 k: 0

IOIOIOIOIOIOIOIOIOIOIOIOIOIOIOIOIOIOIOIOIOIOIOIOIOIOIOIOI

E. Inheritance and Polymorphism

True/False Questions

E1   Inheritance models the 'is-a' relationship between two classes. ***True***
[Inheritance expresses the 'is-a' relationship: if B extends A, then every B object is also an A object]

E2   A strong 'is-a' relationship describes a direct inheritance relationship between two classes. ***True***
[A direct inheritance (extends) relationship between two classes represents a strong is-a relationship]

E3   The 'is-a' relationship is not transitive. ***False***
[The is-a relationship is transitive: if C is-a B and B is-a A, then C is also is-a A]

E4   A weak is-a relationship cannot be represented using interfaces. ***False***
[A weak is-a relationship (e.g., a class 'behaves like' an interface) is expressed using interfaces]

E5   Inheritance is the relationship between an interface and the class that implements it. ***True***
[When a class implements an interface, it establishes an inheritance (is-a) relationship with the interface]

E6   A subclass will not contain more data or methods than in its superclass. ***False***
[A subclass inherits all public and protected members from its superclass and may add new ones, making it more specialized]

E7   A subclass of some class could be a superclass for some other class. ***True***
[A subclass can itself be extended by another class, acting as a superclass in that new relationship]

E8   A subclass inherits the public variables and methods of its superclass. ***True***

[A subclass inherits all public and protected members (variables and methods) of its superclass]

E9 A subclass does not inherit the private variables and methods of its superclass. ***True***
[Private members of the superclass are not accessible directly in the subclass; they are accessed via accessor methods]

E10 A subclass can directly access the public instance variables of its superclass. ***True***
[Public instance variables of the superclass are directly accessible in any subclass]

E11 A subclass cannot directly access the private instance variables of its superclass. ***True***
[Private instance variables of the superclass cannot be accessed directly in the subclass]

E12 A subclass cannot ever access the private instance variables of its superclass. ***False***
[A subclass can use the accessor methods of its superclass to access the private instance variables of its superclass]

E13 A subclass cannot add new private instance variables. ***False***
[A subclass can declare new private instance variables in addition to those inherited from the superclass]

E14 A subclass can add new public or private methods. ***True***
[A subclass can add new methods with any access modifier: public, protected, or private]

E15 A subclass cannot add new static methods. ***False***
[A subclass can add new static methods; static methods belong to the class, not to instances]

E16 A subclass inherits the constructors of its superclass. ***False***
[Constructors are never inherited]

E17 A subclass can inherit the private method of its parent class. ***False***
[Private methods are not inherited by subclasses; they are accessible only within the class that defines them]

E18 A subclass cannot redefine a method that is inherited from its superclass. ***False***

E. Inheritance and Polymorphism

[Public methods of the superclass may be redefined in the subclass]

E19 A private method of a class cannot be overridden by its subclass. ***True***
[A private method is not visible in the subclass; a method with the same name in the subclass is a new, unrelated method]

E20 A static method of a class can be overridden by its subclass. ***False***
[Static methods cannot be overridden; a static method with the same name in a subclass hides (shadows) the superclass method]

E21 A subclass can call a private method defined in its parent class. ***False***
[Private methods of a parent class are not accessible in any subclass; they cannot be called directly from the subclass]

E22 A derived class can call a private method of the base class. ***False***
[Private methods of a base class are inaccessible to any derived class]

E23 A derived class can call a public method that in turn calls a private method when both the methods are in the base class. ***True***
[A derived class can call a public method of the base class; if that method internally calls a private method, it still executes correctly]

E24 A derived class can define a method that invokes a private method of its base class. ***False***
[A derived class cannot invoke a private method of its base class because private methods are not accessible outside their declaring class]

E25 A subclass is more genalized than its superclass. ***False***
[A subclass is more specialized than its superclass]

E26 Given 'Car' is a class, and 'ElectricCar' is a subclass of car, the declaration ElectricCar ec1 = new ElectricCar() is valid. ***True***
[ElectricCar extends Car; declaring and instantiating an ElectricCar variable is always valid]

E27 Given 'Car' is a class, and 'ElectricCar' is a subclass of car, the declaration Car ec1 = new ElectricCar() is not valid. ***False***
[A superclass variable (Car) can hold a reference to a subclass object (ElectricCar) via implicit upcasting]

E28 Given 'Car' is a class, and 'ElectricCar' is a subclass of car, the declaration ElectricCar ec1 = new Car() is not valid. *__True__*
[A subclass variable (ElectricCar) cannot hold a plain superclass object (Car) without explicit downcasting, which would fail at runtime]

E29 A method definition with the `final` modifier may be overridden in a derived class. *__False__*
[A method declared final cannot be overridden in any subclass; it is the final implementation]

E30 The correct method to choose at method invocation is determined by the type of the actual object. *__True__*
[Dynamic dispatch selects the method to invoke based on the actual runtime type of the object, not the declared reference type]

E31 The correct method to choose at method invocation is determined by the type of the object reference. *__False__*
[The reference type determines what methods are accessible at compile time; the runtime type of the object determines which override is called]

E32 Method names cannot be overloaded within a derived class. *__False__*
[A derived class can overload methods inherited from the superclass by defining methods with the same name but different parameters]

E33 The default modifier of a class makes it accessible to a class in the same package, but a class (including a subclass) in a different package cannot access it. *__True__*
[The default (package-private) access modifier restricts access to classes in the same package only]

E34 Java supports polymorphism. *__True__*
[Java supports runtime polymorphism through method overriding and dynamic method dispatch]

E35 Polymorphism does not work with static binding. *__True__*
[Static binding resolves methods at compile time using the declared type; this does not support polymorphic behavior]

E36 Dynamic binding is necessary for polymorphism. *__True__*
[Dynamic binding (late binding) is required for polymorphism so the correct overridden method is called at runtime]

E. Inheritance and Polymorphism

E37 Declaring the data fields to be private facilitates encapsulation. ***True***
[Making data fields private hides internal state from external code, enforcing the principle of encapsulation]

E38 A class extending another class facilitates inheritance. ***True***
[Using 'extends' establishes a superclass-subclass hierarchy, which is the foundation of inheritance]

E39 A method defined in the subclass using the same signature and compatible return type as in its superclass can be overridden. ***True***
[A method in the subclass with the same name, parameter list, and compatible return type overrides the superclass method]

E40 Overloading is valid for methods with the same name but with different signatures. ***True***
[Overloaded methods have the same name but differ in the number, types, or order of their parameters]

E41 Methods in the same class differing only in the return types can be overridden. ***False***
[Two methods in the same class with identical signatures but different return types cause a compilation error]

E42 Methods in the same class differing only in the return type results in run time error. ***False***
[Multiple methods differing only in their return types results in compilation error]

E43 A private method can be overridden. ***False***
[A private method is not visible to subclasses; a method of the same name in a subclass is a new method, not an override]

E44 A method defined in a subclass is unrelated to a method defined as private in its superclass. ***True***
[A private method in the superclass is not inherited, so a method with the same name in the subclass is completely independent]

E45 A static method can be overridden. ***False***
[Static methods are resolved at compile time based on the reference type; they cannot participate in dynamic dispatch (overriding)]

E46　A static method defined in the superclass gets hidden by a method redefined in a subclass. ***True***
[Defining a static method with the same signature in a subclass hides (shadows) the superclass's static method]

E47　An object of a derived class cannot be cast to a type of its base class. ***False***
[An object of a derived class can always be cast up to a base class type (upcasting), which is always safe]

E48　An object of a base class can be cast to a type of its derived class. ***False***
[A base class reference that actually refers to a derived class object can be explicitly downcast to the derived type]

E49　A base class reference value cannot be assigned to a derived class variable. ***True***
[Without explicit casting, the compiler does not allow a base class reference to be stored in a derived class variable]

E50　An object of a derived class cannot be assigned to a variable of any ancestor type. ***False***
[An object of a derived class can be assigned to a variable of any ancestor type. However, the other way is not allowed]

E51　A subclass may not contain more functions than it's parent class. ***False***
[A subclass can add new methods, so it may contain more functionality than its parent class]

E52　A subclass may contain more data members than its superclass. ***True***
[A subclass can declare additional instance variables beyond those inherited from its superclass]

E53　`class A extends B` means B is a subclass of A. ***False***
[In 'class A extends B', A is the subclass (derived) and B is the superclass (base), not the other way around]

E54　The `super` keyword is used only for invoking the constructor, but not a method, of a superclass. ***False***

[The **super** keyword can used for invoking both the constructor and method of a superclass]

E55 A class that implements an interface must define the body for every method specified in the interface. ***True***
[A class implementing an interface must provide concrete implementations for all abstract methods declared in the interface]

E56 A class that implements an interface can define any number of methods. ***True***
[A class implementing an interface must define all interface methods but may also add any number of additional methods]

E57 More than one class may not implement an interface. ***False***
[Multiple unrelated classes can implement the same interface, each providing its own implementation]

E58 An interface will not contain complete method definitions. ***True***
[Traditional Java interfaces contain only abstract method signatures (no bodies); default methods are a later addition]

E59 All interfaces are abstract. ***True***
[Every interface is implicitly abstract; an interface cannot be instantiated directly]

E60 An interface may contain instance variables. ***False***
[Interfaces cannot have instance variables; only constants (public static final fields) are allowed]

E61 An interface is a reference type. ***True***
[An interface defines a reference type; a variable can be declared of an interface type and hold any object of an implementing class]

E62 A class that implements an interface may define more methods than declared in the interface. ***True***
[A class implementing an interface must define all interface methods, and may freely add other methods]

E63 A class cannot implement more than one interface. ***False***
[Java allows a class to implement multiple interfaces, providing a form of multiple type inheritance]

E64 Different classes can implement the same interface. ***True***
[Any number of classes can implement the same interface, each providing its own version of the declared methods]

E65 An interface can be a formal parameter to a method. ***True***
[A formal parameter declared as an interface type can accept any object whose class implements that interface]

E66 An interface can be passed as an argument to a method invocation. ***False***
[An interface itself cannot be passed as an argument; only instances of classes implementing the interface can be passed]

E67 An object of a class implementing an interface can be passed as an argument to a method. ***True***
[A method with an interface as a formal parameter can be supplied with an object that implements the interface]

E68 It is not possible to have a method that is both overloaded and overridden. ***False***
[A mehod can be both overloaded and overridden. Which of the overloaded method to be used is determined by the compiler. Which of the overridden method to be used is determined at runtime]

E69 Invoking an overridden method from some ancesotor class, other than the direct parent class, is not permitted. ***True***
[The super keyword only accesses the direct parent class; you cannot use super.super to reach a more distant ancestor]

E70 An object of a derived class can be referenced by a variable whose type is any one of its ancestor classes. ***True***
[A derived class object is also an instance of all ancestor types; any ancestor type reference can hold it]

E71 A direct subclass cannot be defined until its direct superclass has been defined. ***True***
[A subclass definition depends on its superclass; the superclass must be compiled and available before the subclass can be defined]

E72 Polymorphism does not work with abstract classes. ***False***

E. Inheritance and Polymorphism

[Abstract classes support polymorphism; a variable of an abstract class type can refer to objects of any concrete subclass]

E73 A variable of a subtype can be assigned to a variable of its supertype. ***True***
[Assigning a subtype value to a supertype variable (upcasting) is safe and implicit in Java]

E74 Given x is a variable of a subtype, and y is a variable of a supertype, the assignment x = y is valid. ***False***
[Assigning a supertype variable to a subtype variable requires an explicit downcast; the compiler rejects it without one]

E75 A variable of a supertype can never be assigned to a variable of its subtype. ***False***
[A variable of a supertype can be assigned to a variable of its subtype with explicit casting]

E76 An abstract class cannot have a concrete subclass. ***False***
[A subclass of an abstract class can be instantiated if it overrides each of the abstract methods of its superclass and implements all of them]

E77 Given A is an abstract class, A a = new A() is not a valid statement. ***True***
[An abstract class cannot be instantiated; using 'new' on an abstract class causes a compilation error]

E78 Casting object reference variable affects the contents of the object. ***False***
[Casting changes only how the reference is viewed; the actual object in memory remains identical]

IOIOIOIOIOIOIOIOIOIOIOIOIOIOIOIOIOIOIOIOIOIOIOIOIOIOIOI

Fill-in the-blanks Questions

E1 Only the ***public*** or ***protected*** methods of a class may be overridden by its subclass.
[Only public and protected methods are inherited and can be overridden; private methods are not visible to subclasses]

E2 The ***private*** and ***static*** methods of a class cannot be overridden by its subclass.
[Private methods are not inherited and therefore cannot be overridden; static methods belong to the class and are hidden, not overridden]

E3 Different objects of different methods invoking the same method name, but with different actions, is known as ***polymorphism***.
[Polymorphism allows the same method name to produce different behaviours depending on the actual type of the object invoking it]

E4 A subclass using a call to a method of its superclass in order to override a method of the superclass is known as ***partial overriding***.
[In partial overriding, the overriding method in the subclass calls the superclass method via super and then adds extra behaviour]

E5 Method overriding in the subclass which retains a part of the inherited method from its superclass is known as ***partial overriding***.
[Partial overriding means the subclass method uses super to call the inherited superclass method and adds only the new part]

E6 A class which cannot be used as a base class to derive subclasses must be declared with the modifier `final`.
[Declaring a class final prevents it from being extended (subclassed) by any other class]

E7 A method that has been overridden in at least one subclass is known as ***polymorphic***.
[A polymorphic method is one that is declared (possibly as abstract) in a class and overridden in at least one of its subclasses]

E8 Facilitating the calling (invocation) of the correct method for a subclass object during runtime is facilitated by ***polymorphism***.
[Polymorphism allows the correct overriding method to be selected and invoked automatically at runtime based on the actual type of the object]

E9 A(n) ***abstract*** method has only header, and no implementation code.
[An abstract method has only a signature (header) and no body; the subclass must provide the implementation]

E10 The correct method to choose at method invocation is determined at ***run*** time.
[Dynamic dispatch resolves which overriding method to call at runtime based on the actual type of the object, not the reference type]

E. Inheritance and Polymorphism

E11 Redefining/changing method in a subclass which was inherited from its superclass is known as ***method overriding***.
[Method overriding occurs when a subclass provides its own implementation of a method that it inherits from a superclass]

E12 Casting a superclass to a subclass is known as ***downcast***.
[Downcasting (or narrowing) converts a superclass reference to a subclass type; it requires an explicit cast and may throw ClassCastException]

E13 Conversion of an object to the type of its subclass is known as ***narrowing*** conversion.
[Narrowing conversion goes from a more general type (superclass) to a more specific type (subclass); it requires explicit casting]

E14 Conversion of an object to the type of its superclass (or of any ancestor class) is known as ***widening*** conversion.
[Widening conversion goes from a more specific type (subclass) to a more general type (superclass); it is safe and done implicitly]

E15 Method ***overriding*** occurs when a method in a base class is redefined in its derived class.
[Method overriding occurs when a derived class redefines a method inherited from its base class with the same signature]

E16 Assigning a derived class reference to a base class variable is known as ***upcasting***.
[Upcasting (widening) assigns a reference to a derived class object to a variable of the base class type; this is always safe]

E17 "**class A extends B**" means **A** is a subclass of **B**.
[In Java, 'class A extends B' declares A as a direct subclass of B and B as the direct superclass of A]

E18 Data field of a class referencing another object is known as ***composition***.
[Composition is when a class contains a data field that holds a reference to another class object]

E19 The keyword for invoking a superclass constructor is **super**.
[The super keyword, when used in a constructor, calls the constructor of the immediate superclass]

E20 ***Inheritance*** models the is-a relationship between two classes.
[Inheritance models an is-a relationship: a Dog is an Animal; an Employee is a Person]

E21 A strong is-a relationship describes a ***direct inheritance*** relationship between two classes.
[A strong is-a relationship means that one class is a specific kind of another; it is best represented by direct (single-level) inheritance]

E22 The access modifier required for a member variable of a class so that it is accessible by any subclasses of this class, but not by classes which are not members of the same package is ***protected***.
[protected allows access within the class, its subclasses in any package, and other classes in the same package]

IOIOIOIOIOIOIOIOIOIOIOIOIOIOIOIOIOIOIOIOIOIOIOIOI

Essay-type Questions

E1 Noting the 'String' class is a descendent classes of the 'Object' class, is there a problem with the following statements? If so, what is a fix?

```
Object o = "Example";
String s =  o;
```

The first statement which assigns a string to a variable of type 'Object' is okay. However, the second statement which assigns an object of type 'Object' to a 'String' type is a narrowing conversion, and gives a compilation error. The fix is to use a cast as shown below.

```
Object o = "Example";
String s =  (String) o;
```

E2 Analyze the following code segment. Is there a problem, and if so, what is a fix?

```
class A { }
class B extends A {
```

```
    B (int a) {
      A (a);
    }
}
```

It has a compilation error due to illegal invocation of A's constructor. The super class constructor should be explicitly invoked using super() or super(arg). The fixed code is given below.

```
class A { }
class B extends A {
    B (int a) {
      super ();
    }
}
```

E3 Analyze the following code segment.

```
class A {
    public A () { }
}
public class B extends A { }
```

Works fine. The default constrictor of class A has been defined.

E4 What is the error in the following code segment, and what is the fix?

```
class A {
    public A (int a) {
    }
}
public class B extends A { }
```

It has a compilation error because the default constructor of B invokes the default constructor of A, but A does not have a default constructor. The following modification fixes the problem.

```
class A {
    public A (int a) {
    }
}
```

```java
public class B extends A {
  B (int a) {
    super(a);
  }
}
```

E5   What is the output of the following code?

```java
public class Test {
  public static void main(String[] args) {
    printType (new PC ());
    printType (new Laptop ());
    printType (new Computer ());
    printType (new Object ());
  }

  public static void printType (Object x) {
    System.out.println(x. getType ());
  }
}

class PC extends Laptop {
  public String getType () {
    return "PC";
  }
}

class Laptop extends Computer {
  public String getType () {
    return "Laptop";
  }
}

class Computer extends Object {
  public String getType () {
    return "Computer";
  }
}
class Object {
  public String getType () {
    return "Object";
  }
}
```

```
PC
Laptop
Computer
Object
```

E6 What is the output of the following code?

```
public class Test {
  public static void main(String[] args) {
    new Computer ().printType();
    new Laptop ().printType();
  }
}

class Laptop extends Computer {
  @Override
  public String getType() {
    return "Laptop";
  }
}

class Computer {
  public String getType() {
    return "Computer";
  }

  public void printType() {
    System.out.println(getType());
  }
}
```

```
Computer
Laptop
```

E7 What is the output of the following code?

```
public class Test {
  public static void main(String[] args) {
    new Computer().printType();
    new Laptop().printType();
  }
}
```

```
class Laptop extends Computer {
  private String getType() {
    return "Laptop";
  }
}

class Computer {
  private String getType() {
    return "Computer";
  }

  public void printType() {
    System.out.println(getType());
  }
}
```

      Computer
      Computer

Note that the getType method is private in class Computer and is not known outside of the class. This is the method invoked from the printType() method.

E8   Given the following classes and the declarations:

```
class A { }
class B extends A { }
class C extends B { }
class D extends A { }

A a1 = new A();
A a2 = new B();
A a3 = new D();
B b1 = new B();
B b2 = new C();
```

Which of the following assignments are in error?

```
a1 = a2;
a2 = a1;
a1 = b1;
b1 = b2;
```

E. Inheritance and Polymorphism

```
b2 = b1;
A a4 = a3;
```

All of the above are valid

E9 Consider the following statements:
```
String s = new String("Example");
Object o = s;
String t = (String) o;
```

The number of objects that are created is **3**.

s, o, and d reference the same String object. ***True***

E10 What is the output of the following code segment?

```
Object o1 = new Object();
Object o2 = new Object();
Object o3 = o1;
System.out.println(o1 == o2);
System.out.println(o1 == o3);
```

```
false
true
```

[o1 and o2 are references to to different objects, while o1 and o3 refer to the same object]

E11 What is the output of the following code segment?

```
Object o1 = new Object();
Object o2 = o1;
System.out.println(o1 == o2);
System.out.println(o1.equals(o2));
```

```
true
true
```

E12 What is the output of the following code segment?

```
Object o1 = new Object();
Object o2 = o1;
```

```
o1 = "Example";
System.out.println(o1 == o2);
System.out.println(o1.equals(o2));
```

```
false
false
```

E13 What is the output of the following code segment?

```
Object o1 = new Object();
o1 = "Example";
Object o2 = o1;
System.out.println(o1 == o2);
System.out.println(o1.equals(o2));
```

```
true
true
```

E14 What is the output of the following code segment?

```
Object o1 = new String("Example");
Object o2 = "Example";
System.out.println(o1 == o2);
System.out.println(o1.equals(o2));
```

```
false
true
```

E15 What is the output of the following code?

```
public class Test {
  public static void main(String[] args) {
    Object o1 = new A();
    Object o2 = new A();
    System.out.println(o1.equals(o2));
  }
}

class A {
  int x;

  public boolean equals(Object o) {
    return this.x == ((A) o).x;
```

}
}

true

The equals method in the Object class is overridden by that of class A. o1.equals(o2) invokes the overridden method.

E16 What is the output of the following code?

```java
public class Test {
  public static void main(String[] args) {
    Object a1 = new A();
    Object a2 = new A();
    System.out.println(a1.equals(a2));
  }
}

class A {
  int x;

  public boolean equals(A a) {
    return this.x == a.x;
  }
}
```

false

The equals method in the class A is invoked. There are now two overloaded methods available in the class A – (a) public boolean equals (Object a) and (b) public boolean equals (A a). The method used by a1.equals(a2) is determined at compile time to be the equals method defined in the Object class, which returns false.

E17 What is the output of the following code?
```java
public class Test {
  public static void main(String[] args) {
    A a1 = new A();
    A a2 = new A();
    System.out.println(a1.equals(a2));
  }
}

class A {
```

```
    int x;
    public boolean equals(A a) {
       return this.x == a.x;
    }
}
```

   true

   a1.equals(a2) matches the equals method defined in the class A.

E18   What is the output of the following code?
```
public class Test {
   public static void main(String[] args) {
      Object a1 = new A();
      Object a2 = new A();
      System.out.println(((A)a1).equals((A)a2));
   }
}
class A {
   int x;
   public boolean equals(A a) {
      return this.x == a.x;
   }
}
```

   true

   The ((A) a1).equals((A) a2) matches the equals(A a) method in the class A.

E19   What is the effect of executing the following set of statements?

```
class A { }
class B extends A { }
class C extends B { }
class D extends A { }
A[] arr1 = {new A(), new B(), new C()};
```

An array named arr1 of type A has been declared and initialized with references to three objects each of type A, B, C, respectively.

IOIOIOIOIOIOIOIOIOIOIOIOIOIOIOIOIOIOIOIOIOIOIOIOIOI

E. Inheritance and Polymorphism

F. Exception Handling

True/False Questions

F1　An exception is a method. ***False***
　　[An exception is an object (of some class)]

F2　Java provides predefined exception classes. ***True***
　　[Java's class library provides an extensive hierarchy of predefined exception classes rooted at Throwable]

F3　Java provides some default exception handlers. ***False***
　　[Java does not provide pre-built default handlers that automatically deal with specific exceptions; the programmer must write handlers]

F4　A method must declare all exceptions that it can possibly throw. ***False***
　　[Only checked exceptions (those not descending from RuntimeException or Error) must be declared in a method's signature if they are not handled within the method itself]

F5　Unchecked exceptions can be thrown by any method. ***True***
　　[Any method can throw an unchecked exception at runtime; no declaration is required]

F6　An unchecked exception must be caught in a `catch` block. ***False***
　　[An unchecked exception need not be caught in a `catch` block]

F7　An unchecked exception need not be declared in a `throws` clause. ***True***
　　[An unchecked exception need not appear in any throws declaration; the compiler does not check for it]

F8　User programs cannot define their own exception classes. ***False***
　　[Programmers can create custom exception classes by extending Exception, RuntimeException, or any other exception class]

F9　In case of system error, the user program can handle it by defining an exception handler. ***False***

F. Exception Handling

[In case of system error, invariably, there is nothing more done by the user program than a notification and termination of the program gracefully]

F10 The exceptions can be caught and handled by your program. ***True***
[Exceptions descended from Exception (other than RuntimeException) can be caught and handled in a catch block]

F11 A method may declare to throw multiple exceptions. ***True***
[A method signature may list any number of exception types in its throws clause, separated by commas]

F12 Exception handling can resolve exceptions. ***False***
[Exception handling does not fix the underlying problem; it allows the program to respond gracefully, but the root cause remains]

F13 Exceptions can be thrown by calls from a try block to other methods. ***True***
[Any code within a try block — including calls to other methods — can throw exceptions that the try block's catch handlers will catch]

F14 The try block must be followed by at least one catch block. ***False***
[A try block can be followed by a finally block alone, with no catch block]

F15 You cannot have a try block without a catch block. ***False***
[A try block without a catch block should have a finally block]

F16 A single try block cannot have multiple catch blocks associated with it. ***False***
[A single try block can be associated with any number of catch blocks, each handling a different exception type]

F17 A finally block is placed after the last catch block. ***True***
[The finally block, if present, must appear after all catch blocks associated with the same try block]

F18 If a checked exception occurs in a method, it must be either caught or declared to be thrown from the method. ***True***
[If a checked exception can propagate from a method, the method must either handle it in a try-catch or declare it with throws]

F19 A class that extends **Error** should not be declared, since **Error** raises a fatal error that terminates the program. _**True**_
[Subclassing Error signals unrecoverable JVM-level problems; such classes are not meant to be caught or handled by user code]

F20 An exception cannot be declared in the main method. _**False**_
[Exceptions can be declared in the main method's throws clause, just as in any other method]

F21 In case of system error, the user is notified and the program is attempted to terminate gracefully. _**True**_
[When a system error occurs the JVM prints a diagnostic message (stack trace) and attempts to terminate the program gracefully]

F22 The errors caused by user program and external circumstance can be caught and handled by user program. _**True**_
[Exceptions caused by program logic errors and I/O problems can be caught and handled; only Error subclasses are generally not handled]

F23 Java does not throw any exception for floating point operations. _**True**_
[Floating-point operations follow IEEE 754; they produce NaN or Infinity rather than throwing exceptions]

F24 The division 0 / 0 results in an exception. _**True**_
[Integer division by zero (0/0) throws java.lang.ArithmeticException: / by zero]

F25 The division 0.0 / 0.0 results in an exception. _**False**_
[The result is NaN — Not a Number]

F26 Java does not throw integer overflow exceptions. _**True**_
[Integer overflow in Java wraps silently using two's-complement arithmetic; no exception is thrown]

F27 An instance of **NumberFormatException** is an unchecked exception. _**True**_
[NumberFormatException extends IllegalArgumentException, which extends RuntimeException; it is therefore unchecked]

F28 An instance of **Throwable** is an unchecked exception. _**False**_

[Throwable is the root of the entire exception hierarchy; it is neither purely checked nor unchecked]

F29 A method must declare **throw** for checked exceptions. *True*
[A method that can throw a checked exception must either handle it internally or declare it with the throws keyword]

F30 A method must declare **throw** for unchecked exceptions. *False*
[Unchecked exceptions (RuntimeException and its subclasses) do not need to be declared in a throws clause]

F31 A method must declare **throw** for **RuntimeException**. *False*
[RuntimeException is the root of the unchecked exception hierarchy; methods are not required to declare it in a throws clause]

F32 A method may not have declarations to throw multiple exceptions. *False*
[A method may declare multiple exception types in a single throws clause, e.g., throws IOException, SQLException]

F33 Declaration of an exception cannot be done in the main method. *False*
[Exceptions can be declared in the throws clause of any method, including main]

F34 Upon an exception of type **Error**, the program terminates. *True*
[An unhandled Error causes the JVM to print a diagnostic and terminate the program]

F35 A **try** block can throw only one exception. *False*
[A **try** block can throw any number of exceptions]

F36 A **catch** block can catch exception of only one type. *False*
[Since Java SE7, a single catch block may handle multiple exception types using the multi-catch syntax: catch (ExType1 | ExType2 e)]

F37 A method that does not declare exceptions cannot be invoked inside a try block. *False*
[Any method can be called from inside a try block regardless of whether it declares exceptions]

F38 When an exception is thrown, the code in the remainder of the try block could still be executed. *False*
[Once an exception is thrown, execution of the try block stops immediately; no further statements in the block are executed]

F39 The catch block is not a method definition. *True*
[The catch block looks and behaves like a method, but it is not a method]

F40 A catch block applies to any any preceding try blocks. *False*
[A catch block applies only to an immediately preceding try block]

F41 After execution of the catch-block code, control returns to the try-block (from where it entered the catch-block). *False*
[After execution of the catch-block code, control transfers to the code after the last catch-block]

F42 When no exception is thrown, none of the code in any of the catch blocks get executed. *True*
[Catch blocks are skipped entirely when no exception is thrown; control flows past them after the try block completes normally]

F43 A try-block can contain any number of throw statements (either explicit or invoked in method calls). *True*
[A try block can contain explicit throw statements and calls to methods that throw exceptions; there is no limit on the number]

F44 Unchecked exceptions are descendants of class `RuntimeException`. *True*
[Unchecked exceptions are subclasses of RuntimeException (and Error); they do not need to be declared or caught]

F45 Checked exceptions are descendants of class `RuntimeException`. *False*
[Checked exceptions are descendants of class `Exception`]

F46 `IOException` is a checked exception. *True*
[IOException extends Exception (not RuntimeException), making it a checked exception that must be declared or caught]

F. Exception Handling

F47 Some of the statements in a try{} block may never throw an exception. ***True***
[Not every statement in a try block necessarily throws an exception; only the ones that involve risky operations may do so]

F48 The statements in a try{} block may throw different types of exception. ***True***
[Different statements in a try block may throw unrelated exception types; multiple catch blocks handle each type]

F49 The statements in a try{} block cannot include a loop. ***False***
[A try block may contain any valid Java statement, including loops]

F50 The catch{} block for a child exception class must follow that of a parent execption class. ***False***
[This facilitates more specific actions/messages preceding more general actions/messages]

F51 There must be only one catch{} block in a try/catch structure. ***False***
[A single try block can be followed by multiple catch blocks. This allows handling different types of exceptions with unique logic for each]

F52 Every 'try' block must have a matching 'catch' block. ***False***
[A try block does not need a catch block if it has a finally block]

F53 There must be a finally{} block in a try/catch structure. ***False***
[A finally block is optional; it is not required in every try/catch structure]

F54 There can be more than one finally{} block in a try/catch structure. ***False***
[There can be at most one finally{} block in a try/catch structure]

F55 The finally {} block (if one exists) must be after the last catch{} block. ***True***
[The finally block, if present, must be placed after all catch blocks for the same try]

F56 A try{}/catch{} cannot be nested inside an outer try{} block. ***False***
[There could be a try{} / catch{} block within an outer try block]

IOIOIOIOIOIOIOIOIOIOIOIOIOIOIOIOIOIOIOIOIOIOIOIOIOI

Fill-in the-blanks Questions

F1 The two categories of exception are ***checked*** and ***unchecked***.
[Java exceptions are either checked (must be declared or caught) or unchecked (subclasses of RuntimeException or Error)]

F2 When an exception occurs it is said to have been ***thrown***.
[When an error condition arises and an exception object is created and passed to the runtime system, the exception is said to be thrown]

F3 The ***exception object*** serves as the argument to the catch block.
[The catch clause declares a parameter of the exception type; the thrown exception object is passed as the argument to that parameter]

F4 An exception that must be caught in a catch block or declared in a throws clause, is known as ***checked*** exception.
[A checked exception is one that the compiler enforces: the method must either catch it in a try-catch or declare it with throws]

F5 If a ***checked*** exception occurs in a method, it must be either caught or declared to be thrown from the method.
[The compiler enforces that a checked exception occurring in a method must either be caught locally or declared in the method's throws clause]

F6 The method **getMessage** that returns the descriptive string stored in an exception is provided by the class **Throwable**.
[getMessage() is defined in the Throwable class and returns the detail message string stored in the exception object]

F7 To catch an exception the code that might throw, the exception must be enclosed in a **try** block.
[The try block encloses the code that might throw an exception; a matching catch block handles any thrown exception]

F8 The **try** block should contain statements that may throw an exception.
[Statements that could throw exceptions are placed inside a try block so that the associated catch blocks can handle any exceptions]

F9 The keyword that is used to throw an exception is **throw**.

[The throw statement explicitly throws an exception object; it is used inside a method body]

F10 The keyword that is used to declare exceptions in the method heading is **throws**.
[The throws clause in a method signature declares the checked exceptions that the method may throw but does not handle]

F11 The keyword used to declare exceptions in the method heading is **throws**.
[throws in a method heading lists the checked exceptions the method may propagate to its caller]

F12 The keyword used to throw an exception is **throw**.
[The throw keyword is used inside a method to explicitly throw an exception object]

F13 When an exception is thrown, the code in the *catch* block begins execution.
[When an exception is thrown inside a try block, execution jumps immediately to the matching catch block]

F14 All exceptions are objects of classes that are descendants of the **Throwable** class.
[All exception and error classes in Java extend Throwable; it is the root of the exception hierarchy]

F15 The super class of all exceptions is the **Throwable** class.
[Throwable is the parent class of all exceptions and errors in Java]

F16 The two predefined exception classes, the subclasses of **Throwable**, are **Error** and **Exception**.
[Error and Exception are the two direct subclasses of Throwable; Error represents serious JVM errors, Exception represents recoverable conditions]

F17 Errors that are thrown by the run-time system are associated with the **Error** exception class and its descendants.
[The Error class and its subclasses represent serious problems thrown by the JVM, such as OutOfMemoryError or StackOverflowError]

F18 The keywords related to exception handling are **try**, **catch**, **throws**, **throw** and **finally**.

[Java's exception-handling keywords are: try (guards the code), catch (handles exceptions), throw (throws an exception), throws (declares exceptions), and finally (always runs)]

F19 The statements that may throw exceptions are in the **try** block.
[The try block contains the statements that might throw exceptions; any exception thrown inside is caught by the associated catch block]

F20 The keyword for declaring an exception is **throws**.
[The throws keyword in the method heading declares which checked exceptions the method may propagate]

F21 The keyword for (manually) throwing an exception is **throw**.
[The throw keyword is used in a method body to explicitly throw an exception object]

F22 If an exception occurs, it is caught and handled (processed) by the **catch** block.
[If an exception is thrown in the try block, the matching catch block executes; the catch block implements the exception handler]

F23 All Java exceptions are instances of class **Throwable**.
[Every exception in Java is an instance of a class that is a descendant of Throwable]

F24 A Java system error is an instance of class **Error**.
[A Java system error is represented by an instance of Error or one of its subclasses]

F25 Upon an exception of type **Error**, the user program would terminate.
[When an uncaught Error occurs, the JVM typically terminates the program after printing a stack trace]

F26 Errors caused by both user programs and external circumstances are instances of class **Exception**.
[The Exception class (and its subclasses other than RuntimeException) represents conditions caused by user programs or external factors that can be handled]

F27 **NumberFormatException** is a subclass of **RuntimeException**.
[NumberFormatException is a subclass of IllegalArgumentException, which is a subclass of RuntimeException]

F. Exception Handling

F28 The exception caused by division by 0 is **ArithmeticException**.
[Integer division by zero (e.g., 5/0) throws an ArithmeticException with message '/ by zero']

F29 The exception caused by trying to access elements beyond the array bounds is **ArrayIndexOutOfBoundsException**.
[Accessing an array element outside the valid index range [0, length-1] throws ArrayIndexOutOfBoundsException]

F30 The exception caused by trying to access elements beyond the length of a string is **StringIndexOutOfBoundsException**.
[Accessing a character position beyond the end of a String (e.g., with charAt or substring) throws StringIndexOutOfBoundsException]

F31 The exception type thrown by the following code segment is **ClassCastException**.
[Casting an object to an incompatible type (Object obj = new Object(); (String)obj) throws ClassCastException at runtime]
```
Object obj = new Object();
String str = (String)obj;
```

F32 The exception type thrown by the following code segment is **NullPointerException**.
[Calling a method or accessing a field on a null reference throws NullPointerException]
```
Object o1 = null;
System.out.println(o1.toString());
```

F33 The exception type thrown by the following code segment is **NumberFormatException**.
[Integer.parseInt('3.14') fails because '3.14' contains a decimal point and cannot be parsed as an integer, throwing NumberFormatException]

```
String s = "3.14";
Integer.parseInt(s);
```

F34 An instance of **RuntimeException** class describes programming errors, such as bad casting, accessing an out-of-bounds array, and numeric errors.
[RuntimeException and its subclasses represent programming errors such as invalid casts, array index violations, and arithmetic errors]

F35 The method of an 'Exception' object that prints a list of methods that were called before the exception was thrown, is **printStackTrace()**.
[printStackTrace() prints the sequence of method calls (the call stack) that were active at the time the exception was thrown]

F36 The method of an Exception object returns a message string, is **getMessage()**.
[getMessage() returns the detail message string that was set when the exception object was created]

F37 The only type of exception that is not checked, is **RuntimeException**.
[It is the only type of Exception that is not checked by the compiler]

IOIOIOIOIOIOIOIOIOIOIOIOIOIOIOIOIOIOIOIOIOIOIOIOIOI

Essay-type Questions

F1 Describe the structure and function of a **catch** block in Java.

In Java, a **catch** block starts with the keyword **catch** followed by a parenthesized exception declaration containing optional qualifiers, a type, and an optional variable name. The declaration specifies the type of object that the exception handler may catch. Once an exception is caught, the body of the catch block is executed. If no handler catches an exception, the program is terminated.

F2 Describe the exception handling constructs in Java.

In Java, all exceptions are objects of classes that are derived from **Throwable** class. There are two pre-defined exception classes namely (a) **Error** and (b) **Exception**. **Error** classes are related to errors thrown by the Java run-time system (and not user programs). The **Exception** classes are related to I/O exceptions and run-time errors of user programs. User programs can define their own exception classes.

F3 In Java, which part of code gets executed whether exception is caught or not?

The **finally** block of the code gets executed whether exception is caught or not. The closing of files, database connection, etc., are usually done in **finally** block.

F4 In Java, what do **final**, **finally**, and **finalize()** do?

final: When applied to a variable, the value of the variable cannot change. When applied to a method, the method cannot be overridden. When applied to a class, the class cannot be sunclassed.

finally: The statements in the optinal **finally** block after the **try** or **catch** block will always be executed. This is usually used for clean-up code.

finalize(): Method called by the Garbage collector when it determines that no more references exist for the object.

F5 What is the output of the following code segment?

```
try {
  int x = 0;
  int y = 1 / x;
}
catch (RuntimeException excep) {
  System.out.println("Division by 0");
}
try {
  String s = "3.14";
  Integer.parseInt(s);
}
catch (NumberFormatException excep) {
  System.out.println
      ("NumberFormatException");
}

Division by 0
NumberFormatException
```

F6 What is the output of the following code segment?

```java
public static void main(String[] args) {
  try {
    testMethod();
    System.out.println("After testMethod");
  }
  catch (RuntimeException excep) {
    System.out.println("RuntimeException");
  }
  catch (Exception excep) {
    System.out.println("Exception");
  }
}

static void testMethod() throws Exception {
  try {
    String s = "3.14";
    Integer.parseInt(s);
    int x = 0;
    int y = 1 / x;
    System.out.println("After division");
  }
  catch (RuntimeException excep) {
    System.out.println("RuntimeException");
  }
  catch (Exception excep) {
    System.out.println("Exception");
  }
}
```

```
RuntimeException
After testMethod
```

F7   What is the output of the following code segment?

```java
int x = 0;
int y = 1 / x;
System.out.println(y);
System.out.println("After division");
```

```
Exception in thread "main"
java.lang.ArithmeticException: / by zero
```

F8   What is the output of the following code segment?

F. Exception Handling

```
int x = 0;
double y = 1.0 / x;
System.out.println(y);
System.out.println("After division");
```

> Infinity
> After division

F9 What is the output of the following code segment?

```
try {
  System.out.println("Java is fun");
}
finally {
  System.out.println("In finally clause");
}
```

> Java is fun
> In finally clause

F10 What is the output of the following code segment?

```
try {
  System.out.println("Java is fun");
  return;
}
finally {
  System.out.println("In finally clause");
}
```

> Java is fun
> In finally clause

F11 What is the output of the following code segment?

```
try {
  System.out.println("1: Java is fun");
  int x = 0;
  int y = 1/x;
  System.out.println("2: Java is fun");
}
catch (RuntimeException excep) {
  System.out.println("catch: Exception caught");
}
finally {
```

265

```
      System.out.println("finally: End of block");
}
```

```
      1: Java is fun
      catch: Exception caught
      finally: End of block
```

F12   What is the output of the following code segment?

```
try {
  System.out.println("1: Java is fun");
  int x = 0;
  int y = 1/x;
  System.out.println("2: After div. by 0");
}
catch (RuntimeException excep) {
  System.out.println("catch: div. by 0");
}
finally {
  System.out.println("finally block");
}
System.out.println("End of block");
```

```
      1: Java is fun
      catch: div. by 0
      finally block
      End of block
```

F13   What is the output of the following program?

```
public class Test {
  public static void main(String[] args) {
    try {
      testMethod();
      System.out.println("After method call");
    }
    catch (RuntimeException ex) {
      System.out.println("RuntimeException");
    }
    catch (Exception ex) {
      System.out.println("Exception");
    }
  }

  static void testMethod() throws Exception {
    try {
```

```
      String s = "3.14";
      Integer.parseInt(s);

      int x = 0;
      int y = 1 / x;
      System.out.println("After division");
    }
    catch (NumberFormatException excep) {
      System.out.println
          ("NumberFormatException");
      throw excep;
    }
    catch (RuntimeException excep) {
      System.out.println("RuntimeException");
    }
  }
}
```

     NumberFormatException
     RuntimeException.

IOIOIOIOIOIOIOIOIOIOIOIOIOIOIOIOIOIOIOIOIOIOIOIOIOI

G. Files and I/O

True/False Questions

G1   Data can flow through a given stream in both directions. ***False***
     [No. data in a stream flows in only one direction]

G2   A stream could act as a data source for another stream. ***True***
     [Streams can be chained; for example, a BufferedInputStream wraps a FileInputStream, using it as its data source]

G3   A `File` object is not an actual file. ***True***
     [A `File` object holds information about a disk file or a disk directory]

G4   A file cannot exist without a `File` object. ***False***
     [A file on disk exists independently of any Java File object; you can have a disk file with no File object pointing to it]

G5   A `File` object can exist without a file. ***True***
     [You can create a File object pointing to a path that does not (yet) exist on disk; the object will simply reflect that absence]

G6   An instance of the File class can be used to determine whether the file exists. ***True***
     [File.exists() returns a boolean indicating whether the file or directory named by the path actually exists]

G7   The properties of the file cannot be determined from an instance of the File class. ***False***
     [The File class provides methods such as length(), lastModified(), isHidden(), and canRead() to query file properties]

G8   An instance of the File class can be used to rename the file. ***True***
     [File.renameTo(File dest) renames the file denoted by the abstract pathname]

G9   An instance of the File class cannot be used to delete the file. ***False***
     [File.delete() deletes the file or directory denoted by the abstract pathname]

G. Files and I/O

G10 The **Reader** and **Writer** are abstract classes. *True*

[Reader and Writer are abstract base classes for character-based I/O streams; concrete subclasses provide specific implementations]

G11 The **OutputStream** and **OutputStream** are abstract classes. *True*
[InputStream and OutputStream are abstract base classes for byte-based I/O streams]

G12 Any file type can be read (meaningfully) with FileReader. *False*
[The bytes of Binary files, Bytecode files, etc. have no meaningful character interpretation]

G13 A binary file is generally much smaller than a text file containing an equivalent amount of data. *True*
[Binary files store data in compact native formats; text files add encoding overhead such as field delimiters and newlines]

G14 Input/Output with binary files is slower than with character-oriented files. *False*

[Binary I/O is generally faster than character I/O because it avoids character encoding/decoding conversions]

G15 It is not possible to make a copy of a file without knowing the format of the data it contains. *False*
[By making a byte-by-byte copy, any file can be copied]

G16 Constructing a **File** object automatically creates a disk file. *False*
[In the java.io package, a File object is simply an abstract representation of a file or directory path. No file is created on disk and no existing file is affected]

G17 The use of **fileWriter** constructor with the name of an existing file replaces the file with an empty one. *True*
[Opening a FileWriter on an existing file path truncates the existing content; use FileWriter(name, true) for append mode]

G18 The method **getname** of the class **File** returns the path name of the file. *False*
[It returns the name of the file]

G19 Different types (ex. int, double, String) can be written to the same binary file. ***True***
[DataOutputStream methods writeInt, writeDouble, writeUTF, etc. allow heterogeneous data to be written to the same binary file]

G20 The method **readUTF** should be used only to read a string from a binary file. ***True***
[readUTF() reads a string written by writeUTF(); they use a 2-byte length prefix followed by modified UTF-8; mixing with other read methods is unsafe]

G21 A number written to a file using **writeInt** can be read using **readLong** without error. ***False***
[readLong reads 8 bytes, but writeInt wrote only 4; the extra 4 bytes would come from the next value in the file, corrupting the data]

G22 The **fileInputStream** class has the **readInt** method. ***False***
[FileInputStream provides only raw byte-level read methods; readInt() belongs to DataInputStream]

G23 The **println()** method never throws exceptions. ***True***
[PrintStream (which provides println) catches all IOExceptions internally; it sets an internal error flag instead of throwing]

G24 A 'null' is returned when **readLine()** encounters an error. ***False***
[An **IOException** is thrown when **readLine()** encounters an error]

G25 The value returned by **readLine()** upon encountering end-of-file, is an empty string. ***False***
[Upon encountering end-of-file, **readLine()** returns 'null']

G26 Compressed text files can be read using a **FileReader** stream. ***False***
[Compressed text files are binary files, which are not properly read by **FileReader** stream]

IOIOIOIOIOIOIOIOIOIOIOIOIOIOIOIOIOIOIOIOIOIOIOIOIOIOIOI

G. Files and I/O

Fill-in the-blanks Questions

G1 The connection between a program and a data source or destination is known as ***stream***.
[A stream is a channel connecting a program to a data source (input) or destination (output); data flows through it sequentially]

G2 The character data format used internally by Java programs is ***16-bit char***.
[Java stores characters internally as 16-bit Unicode (char) values using the UTF-16 encoding]

G3 The format of the characters used in text files written by Java programs is ***UTF format***.
[Java text files are written using UTF-8 (or the platform default), which is a Unicode Transformation Format]

G4 The type of the value returned by the method **next** of class **Scanner** is **String**.
[Scanner.next() reads and returns the next token as a String]

G5 The type of the value returned by the method **nextLine** of class **Scanner** is **String**.
[Scanner.nextLine() reads an entire line including the newline terminator and returns it as a String]

G6 The class containing the method for checking if a file exists is **File**.
[The java.io.File class provides the exists() method and other methods to query file system metadata]

G7 **File.pathSeparatorChar** returns the path separator character.
[File.pathSeparatorChar is a static char field holding the path separator for the current OS (';' on Windows, ':' on Unix)]

G8 The class that is used to write data into a text file is **PrintWriter**.
[PrintWriter provides print(), println(), and printf() for writing formatted text to a file or stream]

G9 The class that is used to read data from a text file is **Scanner**.
[Scanner can wrap a File object to tokenise and read text from a file]

G10 The method that is used to write data is **print**.
[PrintWriter.print() writes a value without a trailing newline; println() adds the newline]

G11 The method that is used to read a whole line from a file is **nextLine**.
[Scanner.nextLine() reads one complete line of text (up to but not including the line terminator) from the file]

G12 The method that is used to create an input object for file named 'sales1.dat' is **new Scanner(new File("sales1.dat"))**
[The Scanner constructor accepts a File object; wrapping it provides token-based and line-based reading of the file]

G13 The package that holds the File class is **java.io**.
[The File class is in the java.io package, which must be imported to use it]

G14 The output displaying byte-by-byte contents of a binary file is known as *hex dump*.
[A hex dump shows the raw byte values of a file in hexadecimal, used to inspect binary files]

G15 The failure to open a file for reading results in **FileNotFoundException** exception.
[If the specified file does not exist when opening it for reading, Java throws FileNotFoundException]

G16 The ancestor of all character-oriented input streams is **Reader**.
[Reader is the abstract root class of all character-based input stream classes in java.io]

G17 The ancestor of all character-oriented output streams is **Writer**.
[Writer is the abstract root class of all character-based output stream classes in java.io]

G18 The ancestor of all byte-oriented output streams is **OutputStream**.
[OutputStream is the abstract root class of all byte-oriented output stream classes]

G19 The ancestor of all byte-oriented input streams is **InputStream**.
[InputStream is the abstract root class of all byte-oriented input stream classes]

G20 Convenient methods for output of primitive data types is provided in the class **DataOutputStream**.

G. Files and I/O

[DataOutputStream provides writeInt(), writeDouble(), writeUTF(), etc. for writing Java primitives in portable binary format]

G21 The method of a stream which ensures that all pending output operations are completed is **flush()**.
[flush() forces any data buffered in the stream to be written to the underlying output device or next stream in the chain]

G22 The method that reads 'int' values from a stream is **readInt()**.
[DataInputStream.readInt() reads 4 bytes and reconstructs them as an int value]

G23 The method that writes double precision values to a stream is **writeDouble()**.
[DataOutputStream.writeDouble() writes an 8-byte IEEE 754 double-precision value to the stream]

G24 The method that gives the number of bytes written to a stream so far is **size()**.
[DataOutputStream.size() returns the number of bytes written to the stream so far]

G25 The method that is used to test if a file or directory exists is **exists()**.
[exists() tests whether the file or directory exists. isFile() tests only whether the path is a regular file (returns false for directories)]

G26 The class that is used for input of character data from a disk file is **FileReader**.
[FileReader is a convenience class that opens a character-based stream to read from a disk file]

G27 The class that is used for output of character data to a disk file is **FileWriter**.
[FileWriter is a convenience class that opens a character-based stream to write to a disk file]

G28 The parent class of **FileWriter** is **OutputStreamWriter**.
[FileWriter extends OutputStreamWriter, which wraps an OutputStream with a character encoder]

G29 The **readLine()** is a method belonging to the class **BufferedReader**.

[BufferedReader provides the readLine() method, which reads a full line of text from the underlying Reader]

G30 The return type of **readLine()** is **String**.
[readLine() returns a String containing the content of the line, or null if end of stream is reached]

G31 The value returned by **readLine()** return upon encountering end-of-file is **null**.
[readLine() returns null when it reaches the end of the file, signalling that there is no more data]

G32 The method to create a new disk directory is **mkdir()**.
[File.mkdir() creates the directory named by the abstract pathname; it returns true if the directory was created successfully]

G33 The method to remove a file is **delete()**.
[File.delete() deletes the file or directory; it returns true if deletion succeeded]

G34 The exception that is thrown when the end of a file is reached, is **EOFException**.
[EOFException is thrown by DataInputStream methods when the end of a binary stream is reached unexpectedly]

IOIOIOIOIOIOIOIOIOIOIOIOIOIOIOIOIOIOIOIOIOIOIOIOIOI

H. Programming Problems

H1 Write a program to compute the average of three numbers which are read from the terminal.
```
import java.util.Scanner;
public class Main {
  public static void main(String[] args) {
    Scanner input = new Scanner(System.in);
    System.out.print("Enter three numbers: ");
    double num1 = input.nextDouble();
    double num2 = input.nextDouble();
    double num3 = input.nextDouble();

    double average = (num1 + num2 + num3) / 3;

    System.out.println(average);
  }
}
```

H2 Write a program to compute the volume of a cone whose base radius and height are read from the terminal.
```
import java.util.Scanner;
public class Main {
  public static void main(String[] args) {
    final double PI = 3.14159;
    Scanner input = new Scanner(System.in);
    System.out.print("Enter the radius and height: ");
    double radius = input.nextDouble();
    double height = input.nextDouble();

    double coneVolume = (PI * radius * radius * height) / 3.0;

    System.out.println("Volume of the cone of radius" +
    radius + " and height " + height + " is " + coneVolume);

  }
}
```

H3 Write the code segment to compute the largest of three numbers which are in variables num1, num2, and num3.
```
    if (num1 > num2 && num1 > num3)
       largest = num1;
    else if (num2 > num3)
       largest = num2;
```

```
    else
       largest = num3;
```

H4 Write the code segment to compute the largest of three numbers which are in variables num1, num2, and num3, using the ternary operator ('?', ':').

```
largest = num3 > (num1 > num2 ? num1 : num2) ?
    num3 : ((num1 > num2) ? num1 : num2);
```

H5 Write a program to print the following based on age read from the terminal: (a) less than 3 years → Infant; (b) ≥ 3 and < 13 years → Child; (c) ≥ 13 and < 20 years → Teenager; (d) ≥ 20 and < 30 years → Youth; (e) ≥ 30 and < 65 years → Adult; (f) > 65 years → Senior Citizen.

```
public class Main {
  public static void main(String[] args) {
    Scanner input = new Scanner(System.in);
    int age;

    do {
       System.out.print ("Please type the age [0-120]: ");
       age = input.nextInt();;
    } while (age < 0 || age > 120);

    if (age < 3)
       System.out.println ("Infant\n");
    else if (age < 13)
       System.out.println ("Child\n");
    else if (age < 20)
       System.out.println ("Teenager\n");
    else if (age < 30)
      System.out.println ("Youth\n");
   else if (age < 65)
      System.out.println ("Adult\n");
   else
      System.out.println ("Senior Citizen\n");
  }
}
```

H6 Write a program to determine the least number of coins using quarters, dimes, nickels, pennies to be given as change.

```
import java.util.Scanner;
public class Main {
  public static void main(String[] args) {
    Scanner input = new Scanner(System.in);
```

H. Programming Problems

```
    int amt, quarters, dimes, nickels, pennies;

    do {
        System.out.print ("Type the change amount[1-99]: ");
        amt = input.nextInt();
    } while (amt < 1 || amt > 99);

    quarters = amt/25;
    amt %= 25;
    dimes = amt/10;
    amt %= 10;
    nickels = amt/5;
    pennies = amt % 5;

    System.out.print ("The change is: ");
    if (quarters > 0)
       System.out.print (quarters + " Quarters ");
    if (dimes > 0)
       System.out.print (dimes + " Dimes ");
    if (nickels > 0)
       System.out.print (nickels + " Nickels ");
    if (pennies > 0)
       System.out.print (pennies + " Pennies");

    System.out.println();
  }
}
```

H7 Given two intervals (a_1, b_1) and (a_2, b_2) on the real number line, write a method **overlap** to determine if they overlap or not. For example, (2.7, 5.3) and (4.8, 12.2) overlap, (3.4, 6.6) and (6.6, 7.3) do not overlap, and (2.7, 5.3) and (7.1, 9.5) do not overlap. Each interval is represented by an array of two real numbers, and the method returns a Boolean.

```
public static boolean isOverlap(double[] x, double[] y){
   return !(x[1]<=y[0] || x[0] >= y[1]);
}
```

H8 Write a method which takes as arguments three real numbers representing the sides of a triangle, and determines and returns true or false, based on whether it is a valid triangle or not. **Note:** In a valid triangle, the sum of the lengths of any two sides is greater than the length of the third side. For example, if the given side lengths are 10.7, 5.6, and 2.9, it should return false.

```
public static boolean isValidTriangle (double a, double
     b, double c){
   return (a >= b + c || b >= a + c || c >= a + b);
```

H9 Write a program to print the sequence: 1 2 4 7 11 ....The length of the sequence is read from the terminal.

```java
import java.util.Scanner;
public class Main {
  public static void main(String[] args) {
    Scanner input = new Scanner(System.in);
    int i, num, seqLen;
    i = 1; num = 1;
    System.out.print ("Type in the sequence length: ");
    seqLen = input.nextInt();

    while (i <= seqLen) {
       System.out.print (num + " ");
       num += i;
       i++;
    }
  }
}
```

H10 Write a method which takes two integers 'num' and 'pos' as arguments, and returns the digit at position 'pos' of the number 'num'. Note that pos = 1 denotes the unit's position. For example, Input: (6753, 3), Output: 7; Input: (372514, 4), Output: 2. Assume that the value of 'pos' is > 0.

```java
public static int digitAtPos (int num, int pos) {
  int dgt;
  do {
    dgt = num % 10;
    num = num / 10;
    pos--;
  } while (pos > 0);
  return dgt;
}
```

H11 Write a method which reads an integer limit and determines and prints out all 'Armstrong numbers' within the limit. An Armstrong number is one which equals the sum of the cubes of its digits. A sample output is shown below.

    Enter limit: 1000
    1 153 370 371 407

```java
    public static void main(String[] args) {
```

H. Programming Problems

```
int q, r, s;
Scanner input = new Scanner(System.in);
System.out.print("Enter limit: ");
int lim = input.nextInt();
for (int i = 1; i <= lim; i++) {
  q = i; s = 0;
  while (q != 0) {
    r = q % 10;
    q = q / 10;
    s += r*r*r;
  }
  if (s == i)
    System.out.print(i + " ");
}
```

H12 Write a program that calculates and prints the sequence, as shown below.

```
        9
       89
      789
     6789
      ::
      ::
123456789
```

```
public class Main {
  public static void main(String[] args) {
    int n, nd, ndgts, num;

    for (ndgts = 1; ndgts <= 9; ndgts++ ) {
      nd = ndgts;
      n = 10 - nd;
      num = 0;
      while (nd > 0) {
        num = num*10 + n;
        n++;
        nd--;
      }
      System.out.printf ("%10d ", num);
    }
  }
}
```

H13 Write a method to calculate and print all the well-ordered numbers of a given number of digits. It should take as input the number of digits, and return the number of well-ordered numbers of that many digits. A well-ordered number is one whose digits strictly increase from left to right. A sample output is given below.

```
Type the number of digits [1-9]: 2
12 13 14 15 16 17 18 19 23 24
25 26 27 28 29 34 35 36 37 38
39 45 46 47 48 49 56 57 58 59
67 68 69 78 79 89
Number of well ordered numbers of 2 digits = 36
```

```java
import java.util.*;
public class Main {
  public static int wellOrdered(int nDigits) {
    int    n,   nd,   num,   loLim,   hiLim=1,   cnt=0,   curDigit,
    prevDigit;
    boolean wellOrder;

    for (n = nDigits; n > 0; n--)
      hiLim *= 10;

    loLim = hiLim / 10;

    for (n = loLim; n < hiLim; n++) {
      num = n;
      wellOrder = true;
      prevDigit = num % 10;
      num /= 10;
      while (num != 0) {
        curDigit = num % 10;
        if (curDigit >= prevDigit) {
          wellOrder = false;
          break;
        }
        prevDigit = curDigit;
        num /= 10;
      }
      if (wellOrder) {
        cnt++ ;
        System.out.printf ("%d ", n);
        if (cnt % 10 == 0)
          System.out.println();
      }
    }
    System.out.println();
    return (cnt);
  }
  public static void main(String a[]) {
    int nDigits, cnt;
    Scanner input = new Scanner(System.in);
    System.out.print ("Type the number of digits [1-9]: ");
```

```
    nDigits = input.nextInt();
    cnt = wellOrdered (nDigits);
    System.out.printf ("Number of well ordered numbers of %d
      digits = %d\n", nDigits, cnt);
  }
}
```

H14 Write a method which takes a sorted array of integers, and an integer 'num', and determines and prints out the 'num' elements of the array which are closest to the median.

Note: Given two numbers a and b, a is closer to the median m if $|a - m| < |b - m|$

```
public static void closeToMedian (int arr[], int num) {
  int p = 1, m = arr.length/2;
  int d1, d2, i = m-1, j = m+1;
  while (p <= num && i >= 0 && j < arr.length) {
    d1 = arr[m] - arr [i]; d2 = arr[j] - arr[m];
    if (d1 < d2) {
      System.out.print(arr[i] + " ");
      i--;
    }
    else {
      System.out.print(arr[j] + " ");
      j++;
    }
    p++;
  }
  if (i < 0) {
    while (p <= num && j < arr.length) {
      System.out.print(arr[j] + " ");
      j++;
    }
  }
  else if (j < arr.length) {
    while (p <= num && i >= 0) {
      System.out.print(arr[i] + " ");
      i--;
    }
  }
}
```

H15 Write a program that computes the square root 'r' of a number 'x' using Newton's method, and compare it with the value given by the library function. An example output is given below.

```
Type the number: 57
Square root of 57.000000 using Newton's method is
7.549835
The number of iterations required was 6
Square root computed by library function = 7.549834
```

Newton's method: Start with r = 1. If 'r' is an approximation to the square root of 'x', then a better approximation to the square root is given by: (x/r + r)/2 . This is iterated till the error converges (*i.e.* keep itearating until error becomes less than a small number ε, say 0.001.

```java
import java.util.Scanner;
public class Main {
  public static void main(String[] args) {
    Scanner input = new Scanner(System.in);
    System.out.print ("Type the number: ");
    double x = input.nextDouble();
    double r = 1.0, err;
    int iter = 0;

    do {
      iter++;
      r = (x/r + r)/2.0;
      err = r*r - x;
      if (err < 0.0)
        err = -err;
    } while (err > 0.001);

    System.out.printf ("Square root of %f using Newton's
    method is %f\n", x, r);
    System.out.printf ("The number of iterations required was
    %d\n", iter);
    System.out.printf ("Square root computed by library
    function = %f\n", Math.sqrt(x));
  }
}
```

H16 Write a method which takes as argument a number *N* (integer), and returns the sum of the sequence: 1/2 + 2/3 + 3/4 + ... + *N*/(*N*+1). Note that the sequence sum is a real number. For example, if *N* = 6, it should output 4.4071428 ...

```java
public static double seriesSum (int n) {
  int i;
  double sum = 0;
  for (i = 1; i <= n; i++) {
    sum += (double)i / (i + 1);
  }
```

```
    return sum;
}
```

H17 Write the code segment to determine if a given 'year' is leap year or not. Note that a year is leap year if it is divisible by 4 or if it is a century boundaries, it must be divisible by 400. For example, for an input of 1976, the output should be "1976 is a leap year"; for 1982, it should be "1982 is not a leap year"; for 1900, it should be "1900 is not a leap year"; for 2000, it should be "2000 is a leap year".

```
leapYear = ((year % 400 == 0) || (year % 100 != 0 && year
% 4 == 0));
```

H18 Write a program to determine the value of N when the sum of the sequence: $1/2 + 2/3 + 3/4 + \ldots + N/(N+1)$ exceeds the value 42.7.

```
import java.util.Scanner;
public class Main {
  public static void main(String[] args) {
    Scanner input = new Scanner(System.in);
    int n=1;
    double sum = 0;

    while (sum <= 42.7){
      sum += (double)n / (n + 1);
      n++;
    }
  System.out.println ("The value of N when sequence sum
    exceeds 42.7 is " + (n-1));
  }
}
```

H19 Write a program to read a number N (integer) from the terminal, and compute π using the first N terms of the approximation given below.

$$\pi = 4\left(1 - \frac{1}{3} + \frac{1}{5} - \frac{1}{7} + \frac{1}{9} - \frac{1}{11} + \cdots + \frac{(-1)^{N+1}}{2N-1}\right)$$

```
import java.util.Scanner;
public class Main {
  public static void main(String[] args) {
    Scanner input = new Scanner(System.in);
    int i, seqLen;
    double Pi, den=1, term, sum = 0;
    System.out.print ("Type in the sequence length: ");
    seqLen = input.nextInt();
```

```
    for (i = 1; i <= seqLen; i++) {
      term = 1.0/den;
      if (i % 2 == 0) // even value of i
        term = -term;
      sum += term;
      den += 2;
    }
    Pi = 4.0 * sum;
    System.out.println ("The value of π using " + seqLen + "
    terms is " + Pi);
  }
}
```

H20 Write a program to read a number N (integer) from the terminal, and compute e, the base of the natural logarithm, using the first N terms of the approximation given below.

$$e = 1 + \frac{1}{1!} + \frac{1}{2!} + \frac{1}{3!} + \cdots + + \frac{1}{N!}$$

```
import java.util.Scanner;
public class Main {
  public static void main (String[] args) {
    Scanner input = new Scanner(System.in);
    int i, seqLen;
    double conste = 1, den=1;
    System.out.print ("Type in the sequence length: ");
    seqLen = input.nextInt();

    for (i = 2; i <= seqLen; i++) {
      conste += 1.0/den;
      den *= i;
    }
    System.out.println ("The value of e using " + seqLen + "
    terms is " + conste);
  }
}
```

H21 Write a program prints the first "N" numbers of the Padovan series. "N" is read from the keyboard. The Padovan series is 1,1,1,2,2,3,4,5,7,9,12,16,21,28,37,... Each number is obtained by skipping the previous one and adding the two before that. Have the program also print the ratio of two successive Padovan numbers.

```
import java.util.Scanner;
```

```
public class Main {
public static void main(String[] args) {
  int i, seqLen, prev1=1, prev2=1, prev3=1, num;
  Scanner input = new Scanner(System.in);
  do {
    System.out.print("Enter the Padovan sequence
     length [>=1]: ");
     seqLen = input.nextInt();
  } while (seqLen < 1);

  for (i=1; i<=3 && i<=seqLen; i++)
    System.out.printf ("%10d   %f\n", 1, 1.0);

  if (seqLen <= 3)
    return;

  seqLen -= 3;
  for (; seqLen > 0; seqLen--) {
    num = prev2 + prev3;
    prev3 = prev2;
    prev2 = prev1;
    prev1 = num;

    System.out.printf ("%10d %f\n", num,
     (float)prev1/(float)prev2);
  }
  System.out.println();
}
}
```

H22 Write a program which generates a random integer between 1 and 1,000 and have the user guess the number. Based on the input, it should notify the user whether the guess was lower/higher than the generated number. There should be a maximum of 10 guesses allowed.

```
import java.util.Scanner;
import java.util.Random;
public class Main {
  public static void main(String[] args) {
    Scanner input = new Scanner(System.in);

    final int guessMax = 10;
    int guessCnt=0;
  System.out.println("This generates a random number between
   1 and 1000.");
  System.out.printf("You are allowed %d guesses.", guessMax);
```

```
     System.out.println("It tells you whether your ");
     System.out.println("guess  is    more   or   less   than   the
       generated number.");
       Random rand = new Random();
       int num = rand.nextInt(1000) + 1;
       while (guessCnt < guessMax) {
         System.out.print ("Type your guess: ");
         int guess = input.nextInt();
         guessCnt++;
         if (guess == num) {
           System.out.printf ("Yes! The number is %d.\n", num);
           System.out.printf  ("You  guessed  in  %d  trials\n",
     guessCnt);
           return;
         }
         else if (guess < num)
           System.out.println ("Your guess is low.");
         else
           System.out.println ("Your guess is high.");
       }
       System.out.println  ("You  have  exceeded  the  limit  on
       guesses.\n");
       System.out.printf ("The number was %d\n", num);
     }
   }
```

H23 Write a method which takes as input an Integer N, and prints out N
     down to 1 in the first row, (N – 1) down to 1 in the second row, etc.,
     and 1 in the last row. For example, if the input value of N is 5, the
     output should be:

     5 4 3 2 1
     4 3 2 1
     3 2 1
     2 1
     1

```
import java.util.Scanner;
public class Main {
  public static void printNumTri (int num){
    int j;
    for (; num >= 1; num--) {
      for (j = num; j >= 1; j--)
        System.out.print (j + " ");
      System.out.println();
    }
  }
  public static void main(String[] args) {
    Scanner input = new Scanner(System.in);
```

```
    int num;
    System.out.print ("Type in the number: ");
    num = input.nextInt();
    printNumTri (num);
  }
}
```

H24 Write a method which takes as argument two numbers (rows and columns), and prints a rectangle of '*'s.
```
public static void printRectangle (int nRows, int
nCols) {
  for (int i = 1; i <= nRows; i++) {
    for (int j = 1; j <= nCols; j++)
      System.out.print ("*");
    System.outprintln();
  }
```

H25 Write a method which takes an integer argument which specifies the height of a triangle and prints it using '*'s and spaces.

   Examples:

       height 1:   *

       height 2:   *
                                       ***

       height 3:   *
                                       ***
                                      *****

```
public static void printTriStars (int height) {
  for(int i = 1; i <= height; i++) {
    for(int j = 1; j <= height-i; j++)
      System.out.print (" ");
    for(int j = 1; j <= 2*(i-1)+1; j++)
      System.out.print ("*");
    System.out.println();
  }
}
```

H26 Write a program to read a number (integer) N from the terminal, and print an arrow of '*'s of a given height.

   Examples:

       height 1:   *

height 2:
```
 *
**
 *
```

height 3:
```
  *
 **
***
 **
  *
```

```java
import java.util.Scanner;
public class Main {
  public static void printUpTriangle (int height) {
    for (int i = 1; i <= height; i++) {
      for (int j = 1; j <= i; j++)
        System.out.print ("*");
      System.out.println();
    }
  }
  public static void printDownTriangle (int height) {
    for (int i = 1; i <= height; i++) {
      for (int j = 1; j <= height-i+1; j++)
        System.out.print ("*");
      System.out.println();
    }
  }
  public static void printArrow (int height) {
    printUpTriangle (height);
    printDownTriangle (height-1);
  }
}
```

H27 Write a method which takes two integer arguments (rows and columns), and prints a "hollow" rectangle of '*'s. (The boundary consists of single '*'s)

```java
  public static void hollowRectangle(int rows, int cols) {
    if (rows <= 2 || cols <= 2) {
      for (int i = 1; i <= rows; i++) {
        for (int j = 1; j <= cols; j++)
          System.out.print ("*");
        System.out.println();
      }
      System.exit(1);
    }
    for (int j = 1; j <= cols; j++)
```

```
      System.out.print ("*");
    System.out.println();
    for (int i = 2; i <= rows-1; i++) {
      System.out.print ("*");
      for (int j = 2; j <= cols-1; j++)
        System.out.print (" ");
      System.out.println ("*");
    }
    for (int j = 1; j <= cols; j++)
      System.out.print ("*");
    System.out.println();
  }
}
```

H28 Write a method to print an "X" shape of '*'s of a given height.

h=1   *

                * *
h=2   *
                * *

              *   *
               * *
h=3   *
               * *
              *   *

i	preGap	formula	midGap	formula
1	0	(i–1), i ≤ h	5	(2h–1–2i), i < h
2	1		3	
3	2		1	
4	3		0	
5	2	(2h–1–i), i > h	1	2(i – h) – 1, i > h
6	1		3	
7	0		5	

```
public static void printX(int height) {
  Scanner input = new Scanner(System.in);
  int i, j, preGap, midGap=0;
  for (i = 1; i <= 2*height-1; i++){
    preGap = (i <= height)? (i-1) : (2*height-1-i);
    midGap = (i < height) ? (2*height-1-2*i) : 2*(i-height)-1;
    for (j = 1; j <= preGap; j++)
      System.out.print (" ");
    System.out.print ("*");
    for (j = 1; j <= midGap; j++)
```

```
        System.out.print (" ");
    if (i != height)
        System.out.println ("*");
    else
        System.out.println ();
    }
  }
}
```

H29   Write a method to print an "Z" shape of '*'s of a given height.

```
              **
h=2           **


              * *
h=3            *
              * *


              ****
               *
h=4            *
              ****
```

```
import java.util.Scanner;
public class Main {
  public static void main(String[] args) {
    Scanner input = new Scanner(System.in);
    int i, j, height;
    System.out.print ("Type in the height: ");
    height = input.nextInt();
    for (j = 1; j <= height; j++) // topmost line
      System.out.print ("*");
    System.out.println ();
    for (i = 2; i <= height-1; i++){
      for (j = 1; j <= height-i; j++)
        System.out.print (" ");
      System.out.println ("*");
    }
    for (j = 1; j <= height; j++) // bottommost line
      System.out.print ("*");
    System.out.println ();
  }
}
```

H30   Write a method to print an "N" shape of '*'s of a given height.

```
h=2           **
              **
```

```
h=3              * *
                ***
                 * *

                *   *
h=4             ** *
                * **
                *   *
```

```
import java.util.Scanner;
public class Main {
  public static void main(String[] args) {
    Scanner input = new Scanner(System.in);
    int i, j, height, sp1, sp2;
    System.out.print ("Type in the height: ");
    height = input.nextInt();
    System.out.print ("*");
    for (j = 2; j <= height-1; j++)
      System.out.print (" ");
    System.out.println ("*");
    for (i = 2; i <= height-1; i++){
      sp1 = (i-2); sp2 = height-1-i;
      System.out.print ("*");
      for (j = 1; j <= sp1; j++)
        System.out.print (" ");
      System.out.print ("*");
      for (j = 1; j <= sp2; j++)
        System.out.print (" ");
      System.out.println ("*");
    }
    System.out.print ("*");
    for (j = 2; j <= height-1; j++)
      System.out.print (" ");
    System.out.println ("*");

  }
}
```

H31   Write a method to print an "M" shape of '*'s of a given height.

```
h=2              * *
                ***

                *   *
h=3             ** **
                * * *

                *     *
```

h=4
```
         **   **
         * * * *
         *  *  *
```

```java
import java.util.Scanner;
public class Main {
  public static void main(String[] args) {
    Scanner input = new Scanner(System.in);
    int i, j, height, sp1, sp2, sp3;
    System.out.print ("Type in the height: ");
    height = input.nextInt();
    System.out.print ("*");
    for (j = 1; j <= 2*height-3; j++)
      System.out.print (" ");
    System.out.println ("*");
    for (i = 2; i <= height-1; i++){
      sp1 = sp3 = i-2; sp2 = 2*height-1-2*i;
      System.out.print ("*");
      for (j = 1; j <= sp1; j++)
        System.out.print (" ");
      System.out.print ("*");
      for (j = 1; j <= sp2; j++)
        System.out.print (" ");
      System.out.print ("*");
      for (j = 1; j <= sp3; j++)
        System.out.print (" ");
      System.out.println ("*");
    }
        // last row
        System.out.print ("*");
        for (j = 1; j <= height-2; j++)
          System.out.print (" ");
        System.out.print ("*");
        for (j = 1; j <= height-2; j++)
          System.out.print (" ");
        System.out.println ("*");
  }
}
```

H32 Write a method to print an "V" shape of '*'s of a given height.

h=1
```
        *
```

h=2
```
        * *
         *
```

h=3
```
        *   *
         * *
          *
```

```
h=4            *   *
             *   *
              * *
               *
```

```java
import java.util.Scanner;
public class Main {
  public static void main(String[] args) {
    Scanner input = new Scanner(System.in);
    int i, j, height, sp1, sp2;
    System.out.print ("Type in the height: ");
    height = input.nextInt();
    for (i = 1; i <= height-1; i++){
      sp1=(i-1); sp2=(2*height-1-2*i);
      for (j = 1; j <= sp1; j++)
        System.out.print (" ");
      System.out.print ("*");
      for (j = 1; j <= sp2; j++)
        System.out.print (" ");
      System.out.println ("*");
    }
    for (j = 1; j <= height-1; j++)
      System.out.print (" ");
    System.out.println ("*");
  }
}
```

H33 Write a method to print an "K" shape of '*'s of a given height.

```
h=1            **

                * *
h=2            **
                * *

                *   *
                * *
h=3            **
                * *
                *   *
```

```java
import java.util.Scanner;
public class Main {
  public static void main(String[] args) {
    Scanner input = new Scanner(System.in);
    int i, j, height, spaces=0;
    System.out.print ("Type in the height: ");
    height = input.nextInt();
```

```java
    for (i = 1; i <= 2*height-1; i++) {
      spaces = (i <= height)? (height-i) : (i-height);
      System.out.print ("*");
      for (j = 1; j <= spaces; j++)
        System.out.print (" ");
      System.out.println ("*");
    }
  }
}
```

H34 Write a program to compute the amounts after compounding of interest quarterly, monthly, and daily, over a range of years.

A sample output is given below.

```
Type in the principal: 10000
Type in the Interest rate (%): 6.5
Type in the term range (ex. 5 10): 6 12
Yield on 10000.0 at 6.5%

              Quarterly        Monthly         Daily

6  Years      14,723.58        14,754.27       14,769.30
7  Years      15,704.19        15,742.39       15,761.10
8  Years      16,750.12        16,796.69       16,819.50
9  Years      17,865.70        17,921.60       17,948.97
10 Years      19,055.59        19,121.84       19,154.30
11 Years      20,324.72        20,402.46       20,440.57
12 Years      21,678.38        21,768.85       21,813.21
```

```java
import java.util.Scanner;
public class Main {
  public static void main (String[] args) {
    Scanner input = new Scanner(System.in);
    double amtQty, amtMonthly, amtDaily, principal,
    intRate;
     int term1, term2;
    System.out.print ("Type in the principal: ");
    principal = input.nextDouble();
    System.out.print ("Type in the Interest rate (%): ");
    intRate = input.nextDouble();
    System.out.print ("Type in the term range (ex. 5, 10): ");
    term1 = input.nextInt();
    term2 = input.nextInt();
    System.out.println ("Yield on " + principal + " at " +
    intRate + "% Compounded");
    System.out.println ("     Quarterly     Monthly     Daily
    ");
    for (; term1 <= term2; term1++) {
```

```
            amtQty = principal*Math.pow(1.0 + (intRate /(100*4)),
        4*term1);
            amtMonthly = principal*Math.pow(1.0
        +(intRate/(100*12)), 12*term1);
            amtDaily = principal*Math.pow(1.0
        +(intRate/(100*365)), 365*term1);
            System.out.format ("%d %s %,12.2f %,12.2f %,12.2f\n",
        term1, "Years", amtQty, amtMonthly, amtDaily);

        }
    }
}
```

H35 The formula for the future value of an Annuity is given below:

$$A = \frac{R\left[\left(1+\frac{r}{n}\right)^{nt} - 1\right]}{\frac{r}{n}}$$

Where A is the future value of the annuity, R is the regular periodic payment, r is the annual interest rate, n is the number of payments made per year, t is the term of the annuity in years.

Write a program which reads the values of A, r, and printout a table which gives the monthly payment required to reach the target with the given interest rate over 5, 10, 15, 20, 25, and 30 years.

```
import java.util.Scanner;
public class Main {
    public static void main(String[] args) {
        Scanner input = new Scanner(System.in);
        System.out.print ("Type in the target amount: ");
        double targetAmt = input.nextDouble();
        System.out.print ("Type in the interest rate (%): ");
        double intRate = input.nextDouble();
        int year;
        double numr, denr;
        System.out.format ("Years   Monthly Payment\n");
        System.out.format ("-------------------------\n");
        for (year = 5; year <= 30; year += 5) {
            numr = targetAmt * (intRate/100)/12;
            denr = Math.pow((1 + (intRate/100)/12), 12*year) - 1;
            System.out.format ("%5d %,10.2f\n", year, numr/denr);
        }
    }
}
```

A sample output is given below.

```
Type in the target amount: 35000
Type in the interest rate (%): 7.5

Years    Monthly Payment
-----------------------
  5         482.58
 10         196.71
 15         105.70
 20          63.21
 25          39.90
 30          25.98
```

H36 Write a program which determines the first common element, if any, in three sorted lists and prints that element and the indices of the three arrays where it occurs. Otherwise, it prints a "Not Found" message. (For simplicity you may use arrays initialized at declaration)

```
public class Main {
  public static void main(String[] args) {
    int[] A = {2, 5, 6, 10, 14, 17, 23};
    int[] B = {1, 4, 8, 9, 11, 12, 13, 14, 19, 23};
    int[] C = {3, 7, 14, 20, 24};
    int i=0, j=0, k=0;

    while (i < A.length && j < B.length && k < C.length) {
      if ((A[i] == B[j]) && (B[j] == C[k])){
        System.out.printf("%d %d %d %d", A[i], i, j, k);
        System.exit(1);
      }
      if (A[i] <= B[j] && A[i] <= C[k])
        i++;
      else if (B[j] <= A[i] && B[j] <= C[k])
        j++;
      else if (C[k] <= A[i] && C[k] <= B[j])
        k++;
    }
    System.out.println("Not Found");
  }
}
```

H37 Write a program to check if a given point is (a) inside, (b) on a border, or (c) outside of a given rectangle.

```
import java.util.Scanner;
public class Main {
  public static void main(String[] args) {
    Scanner input = new Scanner(System.in);
```

```java
      double lowerLeftX, lowerLeftY, width, height, Px,
    Py;
    System.out.print ("Type in the lower left corner point
    (x,y): ");
    lowerLeftX = input.nextDouble();
    lowerLeftY = input.nextDouble();
    System.out.print ("Type in the width and height: ");
    width = input.nextDouble();
    height = input.nextDouble();
    System.out.print ("Type in the point coordinates (x,y):
    ");
    Px = input.nextDouble();
    Py = input.nextDouble();
      boolean    inside   =   (Px   >   lowerLeftX   &&   Px   <
    lowerLeftX+width   &&   Py   >   lowerLeftY   &&   Py   <
    lowerLeftY+height);
      boolean    outside  =   (Px   <   lowerLeftX   ||   Px   >
    lowerLeftX+width   ||   Py   <   lowerLeftY   ||   Py   >
    lowerLeftY+height);
    if (inside == true)
       System.out.println ("Point (" + Px + ", " + Py + ") is
    inside");
    else if (outside == true)
       System.out.println ("Point (" + Px + ", " + Py + ") is
    outside");
    else if (Px == lowerLeftX && Py >= lowerLeftY && Py <=
    lowerLeftY + height)
       System.out.println ("Point (" + Px + ", " + Py + ") is
    on the left border");
    else if (Px == lowerLeftX + width && Py >= lowerLeftY &&
    Py <= lowerLeftY + height)
       System.out.println ("Point (" + Px + ", " + Py + ") is
    on the right border");
    else if (Py == lowerLeftY && Px >= lowerLeftX && Px <=
    lowerLeftX + width)
       System.out.println ("Point (" + Px + ", " + Py + ") is
    on the bottom border");
    else if (Py == lowerLeftY + height && Px >= lowerLeftX &&
    Px <= lowerLeftX + width)
       System.out.println ("Point (" + Px + ", " + Py + ") is
    on the top border");
     }
  }
}
```

H38 Write a program to compute the solutions of the quadratic equation
    `ax^2 + bx + c`, given a, b, and c.

```java
import java.util.Scanner;
public class Main {
  public static void main(String[] args) {
```

```java
    Scanner input = new Scanner(System.in);
    double a, b, c, det, root1=0, root2=0;
    boolean complex = false;
    System.out.print ("Type in the coefficients (a,b,c): ");
    a = input.nextDouble();
    b = input.nextDouble();
    c = input.nextDouble();
    det = b*b - 4*a*c;
    if (det == 0) {
      root1 = root2 = -b/(2*a);
    }
    else if (det < 0) {
      complex = true;
    }
    else {
      root1 = (-b + Math.sqrt(det))/2*a;
      root2 = (-b - Math.sqrt(det))/2*a;
    }
    if (complex == true)
      System.out.print ("The roots are complex\n");
    else
      System.out.println ("The roots are: " + root1 + ", " +
  root2);
  }
}
```

H39 Write a program to simulate the tossing of a fair coin for different number of tosses, which is read from the keyboard. A sample output is shown below:

```
Enter the no. of trials: 1000
Number of Tails: 496
Number of Heads: 504
```

```java
import java.util.Random;
import java.util.Scanner;

public class Main {
enum Face
{
    HEAD, TAIL;
}
public static Face tossCoin () {
     return (Math.random() < 0.5 ? Face.TAIL : Face.HEAD);
  }
   public static void main(String[] args) {
     Scanner input = new Scanner(System.in);
     int tailCnt=0, headCnt=0;
     System.out.print("Enter the no. of trials: ");
     int numTrials = input.nextInt();
```

```java
      for (int i=1; i<=numTrials; i++){
        Face faceUp = tossCoin ();
        if (faceUp == Face.TAIL)
           tailCnt++;
        else
           headCnt++;
      }
      System.out.println("\nNumber of Tails: " + tailCnt);
      System.out.println("Number of Heads: " + headCnt);
   }
}
```

H40 Write a program to simulate the tossing of a fair coin for different number of tosses, N: 100, 1,000, 10,000, 100,000. Display the number of outcomes of exactly 3 and exactly 5 consecutive heads coming up.

```java
import java.util.Random;
import java.util.Scanner;

public class Main {

enum Face
{
    HEAD, TAIL;
}
public static Face tossCoin (){
      return (Math.random() < 0.5 ? Face.TAIL : Face.HEAD);
   }
   public static void main(String[] args) {
      Scanner input = new Scanner(System.in);
      int headCnt=0, tailCnt=0;
      int           consecHeadCnt=0,          head3ConsecCnt=0,
    head5ConsecCnt=0;
      System.out.print("Enter the no. of trials: ");
      int numTrials = input.nextInt();
      for (int i=1; i<=numTrials; i++){
        Face faceUp = tossCoin ();
        if (faceUp == Face.TAIL){
           tailCnt++;
           if (consecHeadCnt == 3){
             head3ConsecCnt++;
           }
           else if (consecHeadCnt == 5){
             head5ConsecCnt++;
           }
           consecHeadCnt = 0;
        }
        else {
           headCnt++;
           consecHeadCnt++;
```

```
      }
    }
    System.out.println("\nNumber of Trials: " + numTrials);
    System.out.println("Number of Tails: " + tailCnt);
    System.out.println("Number of Heads: " + headCnt);
    System.out.println("Number of 3 consecutive heads: " +
  head3ConsecCnt);
    System.out.println("Number of 5 consecutive heads: " +
  head5ConsecCnt);
  }
}
```

H41 Write a program to simulate the tossing of a fair coin and determine the minimum number of trials required for exactly 3 consecutive heads coming up. Also determine the number of tails and heads. Have the program to run a certain number of runs as specified by an input. A sample output for 2 runs is shown below.

```
Enter the no. of runs: 2
Run number: 1
T T T H H T T H H H H T H T H T T H H H H T H H H T
Number of Trials: 26
Number of Tails: 11
Number of Heads: 15
Run number: 2
H T H H H T
Number of Trials: 6
Number of Tails: 2
Number of Heads: 4

import java.util.Random;
import java.util.Scanner;
public class Main {

enum Face
{
    HEAD, TAIL;
}
public static Face tossCoin () {
    return (Math.random() < 0.5 ? Face.TAIL : Face.HEAD);
  }
   public static void main(String[] args) {
      Scanner input = new Scanner(System.in);
      System.out.print("Enter the no. of runs: ");
      int numRuns = input.nextInt();
      for (int i=1; i<=numRuns; i++) {
         int headCnt=0, tailCnt=0, numTrials=0;
         int consecHeadCnt=0;
         boolean head3Consec = false;
         System.out.println("Run number: " + i);
```

```java
      while (head3Consec != true){
        Face faceUp = tossCoin ();
        numTrials++;
        System.out.print(faceUp == Face.TAIL ? "T " : "H ");
        if (faceUp == Face.TAIL){
          tailCnt++;
          if (consecHeadCnt == 3)
            head3Consec = true;
          consecHeadCnt = 0;
        }
        else {
          headCnt++;
          consecHeadCnt++;
        }
      }// endwhile
      System.out.println("\nNumber of Trials: " + numTrials);
      System.out.println("Number of Tails: " + tailCnt);
      System.out.println("Number of Heads: " + headCnt);
    }// endfor
  }
}
```

H42 Simulate and determine the number of throws of a single die until all faces have come up. A sample output is shown below. Note that the theoretical expected number of throws: $6/6+6/5+6/4+6/3+6/2+6/1 \approx 14.7$.

```
2 5 2 1 3 4 2 3 4 4 2 4 3 5 6
Number of trials required for all faces to come up was
    15
```

```java
import java.util.Random;
import java.util.Scanner;
public class Main {
  public static int rollDie (){
     return (int)(Math.random()*6)+1;
  }

    public static void main(String[] args) {
      boolean face1Up = false, face2Up = false, face3Up =
    false, face4Up = false, face5Up = false, face6Up = false;
      int faceUp, numTrials = 0;
      boolean allFacesUp = face1Up && face2Up && face3Up &&
    face4Up && face5Up && face6Up;
      while (allFacesUp == false){
        faceUp = rollDie ();
        numTrials++;
        System.out.print(faceUp + " ");
        switch (faceUp){
          case 1: face1Up = true;
            break;
          case 2: face2Up = true;
```

```
            break;
         case 3: face3Up = true;
            break;
         case 4: face4Up = true;
            break;
         case 5: face5Up = true;
            break;
         case 6: face6Up = true;
            break;
      } // switch
      allFacesUp = face1Up && face2Up && face3Up && face4Up
   && face5Up && face6Up;
   } // while
   System.out.print("\nNumber of trials required for all
   faces to come up was " + numTrials);
   }
}
```

H43 Write a program to count the number of times each of the faces of a die has come up in a given number of trials. A sample output is shown below.

```
Enter the no. of trials: 10000
Number of trials = 10000
Face  No. of times
1     1635
2     1714
3     1680
4     1653
5     1675
6     1643
```

```java
import java.util.Random;
import java.util.Scanner;
public class Main {
   public static int rollDie (){
      return (int)(Math.random()*6)+1;
   }

   public static void main(String[] args) {
      Scanner input = new Scanner(System.in);
      System.out.print("Enter the no. of trials: ");
      int numTrials = input.nextInt();
      int face1Cnt = 0, face2Cnt = 0, face3Cnt = 0, face4Cnt
   = 0, face5Cnt = 0, face6Cnt = 0, faceUp;
      for (int i = 1; i <= numTrials; i++){
         faceUp = rollDie ();
         switch (faceUp){
            case 1: face1Cnt++;
               break;
```

```
            case 2: face2Cnt++;
               break;
            case 3: face3Cnt++;
               break;
            case 4: face4Cnt++;
               break;
            case 5: face5Cnt++;
               break;
            case 6: face6Cnt++;
               break;
         } // switch
      } // for
      System.out.println("\nNumber of trials = " + numTrials);
      System.out.println("Face  No. of times");
      System.out.println("1      " + face1Cnt);
      System.out.println("2      " + face2Cnt);
      System.out.println("3      " + face3Cnt);
      System.out.println("4      " + face4Cnt);
      System.out.println("5      " + face5Cnt);
      System.out.println("6      " + face6Cnt);
   }
}
```

H44 Write a method to method to determine if an integer array has duplicates. It takes an array as argument and returns a Boolean.

```
public static boolean checkDupl (int arr[]){
   boolean dupl=false;
   for (int i=0; i<arr.length-1; i++){
      for (int j=i; j<arr.length; j++){
         if (arr[i] == arr[j+1])
            return true;
      }
   }
   return dupl;
}
```

H45 Write a program to determine if the elements of an array of integers are distinct or not (*i.e.* check if there are duplicates), and print out the index of the first element which has duplicate(s).

```
import java.util.Random;
import java.util.Scanner;
public class Main {
  public static void main(String[] args) {
  final int ARR_SIZE = 20;
  int i, j=0;
  int[] numlist = new int[ARR_SIZE];
   boolean duplicate = false;
   for (i = 0; i < ARR_SIZE; i++)
```

```
      numlist[i] = (int)(Math.random()*20);
   for (i = 0; i < ARR_SIZE; i++)
      System.out.print(numlist[i] + " ");
   System.out.println();
   i = 0;
   while (duplicate == false && i < ARR_SIZE-1){
      for (j = i+1; j < ARR_SIZE; j++){
         if (numlist[i] == numlist[j]){
            duplicate = true;
            break;
         }
      }
      i++;
   }
   System.out.println("Loop exited at i = " + (i-1) + " j = " + j);
   System.out.println("First duplicate seen is " + numlist[i-1]);
   if (duplicate == true)
      System.out.println("\nDuplicate(s) present");
   else
      System.out.println("\nDuplicate(s) not present");
 }
}
```

H46 Write a method which takes an array of integers as argument, and prints out the elements such that repeating (duplicate) elements are printed just once. For example, if the input is:
5,2,7,2,4,7,8,12,3,2,3,2,9,2,4 the output should be:
5,2,7,4,8,12,3,9

```
   public static void printDistinctElements(int[] arr){
      for (int i=0; i<arr.length; i++) {
         boolean isDistinct = true;
         for (int j=0; j<i; j++) {
            if(arr[i] == arr[j]) {
               isDistinct = false;
               break;
            }
         }
         if(isDistinct)
            System.out.print(arr[i] + " ");
      }
   }
```

H47 Write a method to determine and return the maximum element in an array.

```
   public static int findMax(int[] arr) {
      int max = arr[0];
```

```
  for (int i=1; i<arr.length; i++) {
    if(arr[i] > max)
      max = arr[i];
  }
  return max;
}
```

H48 Write a program to determine and print out the elements of an array of integers that are repeated, along with the indices of the first occurrence and the repetitions. For example, if the input array is:

```
17 7 18 2 3 18 18 16 3 18 17 4 10 19 3 11 10 8 16 8
```

the output should be:

```
17 at [0] repeated at indices:  10
18 at [2] repeated at indices:  5 6 9
3 at [4] repeated at indices:  8 14
16 at [7] repeated at indices:  18
10 at [12] repeated at indices:  16
8 at [17] repeated at indices:  19
```

```
import java.util.Random;
import java.util.Scanner;
public class Main {
  public static void main(String[] args) {
  final int ARR_SIZE = 30;
  int[] numlist = new int[ARR_SIZE];
  boolean[] dupl = new boolean[ARR_SIZE];
   for (int i = 0; i < ARR_SIZE; i++){
     numlist[i] = (int)(Math.random()*20);
     dupl[i] = false;
   }
   for (int i = 0; i < ARR_SIZE; i++)
     System.out.print(numlist[i] + " ");
   System.out.println();
   for (int i=0; i < ARR_SIZE-1; i++){
     boolean firstSeen = true;
     for (int j = i+1; j < ARR_SIZE; j++){
       if (numlist[i] == numlist[j]){
          if (dupl[i] == false && firstSeen == true){
            System.out.print("\n"+ numlist[i] + " at [" + i
    + "] repeated at indices:   ");
            firstSeen = false;
          }
          if (dupl[j] == false){
            System.out.print(j + " ");
            dupl[j] = true;
          } // inner if
        } // outer if
      } // inner for
```

```
    } // outer for
  }
}
```

H49 Write a method to print 'histogram' based on values in an array. A sample output for array of {5, 3, 2, 7, 4} is shown below.

```
       *
       *
   *   *
   *  **
  **  **
  *****
  *****
```

```
public static void printHist (int arr[]){
  int max=arr[0];
  for (int i=1; i<arr.length; i++){
    if (arr[i] > max)
      max = arr[i];
  }
  for (int h=max; h>=1; h--){
    for (int i=0; i<arr.length; i++){
      if (arr[i] < h)
        System.out.print(" ");
      else
        System.out.print("*");
    }
    System.out.println();
  }
}
```

H50 Write a method to partition an array into ODD and EVEN integers. After partition, the array will have all odd elements followed by all even elements. It takes an array as an argument and partitions it in-place.

```
public static void partitionOddEven (int arr[]){
  int i = 0, j = arr.length-1;
  while (i < j){
    while (arr[i] % 2 != 0 && i<j)
      i++;
    while (arr[j] % 2 == 0 && j>i)
      j--;
    int temp = arr[i]; arr[i] = arr[j]; arr[j] = temp;
    i++; j--;
  }
}
```

H51 Write a method to print common elements in two sorted arrays, each having distinct values

```
public static void printCommonElements (int arr1[], int
   arr2[]){

  int i = 0, j = 0;
  System.out.println("Common elements:");
  while (i < arr1.length && j < arr2.length){
    if (arr1[i] < arr2[j])
      i++;
    else if (arr1[i] > arr2[j])
      j++;
    else {// arr1[i] equals arr2[j]
      System.out.print(arr1[i] + " ");
      i++; j++;
    }
  }
}
```

H52 Write a program to find the longest plateau in a given array of numbers. For example, if array A[10] = [5, 3, 3, 1, 4, 4, 4, 2, 6, 6] the longest plateau is 4, 4, 4 starting at A[4] and of length 3. The output should be:

   Longest plateau starts at A[4]
   Length of the plateau: 3
For simplicity, you may assume the plateau lengths to be unique.

```
public static void longestPlateau (int arr[]){
  int i=0, len=1, maxlen=1, start=0;
  while (i < arr.length-1){
    if (arr[i] != arr[i+1]){
      if (len > maxlen){
        maxlen = len; start = i-len+1;
      }
      len = 1;
    }
    else
      len++;
    i++;
  }
```

```
    System.out.printf("Longest starts at index
      %d\n", start);
    System.out.printf("Length of the longest plateau:
      %d\n", maxlen);
}
```

H53 Mathematically, a matrix A is said to be symmetric if $A(i, j) = A(j, i)$ for all valid i, j. Write a method which takes a 2D array as an argument and returns true/false based on whether the matrix is symmetric or not.

```
public static boolean isSymmetric (int[][] mat){
  for (int row = 1; row < mat.length; row++){
    for (int col = 0; col < row; col++)
      if (mat[row][col] != mat[col][row])
        return false;
  }
  return true;
}
```

H54 Write a code segment to initialize a square matrix represented by an array 'arr' to an Identity matrix. Note that in the Identity matrix all diagonal elements are 1's and all the remaining elements are 0's.

```
    for (i=0; i<arr.length; i++)
      for (j=0; j<arr.length; j++)
        arr[i][j] = (i==j) ? 1 : 0;
```

H55 Write a method which takes a string as argument and determines if it is a palindrome or not.

```
    static boolean isPalindrome(String str) {
      int i = 0, j = str.length() - 1;
      while (i < j) {
        if (str.charAt(i) != str.charAt(j))
          return false;
        i++;
        j--;
      }
      return true;
    }
```

H56 Write a method which takes a 2D array as argument, and determines the minimum and maximum elements, and returns them in an array of two elements.

H. Programming Problems

```java
public static int[] findMinMax (int[][] mat){
  int[] minmax = new int[2];
  minmax[0] = minmax[1] = mat[0][0];
  for (int row = 0; row < mat.length; row++){
    for (int col = 0; col < mat[row].length; col++){
      if (mat[row][col] < minmax[0])
        minmax[0] = mat[row][col];
      else if (mat[row][col] > minmax[1])
        minmax[1] = mat[row][col];
    }
  }
  return (minmax);
}
```

H57 Write a method to check if a given matrix is a unit matrix. An N x N unit matrix is a matrix of N rows and N columns where all the diagonal elements are '1's and all the remaining elements are '0's. The method should take a 2D array of integers as argument and return a Boolean which is true/false depending on whether the matrix corresponding to the 2D array is a unit matrix or not.

```java
public static boolean isUnitMatrix (int[][] mat){

  for (int row = 0; row < mat.length; row++){
    for (int col = 0; col < mat.length; col++){
      if (row != col){
        if (mat[row][col] != 0)
          return false;
      }
      else if (mat[row][col] != 1)
        return false;
    }
  }
  return true;
}
```

H58 A Magic Square is N x N matrix of integers such that the sum of every row, column, and diagonal is the same. Write a method which takes a 2D array as an argument and returns true/false depending on whether the array is a magic square or not.

```java
public static boolean isMagicSquare (int[][] mSquare){
  int sum1=0, sum2;

  for (int col = 0; col < mSquare[0].length; col++)
```

```
      sum1 += mSquare[0][col];
   for (int row = 1; row < mSquare.length; row++) { //
    check rows
      sum2 = 0;
      for (int col = 0; col < mSquare.length; col++)
        sum2 += mSquare[row][col];
      if (sum2 != sum1)
        return false;
   }

   for (int col = 0; col < mSquare.length; col++) { //
    check columns
      sum2 = 0;
      for (int row = 0; row < mSquare.length; row++)
        sum2 += mSquare[row][col];
      if (sum2 != sum1)
        return false;
   }

   sum2 = 0;
   for (int i = 0; i < mSquare.length; i++) // check
    BLTR diagonal
      sum2 += mSquare[i][i];
   if (sum2 != sum1)
      return false;

   sum2 = 0;
   for (int i = mSquare.length-1; i >= 0; i--) // check
    TLBR diagonal
      sum2 += mSquare[i][i];
   if (sum2 != sum1)
      return false;

   return true;

}
```

H59 Write a method which takes an integer 'N' (≥ 1) as argument, and generates the 'Pascal triangle' of height 'N', and returns it. 'Pascal triangle' is a triangular array of binomial coefficients. An example with N = 5 is shown below.

```
    1
    1 1
    1 2 1
```

```
    1 3 3 1
    1 4 6 4 1

public static int[][] pascalTriangle(int N){
  int[][] pascalTri = new int[N][];
  for (int i=0; i<N; i++){
    pascalTri[i] = new int[i+1];
    pascalTri[i][0] = pascalTri[i][i] = 1;
    for (int j=1; j<i; j++){
      pascalTri[i][j] = pascalTri[i-1][j] + pascalTri[i-1][j-1];
    }
  }
  return pascalTri;
}
```

H60 Write a program which determines the maximum distance between two cities, based on the pair-wise distances between 'N' cities given in a triangular array, as shown below. It should printout the pair of cities with the largest distance and their distance. An example of pair-wise distance of 10 cities, and the expected output is given below. (Note: The C's marked in red are not part of the array).

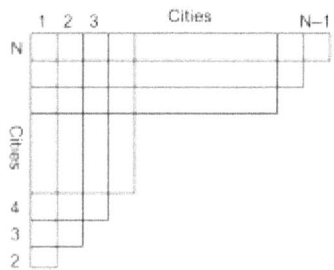

```
        C1      C2      C3      C4      C5      C6      C7      C8      C9
C10  202.26  164.96  134.24  181.28  205.76   77.31   10.87  103.76  240.65
 C9   98.01  167.79   28.84   38.30   41.42  196.61  120.22   83.76
 C8  212.39   86.70  195.99  210.22  227.05   91.37   93.19
 C7  210.84  194.46  153.12   39.87   10.73   59.35
 C6  119.70   51.58  188.96  248.81  124.86
 C5  237.66  239.67   23.41  125.51
 C4  110.72  161.45  103.84
 C3  182.53   39.73
 C2   16.43
```

Max distance is 248.81 between cities 6 and 4

```
public class Main {
  public static void main(String[] args) {
    final int SIZE = 10;
    double[][] distArray = new double[SIZE][];
    for (int i=0; i<SIZE-1; i++){
```

```java
      distArray[i] = new double[SIZE-1-i];
    }
    for (int i=0; i<SIZE-1; i++){
      for (int j=0; j<SIZE-1-i; j++){
        distArray[i][j] = Math.random()*250;
      }
    }
    for (int i=0; i<SIZE-1; i++){
      for (int j=0; j<SIZE-1-i; j++){
        System.out.printf(" %6.2f ", distArray[i][j]);
      }
      System.out.println();
    }
    int i, j, maxIndex1=0, maxIndex2=0;
    double maxDist = 0;
    for (i=0; i<SIZE-1; i++){
      for (j=0; j<SIZE-1-i; j++){
        if (distArray[i][j] > maxDist){
          maxDist = distArray[i][j];
          maxIndex1 = i; maxIndex2 = j;
        }
      }
    }
    System.out.printf("Largest distance is %.2f", maxDist);
    System.out.println(" between cities " + (SIZE- maxIndex1)
     + " and " + (maxIndex2+1));
  }
}
```

IOIOIOIOIOIOIOIOIOIOIOIOIOIOIOIOIOIOIOIOIOIOIOIOIOI

Books on Java

- Starting Out with Java: From Control Structures through Objects (7th Edition). Tony Gaddis. Pearson, 2018. ISBN-13 : 978-0134802213.

- Core Java Volume I – Fundamentals (11th Edition). Cay S. Horstmann. Prentice Hall, 2018. ISBN-13 : 978-0135166307.

- Java: A Beginner's Guide (8th Edition). Herbert Schildt. McGraw-Hill, 2018. ISBN-13 : 978-1260440218.

- Effective Java (3rd Edition). Joshua Bloch. Addison-Wesley Professional, 2017. ISBN-13: 978-0134685991.

- Java: An Introduction to Problem Solving and Programming (8th edition). Walter Savitch. Pearson, 2017. ISBN-13: 978-0134462035.

- Head First Java (2nd Edition). Kathy Sierra and Bert Bates. O'Reilly Media, 2005. ISBN-13: 978-0596009205.

Other Related Quiz Books

This is a quick assessment book / quiz book. It has a vast collection of over 1,100 questions, with answers on Data Structures. Questions have a wide range of difficulty levels and are designed to test a thorough understanding of the topical material. The coverage includes elementary and advanced data structures – Arrays (single/multidimensional); Linked lists (singly–linked, doubly–linked, circular); Stacks; Queues; Heaps; Hash tables; Binary trees; Binary search trees; Balanced trees (AVL trees, Red–Black trees, B–trees/B+ trees); Graphs.

This is a quick assessment book / quiz book. It has a vast collection of over 1,000 questions, with answers on Algorithms. The book covers questions on standard (classical) algorithm design techniques; sorting and searching; graph traversals; minimum spanning trees; shortest path problems; maximum flow problems; elementary concepts in *P* and *NP* Classes. It also covers a few specialized areas – string processing; polynomial operations; numerical & matrix computations; computational geometry & computer graphics

This is a quick assessment book / quiz book. It has a wide variety of over 1,600 questions, with answers on Operating Systems. The questions have a wide range of difficulty levels and are designed to test a thorough understanding of the topical material. The book covers questions on the operating systems structures, fundamentals of processes and threads, CPU scheduling, process synchronization, deadlocks, memory management, I/O subsystem, and mass storage (disk) structures.

This is a quick assessment book / quiz book. It has a wide variety of over 1,700 questions, with answers on Computer Security. The questions have a wide range of difficulty levels and are designed to test a thorough understanding of the topical material. The book covers all the major topics in a typical first course in Computer Security – Cryptography, Authentication and Key Management, Software and Operating Systems Security, Malware, Attacks, Network Security, and Web Security.

This is a quick assessment book / quiz book. It has wide variety of ~1,400 questions on Programming Languages and Compilers. It covers questions on: Bindings and Scopes, Data types, Expressions and Assignment statements, Subprograms and Parameter passing mechanisms, Abstract Data Types, Object- Oriented constructs, and Exception handling. The topics related to Compilers include programming language syntax and semantics, lexical analysis, parsing, and different parsing techniques.

This is a quick assessment book / quiz book. It has a vast collection of over 1,500 short questions, with answers. It covers all the major topics in a typical first course in Computer Networks. The coverage includes, the various layers of the Internet (TCP/IP) protocol stack (going from the actual transmission of signals to the applications that users use) – physical layer, data link layer, network layer, transport layer, and application layer, network security, and Web security.

Other Related Quiz Books

This is a quick assessment book / quiz book. It has a vast collection of over 1,200 short questions, with answers and programs, on C++ programming language. The topical coverage includes data types, control structures, arrays, pointers and reference, classes and objects, inheritance and polymorphism, exception handling, and stream and text I/O.

This is a quick assessment book / quiz book. It has a vast collection of over 1,100 short questions, with answers and programs, on C programming language. It covers all the major topics of C programming – data types, operators, expressions, control structures, pointers, arrays, structures, unions, enumerated types, functions, dynamic storage management, I/O and Library functions.

This is a self–assessment / quiz /exercise book. It has a vast collection of over 1,200 questions, with solutions, in Discrete Mathematics. Questions have a wide range of difficulty levels and are designed to test a thorough understanding of the topical material. The topical coverage includes: Logic and Proof methods, Sets, Functions, Relations, Properties of integers, Sequences, Induction and Recursion, Basic and advanced counting methods, Discrete probability, Graph theory, Modeling computation, and Boolean algebra.

Automata Languages Computability Complexity Quiz Book

A Compendium of over 1,300 questions with answers

S.R. Subramanya

This is a quick assessment book / quiz book. It has a vast collection of a wide variety of over 1,300 questions on Computer Science Theory (Ex. Automata and Formal Languages, Computability, Complexity). The topical coverage includes Finite automata, Regular languages; Context-Free grammars and Context-free languages; Pushdown Automata; Turing Machines, Computability, and Decidability; Computational complexity.

www.ingramcontent.com/pod-product-compliance
Lightning Source LLC
Chambersburg PA
CBHW060823220526
45466CB00003B/953